D0518356

The Epic of Evolution

Advances in Human Evolution
A Prentice Hall Series of Text and Monographs

Series Editor: Prof. Russell L. Ciochon, The University of Iowa

Editorial Board:

Prof. Robert Corruccini, Southern Illinois University—Carbondale

Prof. Dean Falk, Florida State University—Tallahassee

Prof. John Fleagle, State University of New York—Stony Brook

Prof. Henry McHenry, University of California—Davis

Prof. Erik Trinkaus, Washington University, St. Louis

Prof. Mark Weiss, Physical Anthropology Program—National Science Foundation

The Epic of Evolution
Science and Religion in Dialogue

Edited by
James B. Miller

Upper Saddle River, New Jersey 07458

Library of Congress Cataloging-in-Publication Data

The epic of evolution : science and religion in dialogue / edited by
James B. Miller
     p. cm
Includes bibliographical references (p.   ).
   ISBN 0–13–093318–X
I.   Religion and science.   I. Miller, James B. (James Bradley)
   BL240.3 .E65 2004
   201′.65--dc22

                                                          2003018742

Publisher: Nancy Roberts
Editorial Assistant: Lee Peterson
Director of Marketing: Beth Mejia
Senior Marketing Manager: Marissa Feliberty
Marketing Assistant: Adam Laitman
Production Liaison: Marianne Peters-Riordan
Manufacturing Buyer: Ben Smith
Cover Design: Bruce Kenselaar
Composition/Full-Service Project Management: Marianne Hutchinson/
   Pine Tree Composition, Inc.
Printer/Binder: Courier Companies, Inc.

Credits and acknowledgments borrowed from other sources and reproduced, with permission, in this textbook appear on appropriate page within text.

Copyright © 2004 The American Association for the Advancement of Science.
Published by Pearson Education, Inc., Upper Saddle River, New Jersey 07458. All rights reserved. Printed in the United States of America. This publication is protected by Copyright and permission should be obtained from the publisher prior to any prohibited reproduction, storage in a retrieval system, or transmission in any form or by any means, electronic, mechanical, photocopying, recording, or likewise. For information regarding permission(s), write to: Rights and Permissions Department.

Pearson Prentice Hall™ is a trademark of Pearson Education, Inc.
Pearson® is a registered trademark of Pearson plc
Prentice Hall® is a registered trademark of Pearson Education, Inc.

Pearson Education LTD.
Pearson Education Singapore, Pte. Ltd
Pearson Education Canada, Ltd
Pearson Education-Japan
Pearson Education Australia PTY, Limited

Pearson Education North Asia Ltd.
Pearson Educatión de Mexico, S.A. de C.V.
Pearson Education Malaysia, Pte. Ltd
Pearson Education, Upper Saddle River,
   New Jersey

10 9 8 7 6 5 4 3 2 1
ISBN 0-13-093318-X

Contents

Contributors

Francisco J. Ayala, Donald Bren Professor of Biological Sciences and Professor of Philosophy at the University of California, Irvine.

Mary Barber, Consultant, formally on the staff of the Ecological Society of America.

Thomas Berry, former Director of the graduate program in the History of Religions at Fordham University and founder of the Riverdale Center for Religions Research in Riverdale, New York.

Audrey R. Chapman, Director Emeritus of the Program of Dialogue on Science, Ethics, and Religion of the American Association for the Advancement of Science.

Terrence Deacon, Professor, Department of Anthropology at the University of California, Berkeley

Niles Eldredge, Curator in the Department of Invertebrates of the American Museum of Natural History, New York City.

Ursula Goodenough, Professor of Biology at Washington University in St. Louis.

John F. Haught, Landegger Distinguished Professor of Theology at Georgetown University.

Philip Hefner, former Professor of Systematic Theology at the Lutheran School of Theology at Chicago and Editor-in-Chief of *Zygon: Journal of Religion and Science.*

N. Scott Momaday, Regents Professor of English and Comparative Literature at the University of Arizona.

Nancey Murphy, Professor of Christian Philosophy at Fuller Theological Seminary.

Ronald L. Numbers, Hilldale and William Coleman Professor of the History of Science and Medicine, Department of the History of Medicine, University of Wisconsin–Madison.

Stephen J. Pope, Associate Professor, Department of Theology at Boston College.

Joel Primack, Professor of Physics at the University of California, Santa Cruz.

Loyal Rue, Professor of Religion and Philosophy at Luther College in Decorah, Iowa.

Brian Swimme, member of the core faculty in the Program of Philosophy, Cosmology, and Consciousness of the California Institute of Integral Studies.

Ian Tattersall, Curator in the Department of Anthropology of the American Museum of Natural History, New York City.

Mary Evelyn Tucker, Professor, Department of Religion at Bucknell University.

Alaka Wali, Director of the Center for Cultural Understanding and Change of the Field Museum in Chicago.

Preface

The chapters in this volume, with one exception, are based on presentations that were made at a conference, *The Epic of Evolution*, held at the Field Museum of Natural History in Chicago on November 12–14, 1997. The conference was made possible through the generous support of the John Templeton Foundation and the Esther A. and Joseph Klingenstein Fund. The conference also benefited from the endorsement and assistance of the Chicago Academy of Sciences, the Chicago Center for Religion and Science, and the North American Montessori Teachers Association.

The conference was the first national event organized by Program of Dialogue on Science, Ethics, and Religion (DoSER) of the American Association for the Advancement of Science (AAAS). The Dialogue Program enjoyed collaboration in the organization of the event with the Field Museum's Center for Cultural Understanding and Change, and especially its director, Dr. Alaka Wali.

Unfortunately, one of the scheduled presenters, Dr. Ronald Numbers, was unable to attend at the last minute due to illness. However, subsequently he videotaped an interview on his topic and an edited transcript of that interview is included in this volume.

This volume is offered as an example of the potential for dialogue between science and religion that is possible beyond the more popular convictions that science and religion are either inimical or must be kept in hermetically sealed domains. What is manifest in the flow of these chapters is not the end of a conversation but the beginning of one long overdue.

James B. Miller
Program of Dialogue on Science, Ethics, and Religion
American Association for the Advancement of Science

1 The Epic of Evolution: Science and Religion in Dialogue

Alaka Wali *Center for Cultural Understanding and Change,*
The Field Museum

Who are we? Where did we come from? Why are we here? These were among the very first questions that humans asked of themselves as they gained the capacity for abstract thought and expressive language. They compel us to seek explanations for the phenomena we see around us, they inspire us to dizzying creative heights, and they are the genesis of all of our art and storytelling. The rich diversity of answers that humans have proposed to these questions is a testimony to their fundamental significance. They stand at the heart of our inquiry into the processes of evolution.

It is the modern diversity of thought on these questions that was captured in part during a milestone conference held at the Field Museum in November 1997. This volume is a collection of the papers offered at that conference, presented in the informal style of dialogue and discussion that characterized the spirit of the event.

The Center for Cultural Understanding and Change at the Field Museum was proud to collaborate with the American Association for the Advancement of Science on the conference. The idea that the Field Museum could be an appropriate site was first suggested by Anna Roosevelt, at that time a member of the AAAS executive board and a curator at the museum. Indeed, the museum welcomed the opportunity to host the conference because we felt that it was important to promote such a dialogue at a time when there seemed to be a resurgence of polarizing tendency in the United States between two streams of thought: scientific and Christian religious tradition. In Chapter 2 of this volume, Audrey Chapman discusses the context for that polarization and updates its progression since 1997. Our hope in hosting the conference was that through further dialogue, we could all come to better appreciate the complexity of thinking in both scientific and religious traditions on evolution and the fertile common ground that is still in great need of exploration, particularly with respect to how these two modes of inquiry could complement one another. The focus particularly on Christian thought was deemed necessary to counteract the sources of greatest friction between religion and science at the moment in the hope that by demonstrating the value of dialogue among those supposedly the farthest apart we could also encourage dialogue between science and other religious traditions.

The conference unfolded from considerations of evolutionary processes in the macrocosm of the universe to the microcosm of human thought, but then expanded again into consideration of the realm of the future. This volume remains faithful to that sequence. However, the chapters in each section are also self-contained and can be read in nonlinear order.

In the first set of chapters, then, the stage is set for the unfolding of the epic with a look at the cosmos from both the scientific and theological perspective. Primack and Swimme chart the significance of changing perspectives on the origins and evolution of the universe. From here, we leap to the evolution of life on earth. Ronald Numbers discusses Charles Darwin and the impact his work has had, both on science and on society, and places the conflict over evolutionary theory in America in historical perspective. Niles Eldredge discusses recent advances in paleontology on the question of origin of life and the role that mass extinctions play in evolution.

The next three sections of the volume afford an opportunity to delve into the details of the dialogue at the level of specific mechanisms that underlie evolutionary processes. Ursula Goodenough provides a detailed account of how natural selection works and how it led to biological diversity. John Haught then discusses how a Christian theology might build on the insights provided by evolutionary theory (specifically the role of natural selection) to gain more profound insights into the nature of the divine. The discussion then continues with a focus on the origins and evolution of modern humans. Ian Tattersal and Terence Deacon lay the groundwork through detailed analysis of the current anthropological evidence and theorizing on the topic, while Nancey Murphy demonstrates that Christian theology need not be in conflict with a physicalist view of humans. Murphy shows the value of the physicalist approach while at the same time cautioning against an extreme reduction to only physical explanations for central aspects of human behavior. The theme of human behavior and the place of religion are continued in the following section. Here, papers by Sol Katz and Mary Evelyn Tucker begin to reveal the complex underpinnings of the origins of culture and religion. Katz discusses the new frontiers of research on biocultural evolution that is trying to gather empirical evidence on the relationship between biological and cultural processes. He demonstrates that the relationship is one of continual feedback, not a linear vector. Tucker, using examples from religious scriptures of Israel, India, and China, analyzes our fundamental need for religious thought in order to achieve balance between ourselves and nature and to affirm the value of life during vulnerable moments. Philip Hefner discusses the central role of culture in the epic of evolution. He locates religion in culture and culture itself in nature.

In the penultimate section of the volume, we move even deeper into the consideration of culture and human nature by examining the concept of morality. Francisco Ayala provides a coherent analysis of the biological roots of ethical behavior while cogently commenting on the perspective of some sociobiologists to reduce all moral codes to their biological function. He places the development of morality squarely within the realm of culture and history. Loyal Rue approaches the issue from the other side, embracing a sociobiological view of behavior but still locating morality within a socially constructed system of symbolic thought. Symbolic systems, according to Rue, mediate in very powerful ways between genes, where behavior is encoded, and the expression of that behavior. Stephen Pope then offers a Christian theological perspective on the evolutionary roots of morality, attempting to bring together different strands of thought on this topic.

In the concluding section of the volume, we turn outward again to a more macrocosmic perspective by considering the future. Mary Barber reminds us of the considerable impact that we have on the environment and the implications for macrolevel changes if we persist in the present direction of increasing intensive exploitation of natural resources. N. Scott Momaday then tells a powerful set of stories that unfold as a dialogue between Yahweh, the Great Mystery, and Erset, the bear, which remind us that even as we move into the future, we must carry our traditions, the sum of what we know with us. He places the discussion of the conflict between science and the sacred within the context of the nature of creativity. In the final essay of the book, Thomas Berry envisions a great future for both religion and science—not as realms apart but as realms integrated by a broad understanding of our place in the universe.

Taken as a whole, the volume emphasizes the overarching perspective of the Epic of Evolution conference: that much is to be gained by deepening the dialogue between science and religion. A further value of the conference and of this publication is that it highlights the complex nature of the dialogue. Throughout, we see that there is neither one scientific perspective nor one religious perspective. Indeed, debate among scientists on the theory and evidence of evolutionary processes abounds, while theological perspectives, even within Christianity, are equally diverse. This was brought home to us during the conference in the lively exchanges that occurred in the "informal" spaces—after session discussions or in late-night conversations. For this reason, the word *dialogue* is truly appropriate to describe the tenor and intent of the proceedings; for while there has been much polarizing debate on the topic of evolution, we saw through the conference that this need not be the only mode of discourse and that, in fact, there is plenty of common ground on which to base a broader-ranging, more meaningful discussion. While the volume we offer here cannot represent the full exchange that occurred in the conference, it is our hope that as you read the chapters, they will stimulate equally rich dialogue in your classrooms or your living rooms. The chapters presented here hint at the deeper realms of thought that we can all explore together in our ceaseless quest to understand our place in the universe.

2 Evolution and the Science and Religion Dialogue

Audrey R. Chapman *AAAS Program of Dialogue on Science, Ethics, and Religion*

There is a seeming paradox in the recent relationships between science and religion. On the one hand, signs abound of a rapprochement between members of the two communities, even the development of what has been termed a "science and religion movement."[1] The Epic of Evolution Conference, cosponsored by the American Association for the Advancement of Science (AAAS) and the Field Museum, which gave rise to this volume, is but one of several significant conferences and meetings in a science and religion format that have been held in recent years. Many universities and theological institutions now offer courses interfacing science and religion, and several also have programs or centers on the topic. In 1995, AAAS established a program on Dialogue on Science, Ethics, and Religion.[2] Public statements and publications by some leaders and scholars in both fields (for example, the Pope and the President of the AAAS, the world's largest federation of scientific and engineering organizations) evince this warming trend. Yet there are continuing, sometimes escalating instances of conflicts, particularly over issues related to the interpretation and teaching of evolution. The August 1999 decision of the State Board of Education in Kansas to adopt new science standards that failed to include evolution as central to the understanding of biology, which were later overturned, was but the first of a series of skirmishes that are often pointed to as examples of the incompatibility of the two domains. How is it possible then to make sense of these seemingly contradictory trends, and what are their implications?

SCIENCE AND RELIGION: AUTONOMY AND RAPPROCHEMENT

Science and religion have had a complex and multidimensional relationship, and for this reason the warfare imagery often depicted in the media does not convey accurately the historical or contemporary interface between the fields. Recent appraisals of the history of the encounter between various religions, particularly Christianity, and science, based on a careful reexamination of the evidence, portray "a complex and diverse interaction that defies reduction to simple 'conflict' or 'harmony.'"[3] Scholars and scientists, including Alfred North Whitehead, have argued that Christianity, rather than impeding science, provided an essential prerequisite for its development, the belief that nature behaves in a regular and orderly manner.[4] The sociologist Robert Merton claimed that seventeenth-century Puritanism contributed to the origins of modern science by providing a system of values sanctioning scientific effort.[5] Up to and including Leibnitz and Galileo, scientists typically explained their motivation in religious terms. Not until the nineteenth century did science become a fully secularized discipline.[6] So where did the idea of a long-standing war between science and religion originate? Historians suggest that it may have been encouraged by two late nineteenth-century works, William Draper's 1874 *History of the Conflict between Religion and Science* and Andrew Dickson White's 1896 book, *A History of the Warfare of Science with Theology in Christendom.*[7]

That is not to deny that various historical instances of conflict did occur, but they were sporadic, usually occasioned by scientific discoveries that seemingly threatened religious dogma or religious understandings of the place of human beings in the cosmos. The Vatican's condemnation of Galileo in 1633 for holding and teaching the Copernican view of a heliocentric (sun-centered) universe is an oft-cited example. The decision of the church to burn the sixteenth-century astronomer and philosopher Giordano Bruno at the stake because of the tenacity with which he maintained his unorthodox magical ideas and claims for an infinite multiplicity of worlds is often held up as another entry into the warfare archives. The skirmishes over evolution, continuing a century and a half after Darwin published *On the Origin of the Species,* occupy a central position in the perception of a seminal struggle between the fields. The legendary encounter in 1860 between Bishops Samuel Wilberforce and Thomas Huxley, "Darwin's bulldog," came to symbolize this acrimonious relationship. A fifth major entry in the conflict iconography in this country is the 1925 Scopes trial in Tennessee, in which it was argued that the teaching of evolution in the schools should be forbidden because it is contrary to scripture. As unfortunate as these and other incidents may have been, however, they are not representative of the historical or contemporary relationship between the fields.

Moreover, reexamination of the records about these conflicts reveals a far more complex situation than the stereotypical image of progressive science confronting intolerant religious dogma. To cite a few examples, the initial rejection of the heliocentric cosmology of Nicolaus Copernicus that displaced the earth from the center of the universe came from astronomers, not church officials, and were primarily scientific, not theological in nature.[8] Galileo's condemnation was not so much a matter of clear scientific evidence contradicting biblical claims but of ambiguous scientific evidence provoking an intramural dispute within Catholicism over approaches to biblical interpretation, won by the conservative clerics. Moreover, Galileo was more a victim of the complex interplay of political circumstances, personal ambitions, and wounded pride than of the clash between science and religion.[9] Even the nineteenth-century conflicts surrounding Darwinian theory do not fit a simple science-versus-religion formula. The antagonists were, on the one side, persons who wished to retain an older, theologically grounded view of science and, on the other, advocates of a more thoroughly positivistic science. Scientists, as well as clerics, were represented on both sides of the debate, and neither camp was motivated solely by scientific considerations.[10] Nor can the twentieth-century controversy between strict creationists and evolutionists be reduced to the scenario of conservative Christians opposing science.

Instead, the creationists, some of whom are scientists themselves, specifically oppose the social, moral, and theological implications of human evolution.[11]

However one evaluates the historical data, today leaders in both science and religion often express a sense of mutual respect, even admiration, of the contributions of both fields. As a symbol of its changed perception of the world, in 1984 a Vatican commission acknowledged that church officials had erred in persecuting Galileo.[12] Even more significantly, in 1987 Pope John Paul II was instrumental in convening an international research conference at the Vatican Observatory to explore the relationship between theology and science. In a papal message issued in conjunction with the publication of the conference volume, the Pope described a changing relationship between religion and science leading towards greater mutual understanding and a gradual uncovering of common concerns.[13] According to the Pope, "It is crucial that this common search based on critical openness and interchange should not only continue but also grow and deepen in its quality and scope. For the impact each has on the course of civilization and on the world itself, cannot be overestimated, and there is so much that each can offer the other."[14] He called for a new movement of "unity with integrity" in which each discipline would preserve its autonomy and distinctiveness but would also be radically open to the discoveries and insights of the other.[15] His message encouraged theologians to integrate the results of science into their own theological agenda as a matter of some urgency and observed that the vitality and significance of theology will depend on its ability to incorporate these findings.[16] In a later statement touching on the nature of the relationship between science and theology, the Pope optimistically opined that "truth cannot contradict truth."[17] Indeed, this pontiff has been so interested in and supportive of science and religion dialogue that he might be characterized as the "science pope."

Stephen Jay Gould, the well-known Harvard paleontologist and a former elected president of AAAS, eloquently articulated the view that science and religion are complementary rather than conflicting. Gould, who characterized himself as an agnostic, claimed to have an abiding respect for religious traditions and a fascination for religion as a subject[18] and evinced considerable knowledge of church history and biblical exegesis.[19] His writings, particularly his book *Rocks of Ages,* argued that there was a need for tolerance and noninterference between the two realms. While he emphasized that science and religion are logically distinct and fully separate in styles of inquiry and goals, he emphasized the need of the individual to integrate insights from both so as to build a rich and full view of life:[20] "Science and religion should be equal, mutually respecting partners, each the master of its own domain and with each domain vital to human life in a different way."[21]

Most mainstream religious thinkers and probably the majority of scientists share this view of religion and science as independent and autonomous rather than conflicting realms. The prevailing approach reflects a belief that each discipline has its own domain and methods that can be justified on its own terms. Langdon Gilkey, who is a theologian, made the following distinctions in his testimony at a 1982 trial contesting an Arkansas law requiring the teaching of "creation science"[22] in high school biology classes: Science asks objective *how* questions, while religion asks *why* questions about meaning and purpose and about our ultimate origin and destiny. Science seeks to explain objective, public, repeatable data; religion is concerned about the existence of order and beauty in the world and the experiences of our inner life. Logical coherence and experimental adequacy provide the basis of authority in science; God constitutes the final authority for religion with revelation serving as the medium of enlightenment and insight. Science makes quantitative predictions that can be tested experimentally; religion uses symbolic and analogical language.[23] In much the same manner, the theologian John Haught, who is a contributor to this volume, characterizes this dichotomy as follows: "Science is about causes, religion about meaning. Science deals with solvable problems, religion with unsolvable mystery. Science answers specific questions about the workings of nature, whereas religion expresses concern about the ultimate ground of nature. Science is concerned with particular truths; religion is interested in explaining why we should seek truth at all."[24]

Stephen Jay Gould coined the expression "Non-Overlapping Magisteria," or NOMA, as the principle on which to base an appropriate relationship and to overcome and avoid false conflicts between the fields. He used the term *magisterium* as a domain where one form of teaching holds the appropriate tools for meaningful discourse and exclusive teaching authority.[25] According to Gould, the net or magisterium of science covers the empirical realm: what the universe is composed of (fact) and why it works this way (theory). Religion extends over the equally important, but fundamentally different, realm of human purposes, meaning, and value. "To cite the old clichés, science gets the age of rocks, and religion the rock of ages; science studies how the heavens go, religion how to go to heaven."[26] Respectful noninterference, based on the equal status and independence of the two magisteria, acknowledges their fundamental differences and capabilities, and it imposes requirements and limitations. Gould emphasized that science cannot resolve religious questions about God, meaning, and morality; nor can any factual discovery of science lead to ethical conclusions or to convictions about intrinsic meaning.[27] NOMA therefore challenges any attempt to read scripture as a scientific text while also precluding scientific entry into religion, particularly the claims of some scientists that scientific findings disprove the basis of religious belief.[28]

Nevertheless, acknowledgment of the distinctiveness and respective competencies of science and religion does not eliminate the need for meaningful dialogue and exploration of areas of common ground. In an oft-quoted statement, Albert Einstein, perhaps the greatest scientist of the twentieth century, noted that "science without religion is lame, religion without science is blind." Though he acknowledged that the realms of religion and science are clearly marked off from each other, he also pointed to strong reciprocal relationships and dependencies between them.[29] In a statement reminiscent of Einstein, Pope John Paul II observed that "science can purify religion from error and superstition; religion can purify science from idolatry and false absolutes. Each can draw the other into a wider world, a world in which both can flourish."[30]

Recently some religious thinkers and scientists have sought opportunities for constructive dialogue and mutual enrichment between the two fields. These initiatives sometimes reflect the desire to explore boundary questions, such as the relationship between Judeo-Christian religion and the development of modern science. Other advocates of greater interaction anticipate that scientific knowledge can broaden the horizons of religious faith while the perspectives of religious faith can contribute to a fuller understanding of the universe. A desire to explore issues that lie outside of the competence of one's own field often serves as a stimulus. Genetic scientists aware that their research raises ethical dilemmas and fundamental questions as to what it means to be human have sought to pursue these issues. Theologians have become interested in the implications of contemporary physics and cosmology for understanding the nature of the universe and formulating a theology consonant with the findings in these fields. Cosmologists seeking to go beyond the horizons of Big Bang cosmology to investigate the origins of the universe realize that they are dealing with the mysteries of creation long contemplated by religious thinkers.

There are also instances where serious social problems or public issues, such as the perception of an environmental crisis, can encourage cooperation. In 1990, a group of well-known scientists, among them Carl Sagan, Hans Bethe, Freeman Dyson, Stephen Jay Gould, and Jerome Wiesner, issued "An Open Letter to the Religious Community" to encourage a spirit of common cause and joint action to save the earth. Its text states that "as scientists, many of us have had profound experiences of awe and reverence before the universe. We understand that what is regarded as sacred is more likely to be treated with care and respect. Our planetary home should be so regarded."[31] Dissemination of the letter coincided with accelerated activity by many American faith communities and denominations on environmental issues. A group of religious leaders, among them Joseph Cardinal Bernadin, Archbishop Iakovos, Robert Schuller, and Elie Wiesel, therefore welcomed the letter as "a unique moment and opportunity in the relationship of science and religion."[32] This led to a major conference in May 1992 with over 150 religious leaders and scientists entitled the "Joint Appeal Between Religion and Science for the Environment." The conferees issued a statement affirming the possibilities, indeed the need, for collaboration between science and religion to address and resolve the environmental crisis.[33]

Additionally, a small number of theologians and scientists have gone beyond dialogue or accommodation to advocate some form of integration or synthesis between the contents of theology and science. The most traditional approach is natural theology where arguments for the existence of God are based on evidence of design in nature discoverable through science. Scientific discovery can also inspire a sense of the sacred, albeit one stripped of a sense of transcendence or the supernatural, as biologist Ursula Goodenough's book *The Sacred Depths of Nature*[34] shows. Interest in the anthropic principle, the claim that the initial conditions and laws of the universe appear to be "fine-tuned" for the possibilities of life, is a contemporary variant of natural theology. Several of those in the forefront of reformulating religious traditions in light of the findings from contemporary science have training in both science and theology, such as the Jesuit paleontologist Pierre Teihard de Chardin. Others (for example, theologians who work within the philosophical framework developed by Alfred North White-head, known as process theology) draw on both science and religion to formulate a comprehensive metaphysic.

In light of these developments, theologian Ted Peters suggests that the metaphor of revolution would be more appropriate than conflict to characterize the relationship between science and religion. He proposes the term *hypothetical consonance* for these revolutionary efforts to move beyond the boundaries of science and religion so as to explore areas where there may be overlap between what can be said scientifically about the natural world and what the theologian understands to be God's creation. Hypothetical consonance involves identifying common domains of question-asking, particularly the reasking of the "God-question" within the orbit of scientific discussions about the natural world. To be able to do so according to Peters, theologians must be willing to subject their doctrines and ideas to investigation and possible confirmation or disconfirmation by science. On the other side, but apparently not to the same extent, the consonance approach also asks scientists to be open to new religious learning.[35]

There are many tangible manifestations of what has been termed the "science and religion movement." Efforts to find common ground and understand better the implications of scientific methodologies and discoveries for theology and ethics are manifested on an academic level in course offerings, research, and literature. By one count, some 1000 courses on topics interfacing science and faith are now being offered by U.S. institutions of higher learning.[36] A series of centers and programs have been established, many within academic institutions, to promote dialogue and collaboration between scientists and religious thinkers. Pioneering examples include the Center for the Theology and the Natural Sciences at the Graduate Theological Union next to the University of California, Berkeley; the Zygon Center for Religion and Science at the Lutheran Seminary in Chicago; the Institute for Theological Encounter with Science and Technology (ITEST) in St. Louis; and the Faith and Science Exchange linked to the Boston Theological Institute. For the most part, the initiatives for these centers came from the field of religion, but in 1995 AAAS established a Program of Dialogue on Science, Ethics, and Religion[37] to promote understanding of science within the religious community, efforts at dialogue, and collaborative initiatives.

There are also initiatives reaching beyond the university and a specialized community of academics. Each summer the Institute on Religion in an Age of Science (IRAS), a membership organization a half century old, sponsors a conference in a science and religion format on Star Island off the coast of New Hampshire. The American Scientific Affiliation, established in 1941, provides a forum for evangelical scientists to consider the implications of science for their religious faith. Dozens of science and religion conferences and seminars take place each year. Some, like the 1997 "Epic of Evolution Conference," cosponsored by the AAAS and the Field Museum of Natural History in Chicago (which gave rise to this volume), draw a national audience and considerable media attention. The publication field abounds with journals and books interpreting the implications of scientific research for religion, ethics, and philosophy for both academic and broader audiences. *Science and Spirit* magazine, with a circulation of over 50,000 persons, provides a notable example of the latter.

SCIENCE AND RELIGION: CONTINUING CONFLICTS

Despite the constructive statements and creative initiatives taking place, the interaction of science and religion can still give rise to conflicts, particularly over the interpretation and teaching of evolution. Two groups remain locked in combat, one centered in the religious and the other in the scientific community. Both of them reject the principle of NOMA and contest the proper boundaries and the validity of the methods of science. Religious conservatives, particularly biblical fundamentalists or literalists, tend to treat scripture, particularly the Genesis account of creation, as a scientific text. On the other side, scientists, who are advocates of a position that has been termed *scientism,* and others who are militant scientific materialists deny the possibility of religious faith leading to any valid form of truth. It is important to note that this latter position does not characterize the whole of the scientific community. In one survey, for example, some four in ten of the scientists interviewed affirmed a very traditional conception of God and religion, a figure little changed since 1914.[38] Although some scientists adamantly reject conceptions of personal divinity, most seem inclined toward a separate spheres approach.

Fundamentalism arose in the early part of the twentieth century in the United States as a response to the uncertainties and insecurities of modern life. It represents an attempt to overcome the threats, historical relativism, the natural sciences, and the pressures of urbanization that modern life posed to the hitherto accepted certainties of scripture and religious dogma. One group of fundamentalists, biblical literalists, argues that since the Bible is divinely inspired and inerrant, it provides reliable scientific information as well as religious truth. This position contrasts with the view of the overwhelming majority of Jews and Christians, who throughout their history have acknowledged the influence of culture and historical contexts on biblical writings and who often give figurative and allegorical interpretations to problematic passages. One mainline denomination, the Presbyterian Church (U.S.A.), for example, has conducted three surveys with nationally representative samples of members, lay leaders, and ordained ministers that showed that very few Presbyterians believe the earth was created just a few thousand years ago and a majority of the respondents saw no contradiction between belief in God as creator and the theory of evolution (61 percent of members and 85 percent of clergy).[39]

In contrast with the scholars involved with the science and religion movement, conservative Christians from biblical literalist traditions promote an integration of religion and science termed *creation science,* a pseudoscience that seeks to appropriate science to religion. Whenever scientific findings and theories do not correspond with the Bible, particularly in regard to evolution, but also with respect to the creation of the universe, the origin of life, and other issues, they insist that the science must be wrong and religion correct.[40] This has many unfortunate repercussions, among them an effort to move science away from its strict falsification methodology and allow for supernatural explanations, something one commentator quite aptly characterized as a "supreme science stopper."[41] Ironically, literalists frequently misconstrue the intent and message of scripture as well by treating it as a scientific text.[42] Like many contemporary biblical scholars, Roger Timm underscores that Genesis was written to articulate a theological vision of God as Creator, not to present an objective description of how the universe was created. It shows a single God, transcending nature, unlike the mythologies of Israel's neighbors, who had theologies of many gods, each often identified with some aspect of nature. It stresses the goodness of God's creation and the position of humans as the crown of the creation, living in relationship with God.[43]

Commitment to a literal interpretation of the Genesis account (Gen. 1–2:4a), a position usually referred to as *creationism*, has given rise in this country to an emotional opposition to evolutionary theory and an effort to block the teaching of evolution in public schools.[44] In the early 1920s, following a crusade by creationists, several states forbade the teaching of evolution. Then in 1968 the Supreme Court declared these laws unconstitutional on First Amendment grounds. In response, a group of creationists sought to extract their religious affirmations from the biblical text and pass them off as a form of science, labeling their efforts as scientific creationism or creation science, so as to be able to pass legal review. Creation science purports to offer a scientific basis for an instantaneous creation of the universe and life over a six-day, twenty-four-hour human period, 6000 to 10,000 years ago. It generally entails a series of a priori commitments: (1) the creation of the universe out of nothing; (2) the insufficiency of mutation and natural selection to explain the origin and diversity of life; (3) the stability of species and the impossibility of one species evolving out of another; (4) a separate ancestry for apes and humans; (5) catastrophism, especially a worldwide flood, as the explanation for certain geological formations; and (6) a relatively recent formation of the earth (six to ten thousand years ago).[45]

Courts have overturned laws requiring the teaching of scientific creationism or creation science as violating the constitutional separation of church and state because creation science curriculum uses many phrases and ideas taken from scripture. When Arkansas and Louisiana passed laws in the late 1970s requiring that so-called creation science be given equal time in the science curriculum with biological evolution, in a landmark 1982 case dealing with the Arkansas law, the U.S. District Court also ruled that so-called creation science is not legitimate science based on scientific methodologies.[46] Subsequently, the Louisiana law was rejected by the U.S. Supreme Court on the grounds that it was promoting religion.

Because the terms are sometimes used interchangeably, it is important to stress that not all persons labeled as creationists are advocates of creation science and not all theists are creationists. Most religious believers can be characterized as theistic evolutionists who accept the basic scientific account of evolution, with the proviso that God has guided the process.

Historian Ronald Numbers divides creationists into two main camps: strict creationists, who interpret the days of Genesis literally, and progressive creationists, who construe the biblical days to be immense periods of time. Beliefs about the extent and nature of this divine role range considerably among strict and progressive creationists and other theists. At a minimum virtually all theists would attribute the creation of the universe and the emergence of life, and perhaps the human soul, to some form of direct or indirect divine intervention. However, the strict creationists claim a much greater direct divine involvement, extending over numerous acts of specific creation.[47]

Across the disciplinary divide, some aggressively skeptical and atheistic scientists claim that science necessarily conflicts with religion. In doing so, many in this group base their views on a caricature of religion, erroneously equating all religion with fundamentalism and assuming that most believers have the sophistication of ten-year-olds. Adherents of what has been variously termed *scientism* or scientific imperialism make an epistemological claim that there is one reality, the natural world and that science is the only reliable path to knowledge. Others go beyond an epistemological scientism to a metaphysical or ontological assertion that physical matter is the only or fundamental reality in the universe.[48] These scientific skeptics generally assume that modern science disproves religious belief in a purposeful universe created by a benevolent God. By extension, they denigrate religious insight as pseudoknowledge and even deny that religion offers any special expertise on moral questions.

Richard Dawkins, an Oxford zoologist and best-selling author writing for a broad general public, represents with relish the position that there are irreconcilable differences between science and religion. Opposing Gould's principle of NOMA, he argues that there is something patently and dishonestly self-serving in the tactic of claiming that religious beliefs are outside the domain of science. Because religions make what he terms existence claims, Dawkins proposes that religious beliefs and dogma should be subjected to scientific criticism.[49] In his many books, Dawkins delights in savaging traditional religion. *The Blind Watchmaker* puts forward a view of a universe without design or purpose: "Natural selection, the blind, unconscious, automatic process which Darwin discovered, and which we now know is the explanation for the existence and apparently purposeful form of all life, has no purpose in mind. It has no mind and no mind's eye. It does not plan for the future. It has no vision, no foresight, no sight at all. If it can be said to play the role of watchmaker in nature, it is the *blind* watchmaker."[50] The thesis of Dawkins's *The Selfish Gene* is that genes are the central evolutionary driver and that human beings, like all animals, are basically machines created by our genes. Taking the license of writing about genes as if they had conscious aims, he posits that genes control human behavior, "not directly with their fingers on puppet strings, but indirectly like the computer programmer."[51] In a characterization approximating Tennyson's famous phrase, "Nature red in tooth and claw," Dawkins hypothesizes that for a gene to be able to survive for millions of years in a highly competitive world it would have to be ruthlessly selfish. And for him, this gene selfishness usually gives rise to selfishness in individual behavior. "Much as we might wish to believe otherwise, universal love and the welfare of the species as a whole are concepts which simply do not make evolutionary sense."[52] Dawkins's reductionism and biological determinism extend to his interpretation of culture. In his scenario, in the struggle for survival genes produce brains and brains in turn give rise to a new kind of replicator, termed "memes," which serve as units of cultural transmission or mental entities. Dawkins treats the idea of God as a very old meme that probably originated many times by independent "mutation." He attributes its high survival value (i.e., its continued perpetuation across the generations) to its great psychological appeal as a "superficially plausible answer to deep and troubling questions about existence."[53]

Proponents of sociobiology (also known as evolutionary psychology and developmental or behavioral biology) and many geneticists share Dawkins's beliefs. A central tenet of the Harvard biologist Edward O. Wilson's various works is that natural selection shapes human perceiving, thinking, and acting: in other words, we are what we are because of our biology, specifically our genes. Wilson further contends that ethical norms, like other forms of behavior, are shaped by our genes.[54] In *Consilience* he claims that causal explanations of brain activity and evolution already explain most known facts about moral behavior.[55] This understanding of human nature does not leave much room for transcendence or religion. Wilson attributes the predisposition of religious belief, "the most complex and powerful force in the human mind and in all probability an ineradicable part of human nature," to various evolutionary advantages religious beliefs and membership confer.[56] Jay Glass, a neurobiologist, explains belief in God, religions, and the human disposition to praying as the biobehavioral imperative to be part of a dominance hierarchy. Glass describes God as a creation of our need to have a supreme being to whom to submit and asks whether members of a wolf pack, elk herd, or chimp troop also have a God (dominant male) to whom they pray (show submission) for the same purpose.[57] In *The Genetic Gods* John Avise comments that the over the last century the genetic gods would seem to have wrestled from the supernatural gods considerable authority over human affairs and suggests that little, if any room, remains for a metaphysical God.[58]

Some scientists disparage beliefs in God and meaning in the universe. The comment of Steven Weinberg, winner of the Nobel Prize for physics, in his book *The First Three Minutes,* "The more the universe seems comprehensible, the more it also seems pointless,"[59] is well known. He elaborated on his views in a presentation at the 1999 AAAS "Cosmic Questions Conference" arguing that prevalence of evil and misery proves that there are no signs of a benevolent designer. He stated that he was in favor of a dialogue between science and religion, but not a constructive dialogue. "Religion has done some good in the world, but on balance its effects on our lives have been awful . . . the peculiar contribution of religion throughout history has been to allow good people to do evil things."[60]

ISSUES SURROUNDING EVOLUTION

Charles Darwin's 1859 work *On the Origin of Species*, the treatise that gave rise to modern understandings of evolution, has been described as one of the most important books of science ever written. As the eminent biologist Theodosius Dobzansky has said, "Nothing in biology makes sense except in the light of evolution."[61] Evolution also constitutes a major theme or frame of reference for many other disciplines of contemporary science, including cosmology, geology, and physics, as well as biology.

But *On the Origin of Species* and Darwin's 1871 work, *The Descent of Man*, which extended his evolutionary theory to the human species, are more than just contributions to science. Darwinian theory has also had a profound impact on society well beyond the sciences. Commentators have noted that no other intellectual revolution in modern times (with the possible exception of the Copernican) so profoundly affected the way that people viewed themselves and their place in the universe.[62] Before Darwin, it had generally been assumed that nature was essentially static and unchanging. In the evolutionary view, nature is dynamic, changing, and historical in character. Previously, human beings had been considered to be set apart from the rest of nature, their unique status conferred by the capacity for reason and a special relationship with the Creator. Since Darwin, humanity has been understood to be part of nature, the product of a common evolutionary heritage. Prior to Darwin, the universe was assumed to manifest the intentional design of a Creator. Evolutionary biology emphasizes that the genetic variations that lead to change within and the differentiation of species occur randomly, thus assigning chance a central role in the dynamic of evolution. Traditional religious thought assumed that there is an ethical and moral order in nature as well as in human society. Darwinian thought portrays a struggle for survival in nature in which the majority of creatures and species suffer and lose out in the contest, seemingly revealing a basic cruelty in the universe, particularly toward the weak. At first glance this dynamic appears to diminish the role of the loving and compassionate God posited by biblical theism. The idea that humans emerged from an immensely long evolutionary process seems difficult to reconcile with claims that the universe was created for the benefit of human beings.

While evolution does present challenges of interpretation to theistic religions, as well as to Western culture's presumptions of a human-centered universe, the vast majority of mainstream religious communities in this country have accepted evolutionary theory and do not find a contradiction between evolutionary science and religious faith. They generally do so on the grounds that faith affirmations and scientific findings are autonomous, in other words a variant of the principle of NOMA. However, despite the importance of evolution to Western intellectual history during the past century and the issues it raises for traditional theistic religion, until recently evolution has received very little explicit attention from religious thinkers. On the one hand, religious histories acknowledge that "never since the scientific revolution completed by Newton has the humanistic and religious traditions of the West been confronted by a greater need for adjustment and reformulation."[63] On the other hand, only a small number of theologians from mainstream traditions have explicitly addressed the implications of evolution for traditional concepts and doctrines that assume a fixed and unchanging order of creation. Likewise, few theologians and even fewer religious communities make a serious effort to reconcile or integrate evolution with core theological tenets of their faith.

That is not to say that there are no creative and meaningful expressions of theology in evolutionary terms. Process theology is one important example of an approach that is fully consistent with, in fact depends on, an evolutionary perspective.[64] Philip Hefner's *The Human Factor*[65] sacralizes the process of evolution and proposes that God works through evolutionary mechanisms. Like several other thinkers, Hefner presents a biocultural evolutionary paradigm of human beings as two-natured creatures living at the confluence of two major streams of evolutionary information, the genetic and the cultural. A recently published book, *God after Darwin: A Theology of Evolution*,[66] written by John Haught, addresses the challenge that the evolutionary character of reality presents to an intelligent and credible belief in God. The book shows how evolutionary biology can enrich and deepen theological conviction. Haught argues that neo-Darwinian theory, instead of being hostile to religion, provides a fertile setting for a mature reflection on the nature of God. Holmes Rolston, III's *Genes, Genesis and God*[67] integrates biology, philosophy, and theology to evaluate the implications and limitations of recent evolutionary theories for our understanding of science, ethics, and religion. Rolston challenges sociobiological orthodoxy in arguing that genetic processes are not blind, selfish, and contingent and that nature is not value free. As Rolston interprets the role of God, the divine spirit is the giver of life and the metaphysical environment in, with, and under the natural (and later the cultural) environment who orchestrates self-organizing systems and who serves as a force that lures life upward and introduces new possibilities.[68]

But these innovative theologies are few and far between. Moreover, they have only just begun to reach people in the pews or even most of the clergy for that matter.

As further evidence of the concordance between mainstream religion and evolutionary science, I would like to point to the position of the Roman Catholic Church. As early as 1950 in the encyclical *Humani generis* Pope Pius XII defended evolution as a proper field of scientific inquiry and stated that there was no inherent opposition between evolution and the doctrine of the faith about humanity and human vocation. Nevertheless, there were qualifications. The encyclical considered evolution only a serious hypothesis worthy of investigation, not scientific fact.[69] In October 1996 Pope John Paul II made headlines when in his annual message to the Pontifical Academy of Sciences he affirmed that on the basis of knowledge forthcoming in the past half century since *Humani generis* was written biological evolution could be accepted as "more than a hypothesis." In his statement he defended the evidence for evolution and the theory's consistency with Catholic teachings. While he acknowledged that at first sight there are apparent contradictions between Catholic doctrine and scientific evolution, he also expressed confidence that "truth cannot contradict truth."[70]

Recently several prominent organizations in the scientific community have also taken care to express a view that there is not an inherent conflict between evolution and religious belief. A 1998 National Academy of Sciences (NAS) report promoting the teaching of evolution in public schools begins with the statement "Whether God exists or not is a question about which science is neutral." At the news conference at which the report was released, members of the drafting panel emphasized that most religions have no conflict with evolution and that many scientists are religious. Speaking for the National Academy, its president Bruce

Alberts said that "there are many outstanding members of this academy who are very religious people, people who believe in evolution, many of them biologists."[71] Similarly, in 1997 the National Association of Biology Teachers revised its "Statement on the Teaching of Evolution" to remove the words *unsupervised* and *impersonal*, which to some implied atheism.[72]

Voices for Evolution, a compilation of statements published by the National Center for Science Education, includes texts from 15 major religious organizations supporting the teaching of evolution in public schools.[73] These include the Roman Catholic Church, the United Methodist Church, the United Presbyterian Church (U.S.A.), the Lutheran World Federation, the Episcopal Church, the American Jewish Congress, and the Central Conference of American Rabbis.

However, just as religious thinkers until recently failed to deal explicitly with the theological implications of the evolutionary process, religious communities typically do not do a good job of disseminating their views on the lack of conflict between evolution and religious commitment. Nor have they disseminated widely their statements supporting the teaching of evolution. Thus the vast majority of their members tend to be aware of the vocal objections of creationists but are unaware that their religious community disagrees very fundamentally with these claims.

The relative silence of mainstream religious communities leaves a vacuum effectively filled by the opponents of evolution. As on many other social issues, those who are passionately invested in a cause are willing to expend far more time and energy than those who are more peripherally involved. Creationists have been willing to pursue election to school boards while religious proponents of evolutionary science have remained on the sidelines. In addition, passionate advocates often make the kind of emotional and extreme statements that the press finds so newsworthy. Thus, opponents of evolution have received considerable media attention. And in the absence of a more moderate religious voice, the media have come to equate creationism with the position of the majority of the religious communities, assuming that it is the only and necessary option for biblical theism. Media coverage of the "education wars" in turn has become something of a self-fulfilling prophecy by shaping public perception of the issue and the way in which the overwhelming majority of religious Americans relate to evolution. As we are reminded by the media, nearly all Americans (95 percent according to Gallup survey data) affirm a belief in God, and this country is one of the most religious societies in the modern world. One consequence may be that many Americans are reluctant to express views publicly that are considered to be agnostic or atheistic for fear of social isolation. By equating Darwinism and science with atheism and theism with anti-Darwinism, media coverage may have the effect of encouraging support for the creationist option just as it has in maintaining the conformity of public beliefs in other areas.[74] Similarly, many scientists may be reluctant to express religious beliefs publicly for fear of professional ostracism.

These trends are reflected in opinion surveys taken during the past twenty years regarding views on evolution and creation, many of which have used similar instruments so as to be able to compare results. Despite rising levels of education, Americans' beliefs about evolution and human origins have remained remarkably stable during this period. Typically these probes show that, although only a minority identify themselves as biblical literalists, nearly half of adult Americans reject the scientific theory of evolution in favor of some form of a creationist explanation.[75] Surveys also reveal an alarming degree of ignorance or lack of acceptance of common scientific facts related to evolution by the general public.[76] Currently, some 44 percent of Americans identify themselves with the biblical, creationist worldview that humans were created specially by God 10,000 years ago; another 39 percent subscribe to the theistic evolutionist position that "humans developed over millions of years from less advanced forms of life, but God guided this process"; and only 10 percent endorse the position that "humans developed over millions of years from less advanced forms of life. God had no part in this process."[77] In international comparisons of belief, American adults were ranked as the least likely of any of the 21 nationalities surveyed to accept the theory of evolution.[78] Ominously, in a recent poll, 68 percent of respondents favored teaching creationism along with evolution in public schools, and 40 percent supported teaching creationism instead of evolution.[79]

The August 1999 decision by the Kansas Board of Education to delete mention of evolution from the state's science curriculum standards along with related concepts, such as Big Bang cosmology, natural selection, and common ancestors shows how the assumption of conflict with religion can affect science education. The standards adopted at that time did not prohibit the teaching of evolution, but effectively discouraged doing so by eliminating evolution from the state assessment tests evaluating students' performance in various grades. This decision was likely to embolden conservative school districts in Kansas to end all teaching of evolution and, even where that did not happen, made it increasingly difficult for science teachers to justify time spent on evolution. The Kansas decision was also likely to intimidate many science teachers, who already considered themselves under pressure to accommodate to antievolutionary views.[80] It also encouraged other states to follow the Kansas model as a way to avoid legal review. However, Kansas voted in the election of 2000 to replace several of the antievolution members of the State Board of Education with persons supporting the teaching of evolution. As a result the originally proposed set of science education standards in which evolutionary theory was an integral part were adopted by the new Board in early 2001.

Kansas is but the latest state to experience efforts by biblical literalists to restrict or eliminate the teaching of evolution in public schools. In the 1990s, school boards in at least seven states (Arizona, Alabama, Illinois, New Mexico, Texas, Kansas, and Nebraska) tried to remove evolution from the state science standards or water down the concepts. Ironically, the effort to develop national science education standards has brought increased attention to the teaching of biology and thereby accelerated the activity of opponents of evolution. In 1995, Alabama mandated that all biology books used in public schools be given a sticker describing evolution as "a controversial theory some scientists present as a scientific explanation for the origin of living things." The disclaimer adds, "No one was present when life first appeared on earth. Therefore, any statement about life's origins should be considered as theory, not fact."[81] In 1997, the Texas Board of Education nearly voted to replace all biology books in the state with new ones that do not mention evolution. Bills were introduced in state legislatures in Georgia and Ohio that required educators who teach about evolution to also teach the creationists' critique of evidence inconsistent with it. Even in communities and states where the curriculum does not explicitly prohibit the teaching of evolution, science teachers, particularly biologists, are reluctant to do so because they anticipate they will come under attack.[82]

This trend and the decision in Kansas, described in an editorial in *Science* magazine as an "intellectual cleansing atrocity"[83] and subsequently reversed in 2001 represent a tragedy for the teaching of science. In a country whose students already compare unfavorably with the science achievement of students in other economically advanced nations, removing all mention of evolution and related concepts can only further reduce the level of scientific understanding. As one frustrated member of the Kansas committee that worked on revising the science curriculum stated, if you believe the earth is only 10,000 years old, how can you understand geologic time, plate tectonics, or even mineral exploration?[84] If the effort to eliminate evolution from the science standards had prevailed, Kansas students, and those of any other state that followed the Kansas example, would have been woefully unprepared to take national science examinations or to go on in any field requiring a strong scientific background.

Like the strict creationists, the Kansas decision also misconstrued the nature of scientific theory. For scientists the "theory" is the term used for explanations of structures and processes in nature supported by broad bodies of evidence and held with a high degree of confidence. Although in science all theories are provisional and can always be refined or replaced in light of new data and understanding, the evidence for unity of life by common descent over billions of years is overwhelming. The theory of evolution is one of the best-supported theories in all of science. Unfortunately, the Kansas board held that evolution is a speculation about the past that no observer can verify directly. By extension, this form of reasoning would eliminate not only the theory of evolution but almost all of science, including the atomic theory of matter and the heliocentric model of the solar system.[85]

TOWARD A MORE MEANINGFUL RELATIONSHIP

Clearly a coherent and meaningful worldview requires that we bring science and religion into better dialogue, and there is a particular need to do so on the topic of evolutionary theory. Thoughtful communication across the science and religion cultural gulf is essential to interpret the implications of the evolutionary paradigm.

As significant as the pioneering initiatives to foster dialogue across the science and religion boundaries are, they have involved small numbers of people, and the insights garnered from them have not been well disseminated. The interface between science and religion appears on the way to becoming a separate subdiscipline within the fields of religion and ethics rather than a perspective pervading teaching and research across the disciplines. Those who are interested in dialogue or accommodating theology and ethics to science are also becoming specialists in a special academic niche. And very few scientists, particularly bench researchers, are willing to take the time away from their scientific endeavors to participate in such dialogue.

I believe that the public skirmishes over evolution derive in large part from a vacuum in interpretation showing ways of reconciling the science with religious faith. As Eugenie Scott, the Executive Director of the National Center for Science Education notes, "Antievolutionism in the US and Canada is sustained by the idea that evolution and religion (Christianity) are incompatible."[86] Thus, railing against creationists or even attacking unwise decisions by school boards will not resolve the problem. Instead, at least some of that energy needs to be invested in religious and scientific collaborations leading to broader understanding of science and more sustained efforts by religious thinkers to deal with the theological issues that evolution raises.

Further dialogue and collaboration is in the interests of both communities. Unless religious thinkers are able to undertake scientifically informed theological and ethical analysis, they risk becoming irrelevant to modern society. Scientific knowledge can broaden the horizons of religious faith and enable people of faith to interpret scientific discoveries within a framework of religious meaning. In the public sphere, the near silence of the religious mainstream in the face of the vocal fundamentalist and biblical literalist positions is discrediting the entire religious community, as well as contributing to the scientific illiteracy of their members. That virtually all mainstream religious thinkers and religious communions nominally affirm evolutionary theory is not sufficient. They need to deal explicitly with the implications of evolution for faith and religiously informed values. Otherwise, persons of faith will assume, at best, that science is irrelevant to them and, at worse, that there is an inherent conflict between science and religion over evolution. To foster the needed engagement will require that many more theologians and religious thinkers become scientifically aware and willing to address scientifically based issues, and particularly to turn their attention to evolution. It also will call for a sense of theological humility, comparable to that required by science itself, in the face of scientific discoveries, or, to put it another way, an openness to rethinking and revising religious doctrines dependent on worldviews that are no longer scientifically viable. And I say this as an ordained minister and a religious ethicist.

On the other side of the dialogue, it is also in the self-interest of scientists to deal seriously with interpretive issues, particularly related to evolutionary science, and to do so in a way respectful of the broad spectrum of religious belief. Interpretation of evolution necessitates a deep dialogue between members of the science and religion communities: Dialogue by its very nature must be two sided. Complicating the already complex nature of such multidisciplinary initiatives on evolution, biologists generally seem considerably less interested in participating in such collaborative efforts than members of other fields of science. Serious dialogue will also require a changed mind-set among scientists. Scientists will need to distinguish very clearly between methodological reductionism, the scientific method of breaking complex things down analytically so as to study them at the simpler level of their constituent parts, and metaphysical reductionism, the claim that equates the reality of complex things with the sum of their parts. It also requires that scientists exhibit greater humility, particularly in public pronouncements. Writing in *Discover* magazine in 1998, the president of the American Association of Physical Anthropologists reminded his colleagues that "many scientists are atheists or agnostics who want to believe that the natural world they study is all there is, and being only human, they try to persuade themselves that science gives them the grounds for that belief. . . . It's an honorable belief, but it isn't a research finding."[87] If scientists continue to disdain religious belief, there will be continuing opposition to the teaching of evolution in public schools and the crisis of scientific illiteracy will eventually threaten the future of the scientific enterprise in this country. And I state this as someone who is also a Ph.D. social scientist and a staff member of a scientific association.

EPIC OF EVOLUTION CONFERENCE AND VOLUME

Given the situation just described, when the AAAS Program of Dialogue on Science, Ethics, and Religion was established, evolutionary theory was designated as one of its priorities for all of the reasons identified in this chapter. The Program quickly set up a Web site on evolution that provides access to scientific and interpretative resources on evolution. It also produced an edited volume entitled *An Evolving Dialogue: Scientific, Historical, Philosophical and Theological Perspectives on Evolution.*[88] But both of these efforts were based on existing work. However, we also wanted to stimulate fresh new thinking and to attract attention to existing constructive efforts of dialogue on evolution across the science and religion boundary so as to counter the stereotypes in the media. This suggested the possibility of organizing a conference in a dialogue format, preferably in a high-visibility venue, like a major museum.

This then brings us to the 1997 Epic of Evolution Conference and the essays in this volume. The conference was organized in collaboration with the Center for Cultural Understanding and Change of the Field Museum in Chicago and endorsed by the Chicago Academy of Sciences and the Zygon Center for Religion and Science. It took place on November 12 through 14 in the Field Museum and had some 600 participants. The conference was also videotaped to provide a foundation for developing a set of educational video resources on evolution and religion that are now available from AAAS.

Perhaps something should be said about the name of the event. The title "The Epic of Evolution" originated with the biologist E. O. Wilson and had been the title of an earlier conference sponsored by the Institute for Religion in an Age of Science (IRAS) on Star Island, New Hampshire, the site of its annual summer meetings. In using the title, the Program of Dialogue did not intend to convey that evolutionary history was an epic in the usual sense of the word. Nor did the

Program endorse proposals by IRAS members and others that evolution become the basis of a new religious story or myth. Finally, the conference was not intended to promote a single interpretation of evolution but instead to provide insight into the richness of a variety of types of interpretations at different levels of existence: cosmic, biological, human, and cultural.

The AAAS Epic of Evolution Conference was a unique, perhaps historic event, attempting a meaningful public dialogue between science, religion, ethics, and philosophy on the subject of evolution. There have been many conferences on evolution, even a few which have dealt with evolution in a very broad multidisciplinary framework, and here I would like to acknowledge the pioneering work of IRAS. But none, at least to my knowledge, have systematically placed the exploration of the findings of science with respect to the development of the cosmos, life, humankind, and human culture, step by step in a dialogue with religious perspectives. Each session included both scientific presentations and philosophical and/or religious reflections from a variety of perspectives. The conference and this volume provide a series of presentations in a wide range of specializations, including cosmology, evolutionary and cell biology, paleontology, anthropology, ecology, philosophy, history, and theology. This provides an intellectual feast of a multidisciplinary scientific approach to evolution from cosmic origins, through the evolution of life on earth, the appearance of *Homo sapiens,* and the evolution of culture, society, religion, and morality with religious reflections upon each component.

NOTES

1. Eugenie C. Scott, "The 'Science and Religion Movement': An Opportunity for Improved Public Understanding of Science?" *Skeptical Inquirer* 23 (July/August 1999): 29–31.

2. The original name, the Program of Dialogue Between Religion and Science, was revised in 1999 to reflect the work the Program was doing that involved an ethical dimension.

3. David C. Lindberg, "Introduction," in David C. Lindberg and Ronald L. Numbers, eds., *God and Nature: Historical Essays on the Encounter between Christianity and Science* (Berkeley and Los Angeles: University of California Press), p. 10.

4. Alfred North Whitehead, *Science and the Modern World* (New York: Macmillan, 1925), pp. 12–13.

5. Lindberg, "Introduction," p. 4.

6. Frank M. Turner, "The Victorian Conflict between Science and Religion: A Professional Dimension," *Isis* 69 (1978): 356–376.

7. Lindberg, "Introduction," pp. 1–3.

8. Ibid., p. 11.

9. William R. Shea, "Galileo and the Church," in David C. Lindberg and Ronald L. Numbers, eds., *God & Nature: Historical Essays on the Encounter between Christianity and Science* (Berkeley and Los Angeles: University of California Press, 1986), pp. 114–135, particularly p. 132.

10. Lindberg, "Introduction," p. 14.

11. Ibid., p. 14.

12. Ian Barbour, *Religion in an Age of Science: The Gifford Lectures,* Vol. I (New York: HarperCollins, 1991), p. 8.

13. "Message of His Holiness John Paul II," Robert John Russell, William R. Stoeger, and George V. Coynes, S.J., eds., *John Paul II on Science and Religion: Reflections on the View from Rome* (Vatican City State: Vatican Observatory Publications, 1990), pp. m4–7.

14. Ibid., pp. m4–5.

15. Ibid., pp. m8–9.

16. Ibid., p.m12.

17. Pope John Paul II, "Evolution and the Living God," presented in 1996 the Pontifical Academy of Sciences and reprinted in Ted Peters, ed., *Science and Theology: The New Consonance* (Boulder, Colorado: Westview Press, 1998), p. 149.

18. Gould, *Rocks of Ages,* pp. 8, 59.

19. Ibid., pp. 130–131.

20. Ibid., p. 59.

21. Stephen Jay Gould, "Dorothy, It's Really Oz," *Time* 154, August 23, 1999, p. 59.

22. Creation science is the dubious claim that there is scientific evidence for the recent creation of the world so as to support literal interpretations of relevant portions of scripture.

23. Langdon Gilkey, *Creationism on Trial* (Minneapolis: Winston Press, 1985), pp. 108–116.

24. John F. Haught, *Science and Religion: From Conflict to Conversation* (New York: Paulist Press), p. 15.

25. Gould, *Rocks of Ages,* p. 5.

26. Ibid., p. 6.

27. Ibid., pp. 13–19; Gould, "Dorothy, It's Really Oz," p. 59.

28. Gould, *Rocks of Ages,* p. 93.

29. Albert Einstein, "Science and Religion," delivered to a conference in 1940 and reprinted in James Huchingson, ed., *Religion and the Natural Sciences: The Range of Engagement* (Orlando: Harcourt Brace Jovanovich College Publishers, 1993), p. 149.

30. Ibid., p. m13.

31. "An Open Letter to the Religious Community," dated January 1990. This letter is available from the Science Office of the National Religious Partnership for the Environment, P.O. Box 9105, Cambridge, Massachusetts 02238.

32. Peter W. Bakken, Joan Gibb Engel, and J. Ronald Engel, *Ecology, Justice, and Christian Faith: A Critical Guide to the Literature* (Westport, CT: Greenwood Press, 1995), p. 4.

33. "Declaration of the Mission to Washington: Joint Appeal by Religion and Science for the Environment," reprinted in Roger S. Gottlieb, ed., *This Sacred Earth: Religion, Nature, Environment* (New York and London: Routledge, 1996), pp. 640–642.

34. Ursula Goodenough, *The Sacred Depths of Nature* (New York: Oxford University Press, 1998).

35. Peters, "Science and Theology: Toward Consonance," pp. 11–12, 18–19.

36. Edward J. Larson and Larry Witham, "Scientists and Religion in America," *Scientific American* 281 (September 1999): 89.

37. When initially established the name was the Program of Dialogue Between Science and Religion.

38. Larson and Witham, "Scientists and Religion in America," p. 90.

39. Research Services, "Science, Technology, and Faith—The November 1998 Survey," Louisville: Presbyterian Church (U.S.A.): 11–12.

40. Haught, *Science and Religion,* pp. 11–13.

41. Scott, "The 'Science and Religion Movement,'" p. 31.

42. Roger E. Timm, "Scientific Creationism and Biblical Theology," in Ted Peters, ed., *Cosmos as Creation: Theology and Science in Consonance* (Nashville: Abingdon Press, 1989), p. 253.

43. Ibid., p. 254.

44. Ronald L. Numbers, *The Creationists* (Berkeley: University of California Press, 1993).

45. Ibid., pp. 248–249.

46. *McLean v. Arkansas Board of Education* (1982) 529 F. Supp. 1255, 50.

47. Ronald L. Numbers, "The Creationists," in Lindberg and Numbers, *God & Nature,* pp. 391–392.

48. Ibid., pp. 4–8.

49. Richard Dawkins, "You Can't Have It Both Ways: Irreconcilable Differences," *Skeptical Inquirer* (July/August 1999): pp. 62–64.

50. Richard Dawkins, *The Blind Watchmaker* (New York and London: W.W. Norton & Company, Inc., 1986, 1987), p. 5.

51. Richard Dawkins, *The Selfish Gene* (Oxford and New York: Oxford University Press, 1976, 1978), p. 56.

52. Ibid., p. 2.

53. Ibid., p. 207.

54. Edward O. Wilson, *On Human Nature* (Cambridge: Harvard University Press, 1978), p. 208.

55. Edward O. Wilson, *Consilience: The Unity of Knowledge* (New York: Alfred A. Knopf, 1998).

56. Wilson, *On Human Nature,* p. 169.

57. Jay D. Glass, *The Animal within Us: Lessons about Life from our Animal Ancestors* (Corona del Mar, CA: Donington Press, Ltd., 1998), pp. 147–148.

58. Avise, *The Genetic Gods,* pp. 208–217.

59. Steven Weinberg, *The First Three Minutes: A Modern View of the Origin of the Universe* (New York: Basic Books, Inc., 1977, 1988), p. 154.

60. Steven Weinberg, "A Universe with No Designer," *Cosmic Questions: Annals of the New York Academy of Science, No. 950,* James B. Miller, ed. (New York: New York Adacemy of Science, 2001), p. 174.

61. Theodosius Dobzhansky, "Nothing in Biology Makes Sense Except in the Light of Evolution," *American Biological Teacher* 35 (1973): 125–129.

62. Michael Denton, *Evolution: A Theory in Crisis* (Bethesda, MD: Adler & Adler, 1986), p. 67.

63. Sydney E. Ahlstrom, *A Religious History of the American People,* Vol. 2 (New Haven, CT: Yale University Press, 1975), p. 229.

64. Ewert H. Cousins, *Process Theology* (New York: Newman Press, 1971).

65. Philip Hefner, *The Human Factor: Evolution, Culture, and Religion* (Minneapolis: Fortress Press, 1993).

66. John F. Haught, *God after Darwin: A Theology of Evolution* (Boulder, CO: Westview Press, 1999).

67. Holmes Rolston, III, *Genes, Genesis and God: Values and their Origins in Natural and Human History* (Cambridge: Cambridge University Press, 1999).

68. Ibid., pp. 365–367.

69. Pope John Paul II, "Evolution and the Living God," pp. 149–150.

70. Ibid., p. 149.

71. Larson and Witham, "Scientists and Religion in America," p. 91.

72. Ibid.

73. Molleen Matsumura, ed., *Voices for Evolution* (Berkeley: The National Center for Science Education, 1995).

74. George Bishop, "The Religious Worldview and American Beliefs About Human Origins," *The Public Perspective* (August/September 1998): 43.

75. Ibid., p. 39.

76. National Center for Science Education, "Science and Religion in America (Poll and Survey Data)," photocopy made available in July 1999.

77. Bishop, "The Religious Worldview and American Beliefs about Human Origins," p. 40.

78. Ibid., p. 41.

79. "Doubting Darwin," *The New York Times,* August 15, 1999, p. C4. This source was a CNN/USA Today/Gallup Poll conducted June 25–27, 1999.

80. Pam Belluck, "Board for Kansas Deletes Evolution from Curriculum," *The New York Times,* August 12, 1999, pp. A1, A13.

81. Ibid., p. A13.

82. Hanna Rosin, "Creationism Evolves," *The Washington Post,* August 8, 1999, pp. A1, A22.

83. R. Brooks Hanson and Floyd E. Bloom, "Fending off Furtive Strategists," *Science* 285, September 17, 1999: 1847.

84. Brad Williamson, "I Teach, Therefore I Worry, in Kansas," *The Washington Post,* August 29, 1999, pp. B1, B5.

85. George Johnson, "In the Beginning, It's a Fact: Faith and Theory Collide Over Evolution," *The New York Times,* August 15, 1999, p. C1.

86. Scott, "The 'Science and Religion Movement,'" p. 31.

87. Matt Cartmill, "Oppressed by Evolution," *Discover,* March 1998, p. 83.

88. James B. Miller, ed., *An Evolving Dialogue: Scientific, Historical, Philosophical and Theological Perspectives on Evolution* (Washington, DC: American Association for the Advancement of Science, 1998).

3 Cosmic Evolution

Joel Primack   *Department of Physics, University of California–Santa Cruz*

My topics are evolution on the grand scale and how to picture the entire universe. My goal is to try to provide images of the universe that are consistent with what we now know. I will first discuss some older pictures of the universe and then introduce the geography of the universe as we currently understand it. I will summarize the evidence for the Hot Big Bang, the modern theory of the beginning of the universe. Then I will tell our best modern story of the evolution of the universe, according to the standard theory. Finally, I will present a unique way of visualizing the universe as a whole.

OLDER PICTURES OF THE UNIVERSE

There have been countless pictures of the universe in different cultures (Figure 3.1). One of the most common, used by peoples as varied as Nigerian, Hindu, Chinese, and Northern European, has been the symbol of a snake swallowing its tail. The biblical Middle East, on the other hand, had not so much a symbol as a picture of what they believed was the real structure of the world.

The Old Testament picture was of water below the land, flat earth, and a solid dome called the firmament holding up the water of the sky. This picture is presented in the first of the two Biblical creation stories (Gen. 1.1–2:4a). Then a little later there is the Noah story, where "the windows of heaven" open as well as "the foundations of the deep," and waters flood the land. This is not an ordinary rain but a cosmic catastrophe—God is changing the organization of the cosmos with the flood. But you cannot really understand this biblical story unless you know the picture of the universe that people had in mind in the ancient Middle East, according to stories told for thousands of years.

The Medieval picture had the moon, sun, planets, and stars riding on concentric spheres all revolving daily around the earth at the center. This was based on Greek ideas. It is completely different from the biblical picture but was not regarded as being in contradiction to it. The Newtonian picture is of a vast, infinite space in which stars are scattered randomly. Newtonian space is an arena, and time is absolute. What is our modern picture?

THE GEOGRAPHY OF THE VISIBLE UNIVERSE

One of the ways to visualize the modern universe is by a series of cosmic leaps (Figure 3.2).

We know that we live on the third rock from the sun, the third of the rocky planets that are the inner planets of the solar system. The fourth is Mars. Then

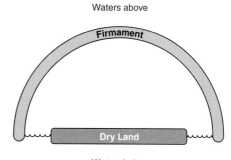

(a) Traditional Uroboros

(b) Biblical

M. C. Escher's "Cubic Space Division"
© 2002 Cordon Art B.V. — Baarn — Holland.
All rights reserved.

(c) Medieval

(d) Newtonian

FIGURE 3.1   *Traditional pictures of the universe. (**3.1a** From* Antique works of art from Benin, *Augustus Pitt-Rivers (London, 1900), reprinted (New York: Dover Publications, 1976), p. 37, plate 18, figure 102.* **3.1b** *From* The Disappearance of God: A Divine Mystery, *Richard Elliott Friedman (Little, Brown and Co., 1995), Figure 1, p. 232. Used with permission.* **3.1c** *From Peter Apian,* Cosmographicus liber, *ed. Gemma Frisius (Antwerp, 1533) in* The Cosmological Glass: Renaissance Diagrams of the Universe *(San Marino, CA: The Henry E. Huntington Library, 1977), Figure 28, p. 38.)*

comes the asteroid belt, then four giant gaseous planets, small icy Pluto, and the much smaller icy comets. Light takes about half a day to cross the solar system, but it takes four years to get to the nearest star, and 100,000 years to cross the Milky Way (our galaxy). We live about two-thirds of the way out from the center of the Milky Way, near one of the spiral arms of our fairly large but typical spiral galaxy. Our galaxy is one of the two big galaxies of the thirty or so galaxies we call the Local Group, which is about 3 million light years across.

Hardly any galaxies are isolated. They usually come in little groups, or bigger groups, or clusters, which are then grouped into superclusters with voids in

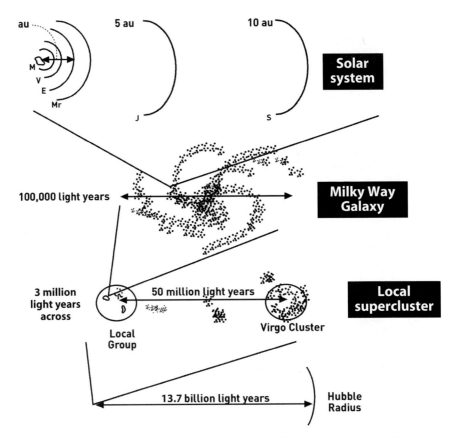

FIGURE 3.2   The "cosmography" of the universe. (au = astronomical unit—distance from Sun to Earth.)

between. The Local Group itself is part of a very large collection of roughly 10,000 galaxies that we call the Local Supercluster. About 50 million light years away from us, there is a cluster of perhaps 1000 galaxies, called the Virgo Cluster, which is more or less the center of the Local Supercluster. And all of this is but a dot on the scale of the whole visible universe—everything we can see out to the Hubble Radius.

How far is that? Well, we think that the universe started about 13.7 billion years ago. So we cannot see any farther back than about 13.7 billion light years. As we look out in space, we look back in time. In order to picture the universe, we have to think in both space and time. Now that is a tricky thing to do. Let me try to give you a sense of how you can picture that.

First, as we look back in space, we see light that has been traveling through expanding space. As space expands, the wavelength of the light expands. When we see it, the wavelength is bigger—sometimes much bigger. The red light in our spectrum has a bigger wavelength than blue light, and so this increase in wavelength is called "redshift." The amount of redshift tells us how much the universe expanded while the light was traveling.

You can picture space in many different ways, but spacetime you can only picture by slicing it. If you want to make a picture in two dimensions, you have to just represent two dimensions. Let one dimension, the radial distance outward, represent time. And the other dimension, around, represents space. If you want to imagine a second dimension of space, think of these circles as representing spheres that come out of this two-dimensional surface. But the full three dimensions of space and one dimension of time, a four-dimensional picture, we cannot represent on two dimensions. So think of a slice through it (Figure 3.3).

The first circle (dashed lines) represents all of space at an early time. Now consider a later time, let us say today. The point where the line labeled "lightcone" crosses another similar line represents "us"—our galaxy, now. We look back in time as we look out in space along our lightcone, and we see a galaxy as it was a long time ago. The light was emitted when the galaxy was far away from our galaxy. That distance is labeled "emission distance." The light then traveled toward us as space expanded. The galaxy that emitted the light is now farther away than when it emitted it, because space has expanded. Figure 3.3 also shows its distance now as we receive the light ("reception distance"). Note that at early times the lightcone approaches the origin of coordinates (the "Big Bang").

THE THREE PILLARS OF THE BIG BANG

Why should anybody believe that this curious picture is accurate? There are basically three main arguments in favor of this standard Big Bang picture: the Hubble expansion, the cosmic background radiation, and the abundance of the light

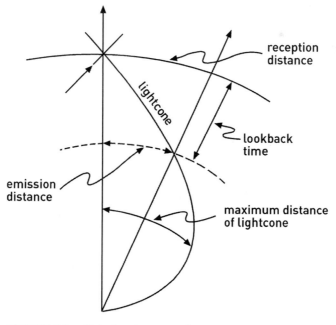

FIGURE 3.3   *Picturing the expanding universe.*

elements. I am going to go through these arguments in a little bit of detail. The conclusion is going to be that the universe, when it started, was filled with hot, dense, and very homogeneous gas.

The Hubble Expansion

The first piece of evidence is based on the Doppler effect. If you have a light source that is moving toward an observer, the light waves are squeezed together. To an observer watching from the opposite side, from which the source is moving away, the wavelength is expanded. We all have heard this effect. When an ambulance is coming toward us, we hear the sound or the siren at a higher pitch. As the vehicle passes us, the sound drops in pitch. This was demonstrated by the Dutch meteorologist Christopher Buijs-Ballot in 1845 by having trained musicians stand on the side of a railroad track while other musicians on a passing train played particular notes. The notes sounded sharp as the train approached and flat as it receded, just as Doppler's theory had proposed.

What makes this useful for astronomy is that chemical elements have characteristic energies. Hydrogen is the simplest of all. There is a certain characteristic pattern of energies, so that there are certain characteristic kinds of light that are emitted when transitions between energy levels take place. Light of characteristic colors is emitted when there is a transition downward, and the same wavelengths are absorbed when there is a transition upward. The pattern is unique for each chemical element. Light from a star like the sun has particular absorption lines indicating the presence of certain elements (for example, sodium). If you heat sodium, you see these same bright lines emitted as you see being absorbed in sunlight. And it is the pattern that is important. Now if you see those very same lines, but with the wrong colors, with the colors shifted, then you know that the source is moving toward you or away from you. If they are shifted toward the blue, then the source is moving toward you. If they are shifted toward the red, the source is moving away from you. This is the Doppler effect for light. And this is how we can measure the speed with which galaxies are moving toward or away from us.

Does this mean that we are at the center of an expanding system? Well, yes it does. Does this mean we are in an unusual position? No. Any other galaxy is also at the center. How can that be (Figure 3.4)?

Well, let us suppose we live in Galaxy A. You see on opposite sides Galaxies B and Z moving away. They are the same distance away moving at the same speed in opposite directions. Twice as far away is Galaxy C moving twice as fast. Galaxy D, three times as far away, is moving three times as fast.

Suppose we were instead sitting on Galaxy B. We would see exactly the same pattern. Galaxy A is moving away at the same speed that we thought Galaxy B was moving away. Galaxy Z, twice as far away, is moving twice as fast. Galaxy D is moving in the opposite direction twice as fast. I hope you can see that there is only one way that the universe can be homogeneous and also expanding. And that is for every point to be the center of expansion. Every point and no point. There is no center or, equally well, we are all at the centers. Nicholas of Cusa said something very much like that a hundred years before Copernicus.

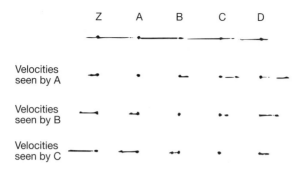

FIGURE 3.4   *Every galaxy is at the center in a uni-
formly expanding universe.   From* The First Three Minutes *by Steven Weinberg (Basic Books, 1977), p. 22.
Used with permission.*

Of the three pieces of evidence that I mentioned before, the one I have been discussing so far is the expansion of the universe, discovered by Edwin Hubble in 1929 by the method I have described, measuring the speed of a galaxy and relating that to its distance from us (Figure 3.5a). What one finds, even going out to much greater distances than Hubble could reach, is that the speed remains proportional to distance.

The Cosmic Microwave Background Radiation

At the turn of the twentieth century, Max Planck discovered the law of heat radiation, of the brightness versus the frequency of light. The dark line on Figure 3.5b is the Planck heat law. Heat radiation always follows that pattern. The little boxes represent the measurements of the Cosmic Background Explorer Satellite (COBE), which was put up in 1989 and was still working until 1993, when it was turned off. You will notice that the boxes fit perfectly on the line. Usually when you see a picture like this, the boxes represent the uncertainty. But if you actually represent the uncertainty in the measurements, the boxes would be much smaller than the line. They have been magnified 100 times. The data points fit so perfectly on the predicted line that you cannot see any deviation. In fact, the fit is better than a part in 10,000, which means that the radiation is definitely heat radiation.

What could have filled the entire universe with uniform heat radiation? No one has come up with an explanation other than the one proposed by George Lemaître in 1927: It is the heat left over from the Big Bang. Today we measure the temperature as about 2.7 degrees Kelvin. As you go back the temperature must go up.

The Abundance of the Light Elements

At a time of around a minute after the Big Bang, the great fusion took place. Today fusion takes place inside the stars. But only a few percent of all the fusion that has occurred happened in the centers of stars. Almost all occurred within a

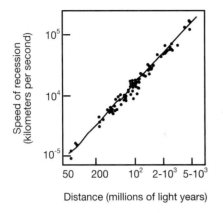

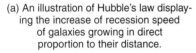

(a) An illustration of Hubble's law display-
ing the increase of recession speed
of galaxies growing in direct
proportion to their distance.

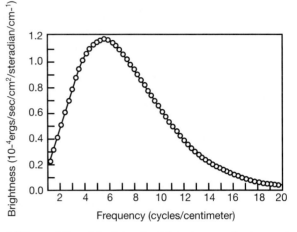

(b) The variation of the intensity of the microwave background
radiation with its frequency as observed by the COBE satellite.
The observations (boxes) match almost exactly the (solid) curve
expected from pure heat radiation with a temperature of 2.73 K.

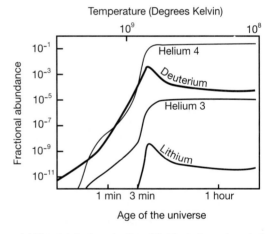

(c) The detailed production of lightest elements out of
protons and neutrons in the first three minutes. The nuclear reactions occur rapidly when the temperature
drops below a billion degrees Kelvin and then shut
down because of the rapidly falling temperature
and density of the expanding universe.)

FIGURE 3.5   *Three pillars of the Big Bang.*

few minutes after the Big Bang, when almost all of the helium in the universe was
formed. First, deuterium (heavy hydrogen) formed, and then it was mostly
locked up in helium. A mix of mostly hydrogen and helium, much less deuterium, then even less helium 3 and lithium, is the pattern predicted by standard
Big Bang nucleosynthesis. That is exactly the pattern we see in the universe in the
same ratios as predicted. These light elements are the relics of a few minutes, and

as far as we can tell, the observed ratios agree very well with the predictions. If a theory is going to be right, it has to make lots of predictions—and lots of evidence must fit the predictions. That is the case with the Big Bang theory.

NEW PIECES OF EVIDENCE

Fluctuations in the Cosmic Microwave Background Radiation

Beside these three pillars of the Big Bang theory, there have been many recent discoveries that confirm predictions of the theory. One of the most important was the discovery that the temperature of space is not uniform in all directions. Although it is generally 2.7 degrees Kelvin in all directions, in the fifth decimal place there are slight differences in different directions. The size of these little temperature fluctuations was predicted in the early 1980s by the theory of cold dark matter (which I helped to invent and develop). COBE and subsequently a dozen more instruments have seen the differences just as they were predicted.

Supernovas of a particular kind, the brightest of all, can be seen at high redshift. They evolve more slowly than they are seen to evolve in the nearby universe by exactly the factor—1 plus the redshift—that they were predicted to have. We can now see them at a redshift of 0.9. They evolve almost a factor of 2 more slowly. They reach a maximum brightness; then the light falls off as much twice as slowly as nearby supernovas because of the expansion of the universe.

As I mentioned, temperature is predicted to increase with redshift. This increase is by the same factor I just mentioned, 1 plus the redshift. The temperature can be measured in galaxies in high redshift. The temperature should be higher, and sure enough it is exactly as predicted.

Gravitational Lensing

The final evidence that I will mention in support of the Big Bang is gravitational lensing (Figure 3.6). Telescopes on earth looking through clusters of galaxies see distorted images of more distant galaxies. In every case the distorted galaxies have a higher redshift. The distortion is caused by the huge gravitation of the cluster of galaxies through which the light of the distant galaxy passes. We have many such examples. They always fit the same pattern.

Let me give you a beautiful example of the gravitational lensing phenomenon. This is a picture from the Hubble Space Telescope. It is a cluster of galaxies at a redshift of 0.171, and we are looking back at much more distant galaxies when we see these arcs. Such an arc is not a galaxy in the cluster, but instead a distorted image of a galaxy far beyond the cluster, at 5 to 10 times greater distance than the cluster itself. How do we know? Because we can measure the redshift of the light. We can reconstruct what the galaxy looks like by undoing the effect of the lensing by the cluster. Einstein first discussed gravitational lensing in 1936, and we are

FIGURE 3.6   Gravitational lensing by a cluster of galaxies. (Hubble Space Telescope image of gravitational lensing in Abell 2218, April 5, 1995, STScI-1995-14. Credit: W. Couch [University of New South Wales], R. Ellis [Cambridge University], and NASA.)

using the formulas of Einstein's theory of general relativity, our modern theory of gravity. Clusters of galaxies are the greatest telescopes in the universe.

A BRIEF HISTORY OF THE EARLY UNIVERSE

I have described older pictures of the universe, introduced the geography of the visible universe, and presented evidence for the Big Bang. Now I want to summarize briefly what we think the history of the universe was according to the Big Bang. The first few steps are speculative. We have no direct evidence that there ever was symmetry breaking, but what we see now is what particle physicists call a broken symmetry. Only electromagnetic symmetry is still unbroken. We think there was a standard model symmetry, which broke to make the laws of physics that we see today. And at an earlier stage, the universe perhaps had what we call the grand unified symmetry. Such theories make predictions that are testable, but they have yet to be tested. We hope to see direct evidence of some of this symmetry breaking when we can get to temperatures that the universe reached 10^{-8} to 10^{-10} seconds after the Big Bang with the next generation of accelerators. The great accelerator called the Large Hadron Collider being built in Geneva should allow us to do that. We are also looking for evidence for "baryogenesis," for the creation of a slight asymmetry between the amounts of ordinary matter and antimatter. The picture is that at about 10^{-4} seconds there was a great annihilation when all the antimatter annihilated with almost all the matter. Roughly for every billion antiquarks, there were a billion and one quarks. The billion annihilated with the billion, and the one quark left over is what we are made of. We have good evidence that that is about what the right numbers were. There was a subsequent annihilation of the electrons and antielectrons, which happened in the first few seconds. That is pretty secure, based on physics we understand and can duplicate in the laboratory.

WHAT BIG BANG THEORY DOES NOT EXPLAIN

Nuclear fusion is understood very well. People who learned to make nuclear bombs did lots of measurements and calculations, and we understand how the stars work based on the same calculations. The question we are working on now is, How do galaxies and larger structures form? There is a lot that the Big Bang theory does not explain. For example, what made the universe have these little ripples? There were until recently two competing theories, cosmic defects and cosmic inflation. Not long ago in *Science* magazine a figure appeared (shown here as Figure 3.7).

The data on the magnitude of the temperature fluctuations of different angular scales lie in the band between the two lighter lines. The cosmic inflation theories make predictions that agree with the data. The cosmic defects predictions lie outside the range of the new observations, so now the defects model is dead. Only inflation is left of the two models. But inflation is also at risk. The pattern of wiggles is crucial. The predictions have been clear for several years. The crucial data will be coming in very soon. In the year 2001, NASA launched the MAP satellite. In 2007, there will be a European satellite, called Planck. These satellites, together with several ground-based and balloon-borne instruments, will be able to measure fluctuations at even higher angular scales. They will see all the wiggles if they are there. So we will know pretty soon if inflation is right.

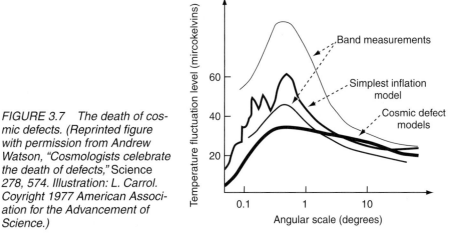

FIGURE 3.7   The death of cosmic defects. (Reprinted figure with permission from Andrew Watson, "Cosmologists celebrate the death of defects," Science 278, 574. Illustration: L. Carrol. Coyright 1977 American Association for the Advancement of Science.)

A NEW PICTURE OF THE UNIVERSE

The Universe Is Mostly Invisible, so the "Picture" Is Metaphorical

I promised that I would help you try to visualize the modern picture of the whole universe. We cannot visualize it with our eyes alone because we cannot see it from outside. When you visualize something, you stand outside it and look at it. But we cannot stand outside the universe because it surrounds us. We are in it, and indeed we *are* it, on our scale. We cannot see all times; we only see a snapshot. We see farther back as we see farther out. The universe is all times. And what is more, most of the matter in the universe is invisible—it is dark matter. Probably 90 percent of all the matter in the universe is something we cannot see. We are trying to discover what it is. Theorists like me make suggestions for what it might be, but we will not know until we actually discover the particles. What I want to do is come up with a picture that suggests all of this.

Importance of Size Scales in Developing a New "Picture"

Let me give you another way of thinking about this by showing you all the sizes versus all the masses that we see. In Figure 3.8, objects are arrayed on a logarithmic scale from the size of people, which is about a meter, to smaller and larger sizes. We can plot all of living things on a diagram like this. Interestingly enough, they form a straight line because we are practically all made of water, and that is just the line of water density. Incidentally, planets and ordinary stars have about the same density as water. Galaxies are much less dense, and some stars are much more dense. But when a star gets even more dense than that and it reaches the upward-sloping line *AB,* it collapses to no size at all. Anything to the left of the line has a mass that is too great for its size and collapses to no size at all, according to general relativity. It becomes a black hole.

An interesting question then is this: Does the universe lie inside this forbidden region? If so, it will expand to the maximum size and then collapse. The uncertainty is represented by the little cross. We do not know how massive the universe is. That measurement is being made today, and the present indications are that the universe will expand forever. In the next 2 to 3 years I think we are going to know for sure. That will tell us the ultimate fate of the universe.

There is another line on the diagram, *AC,* which slopes downward. The uncertainty principle of quantum mechanics says that everything must lie to the right of that line. These two lines cross. That tells us there is a smallest scale, according to our present understanding of the laws of physics. This smallest size is called the Planck length, about 10^{-33} cm. There is also a largest size that we can see, the Hubble radius, about 10^{28} cm. It is the distance to the farthest things we can see, to the things that were emitting light close to the beginning of the universe (actually about 150,000 years after the Big Bang, when the universe first became trans-

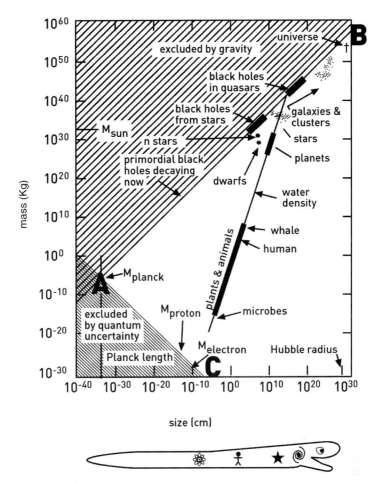

FIGURE 3.8   *Size versus mass in the universe.* (From J. R. Primack, "Dark Matter, Galaxies, and Large Scale Structures in the Universe," in *Proceedings of the International School of Physics,* "Enrico Fermi" XCII, Varenna, Italy, June–July 1984, N. Cabibbo, ed. [North-Holland, 1987], pp. 137–241.)

parent). All the sizes in the visible universe lie between the Planck length and the Hubble radius.

THE COSMIC UROBOROS

Let me come back to the ancient symbol of the snake swallowing its tail, called in the Greek the "uroboros" (Figure 3.9). I represent all the possible length scales from the smallest to the largest along the serpent. We now have a cosmic uroboros around which are arrayed all the length scales of the universe, from the smallest scale up to the Hubble scale, a range of 10^{60} to 60 orders of magnitude.

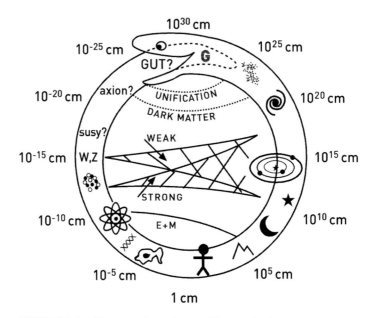

FIGURE 3.9   *The cosmic uroboros.* (From J. R. Primack, "Dark Matter, Galaxies, and Large Scale Structures in the Universe," in *Proceedings of the International School of Physics,* "Enrico Fermi" XCII, Varenna, Italy, June–July 1984, N. Cabibbo, ed. [North-Holland, 1987], pp. 137–241.)

This idea of representing it as a snake swallowing its tail is due to Sheldon Glashow, a physics professor at Harvard, a Noble Prize winner, and an originator of the idea of Grand Unification. Something I pointed out several years ago is that there are some interesting connections across the diagram of Figure 3.9. Electromagnetism controls the physics from atoms to mountains. Mountains are as high as they are because if they were any higher they would flow plastically or break, through earthquakes. On a smaller planet like Mars, mountains can be higher. It is where gravity, which controls the large side of the diagram, meets electromagnetism, which determines the strength of materials. What we call the weak and strong interactions control the physics of atomic nuclei and determine whether they are stable or not. They also control the composition and burning of the sun. The sun burns by a combination of weak processes turning protons into neutrons, and fusion, a strong interaction process combining two protons and two neutrons into helium.

On still smaller scales, there are forces we are trying to understand with our latest accelerators. And those are probably connected to the dark matter, which controls the structure of galaxies and all the larger things of the universe. Glashow's hope is that perhaps gravity controls both the smallest as well as the largest scales and there is only one way to close the circle and let the serpent swallow its tail.

What Does the Cosmic Uroboros Mean?

Humans are in a very interesting position, almost exactly in the middle of the cosmic uroboros, between the largest scale and the smallest scale. There are arguments that this is the only place we could be. We could not be much smaller because there would not be enough complexity for us to have brains enough to think. We could not be much larger because communication times would get too long between the parts of our brains. So we do live in a special place in the universe, but only if you think of it symbolically rather than geographically.

4 The Cultural Significance of the Story of the Universe

Brian Swimme   *California Institute for Integral Studies*

On the basis of the evidence it was at least one and a half million years ago that our hominid ancestors first became fascinated by fire. Perhaps a lightning strike lit up a tree in the middle of the night on the African plains and some creative genius of the *Homo erectus* tribe was too mesmerized to hold herself back from touching it, kicking it, grabbing it. While all or most of her kin kept their distance, she sat pondering the strange presence engulfing the branch, and as the flames slowly puttered out there flickered in her mind images that we today cannot even guess at except to say that whatever they were they could not have been anything like a civilization of blast furnaces and skyscrapers and jet transport that her daring with the smoldering branch eventually gave birth to.

In our own time a small band of her descendants now explore in a similarly hesitant manner a new power that has erupted into the playing field of the present, a power that carries within it the promise of changing world history. This power comes in the form of an idea that we are calling the Epic of Evolution, and although compared with a physical energy such as a flaming tree a single idea might seem a paltry thing, an ephemeral, ethereal thing, it is in fact far more powerful than any form of energy we know, precisely because of the chain of events following upon our domestication of fire; for any idea that seeps into the interstices of the human cerebral cortex suddenly draws into its reach all the developments of the physical energies released from the universe into the hands of the human. In this chapter I explore some considerations concerning the Epic of Evolution and its possible effects of the course of human history.

By the phrases *Epic of Evolution* or the *Story of the Universe* or simply the *New Story* I mean to indicate our contemporary account of how 13.7 billion years of universe evolution, 5 billion years of earth evolution, and 3 million years of human evolution have led to our present condition of life within the earth community. This comprehensive narrative can be considered a single though complex idea that is the construction of millions of humans working ceaselessly for at least four centuries on every continent of earth. It is without any doubt one of the monumental accomplishments of the human species, a crowning intellectual achievement of the modern age.

I would like to begin with a series of observations concerning the Epic of Evolution so that my remarks concerning the implications of the Epic will have a basic context for understanding. The first is simply the obvious parallel between our discovery of fire and our discovery of the Epic. In both cases it was impossible for the humans to have any clear idea in what they were getting involved. During the four centuries of the modern science enterprise nothing could have been further from Copernicus's or Newton's or Curie's mind than the idea that they were in the process of giving birth to a new and comprehensive narrative of the universe's birth and development. Even today, the vast majority of scientists, attending to their own specializations, have neither the time nor the inclination to ponder the transcientific and historical impact of this epic narrative. And in this we are entirely similar to the first hominids dealing with fire, unaware of the vast consequences of the thing they held in their hands.

My second observation concerns the relative permanence of the idea of the Epic of Evolution. No one can predict the future in any detail, but there are reasons to believe that some general features of our future can be pointed to concerning our discovery of evolution, and one of these is the unstoppable nature of this idea. I think this is worth noting. It is hard to imagine that any government or corporation or organization could eliminate the spread of this new story precisely because arriving at an evolutionary understanding that previous generations of humans did not and could not enjoy is so deeply satisfying for the human mind. For this reason alone the Epic has drawn humans from every cultural and national and racial background. It is a human achievement; it is an understanding that will continue to permeate through the earth's humans regardless what any individual states or other subgroups might decide. The unstoppable nature of this idea means that the appearance of the Epic of Evolution can be considered an irreversible transformation of the earth's process. Certain subgroups will attempt to control the Epic, or will attempt to suppress it, but the river of time will flow right on past them and isolate them as living fossils left over from a former era of humanity.

Although the discovery of cosmic and terrestrial evolution has involved humans from a diversity of cultural backgrounds and can thus be considered primarily as a human achievement rather than, say, an American or a French or a Chinese achievement, it is of course true that the representation from the various human subgroups is skewed. In particular there has been a disproportionate number of European males involved. It seems important to state the obvious here, that this disproportion is fundamentally a historical accident, one with some unfortunate consequences that must be addressed. In particular, this overrepresentation leads to an illusion that the scientific enterprise is *Western*, when in truth it is human. Within the scientific tradition there are growing pressures to correct this condition by involving a far greater number of women and individuals from traditionally underrepresented groups. Scientists themselves do not labor under the illusion that science is the creation or the province of any particular civilization but is instead one of the truly universal human activities that we can do.

Concerning all this, my third and final general observation is that, as this enterprise that is focused on observing, analyzing, speculating, theorizing, and articulating the universe story expands to include greater numbers of humans from all the cultures of earth, our understanding will deepen considerably. We do not have a fixed Epic of Evolution that we now announce as any final truth. We have rather a profound grasp of some central moments in the Epic, and we regard this knowledge for all its splendor as sketchy and incomplete at best. It has required

3 million years of human development to arrive at our current understanding of the universe story, and we have simultaneously a tremendous respect for what we have thus far learned and a deep certainty that what is yet to come is equally important.

In turning now to my discussion of the cultural significance of the universe story I would like to draw a comparison with an earlier moment in our history that can shed light on the way in which the Epic of Evolution might guide our civilization through a profound restructuring of its fundamental forms. If we consider the political situation of humanity in the year 1000 we find a series of settlements around the planet with a smaller number of hunter-gatherer bands that are diminishing with every new century. Among the largest settlements in Europe or Africa or India or China we find a common organization, that of the monarchy. So pervasive is the presence of the monarchy that it is difficult for these humans even to imagine a different structure of existence.

Into this situation there emerged an idea, just an ephemeral idea, democracy. What was that but a flickering flame in the neural nets of a small number of *Homo sapiens?* But over the course of a few centuries this idea jumped from mind to mind and eventually organized human consciousness with an intensity sufficient to restructure nearly every civilization by tossing the King onto the junkyard of human history. To complete my analogy I need to indicate what, in our current situation, corresponds to the monarchy that was junked, and what corresponds to the democracy that began to organize human energies once the King was removed.

The difficulty in characterizing the structures of existence in which we live is that the mainstream discourses are themselves so skewed as to be rendered almost useless for our purposes. It would be as if, in the year 1000, we attempted to describe the inadequacies of the monarchy by using the language and the ideas of the theologians of that time. This earlier theology was permeated with an admiration of the King, since the King who ruled on earth was understood to be a representative of the King who ruled in heaven. One could say that the theology of the year 1000 had basically been written by the King, so it would not be a great source of ideas helpful in identifying the more horrific aspects of monarchy.

The way to formulate a clear understanding of the inadequacies of our present condition is by attending to those groups that have been excluded from the benefits of our modern society. One has a tragically long list to choose from. We could take the perspective of one of the 13 million children under five who are starving to death each year; or the 100 million humans murdered in one of our twentieth-century wars; or the billions of women who have been systematically excluded from political and financial power; or the 5 billion humans and people of color from the southern hemisphere who have suffered neocolonization and control; or the trillions of other-than-human beings who have been exterminated during the twentieth century. Any one of these perspectives enables us to see more clearly the essential nature of the structure of our time. The perspective I will take is one that is in some sense the one with which we are least familiar, is one that is meant to include in some sense all the others. I am speaking of the animals. What sort of assessment of our time do we arrive at if we examine the conditions of our existence from the point of view of the animals?

One of the most important conclusions from the Epic of Evolution is that we exist in a very rare moment of earth's history. Animal species are going extinct at an unusually high rate, between 100 and 1000 times as rapidly as normal. From the perspective of the animals, this moment is the worst time in the last 65 million years. Of all the negative effects humans are having on the earth community, nothing else compares to this in terms of ultimacy. If the structures of human existence do not change, we will have eliminated fully 50 percent of all species of life on this planet in a mere fifty years.

To terminate an entire era of earth's life, one that required 65 million years of earth's creativity for its development, is surely the most awesome thing humans have ever done. From within the orientation of the universe story we can begin to fathom the full tragedy of this undertaking. By eliminating a certain degree of the earth's fecundity we are determining in various ways the very nature of what is possible for life for all future eons. But, encased in a modernist consciousness, a human cannot see or feel this tragedy any more than a monarch, encased in a theology that justified his kingship, could see the tragedies inherent to the very structure of monarchy. The modernist sensibility takes economics as its primary ideology; but modern economics does not notice species or their extinction. Throughout the development of classical modern economic theory, all species were lumped under "resources," with the assumption that resources were infinite. *Animal* and *extinction* are not categories in modern economics.

The power of the Epic of Evolution to alter history begins with its capacity to deconstruct the hold of the economics ideology, to disillusion us, to give us eyes to see what is really taking place. Our destruction is fueled by our militarism, our anthropocentrism, our sexism, our racism, but all of these are manifestations of a fundamental structure of the modern human being. While there are a variety of ways to articulate this condition, the one that I would like to explore attempts to capture both the mistake we are making and the justification for the mistake. Our unspoken aim has been to *disconnect because superior.* The destruction that the Epic condemns is the outgrowth of the prior decision to separate ourselves from a select other, and to regard this other as inferior.

With respect to our relationship with animals, our cultural tradition is quite clear. When we examine the positions of nearly all the philosophers and religious personalities of Western civilization the message is simply to disconnect because we humans are superior. The rare, shining counterexamples such as St. Francis of Assisi only cast a glaring spotlight on the vast line-up of cultural heroes and their sad insistence that we need not take animals as seriously as we take humans. In just the same way we find that the essential message given to males is to disconnect because we men are superior. Or to Westerners in general: Disconnect because we Greco-Roman-European races are superior.

The vast majority of the structures and activities of twentieth-century civilization carry this orientation. A fishing fleet with nets 30 miles long scooping up and destroying the vitality of the oceans and driving one-third of all marine life toward extinction does not have "disconnect because we industrial humans are superior" stenciled on its equipment, but all such equipment shouts it out just the same. So too with the vast volume of modern technology. And with the forms of our religious institutions. And with the functioning of our media. And with the business plans of our corporations. The essence of our structures of existence, driving so much of our destruction, is the simple imperative: "Disconnect from the rest of the earth community. For we are the King."

The power of the new story is its capacity to dissolve this enabling assumption of modern civilization, for the new story asserts nearly its opposite. The quintessential wisdom of the new story is that we are all kin. We have all evolved over 13.7 billion years from the same origin moment, so that every being that exists is cousin to every other being. So, the ultimate meaning of the universe is the ecological community. It is redundant to say the ecological community, but it is necessary given the extent to which the modernist confusion has penetrated English. Over the past centuries we allowed ourselves to become convinced that *community* meant "human community," even though strictly speaking there is no such thing as an exclusively human community separate from the earth community. The only community that exists is the life community, the ecological community. And within the new story it is this community that is the ultimate meaning and ultimate wisdom of the universe.

The aim to *disconnect because superior* is replaced by a new and healing aim, to *reinvent the human so that our presence is mutually enhancing within the earth community*. It required 13.7 billion years for the emergence of our present existence, and all these billions of years of creativity are carried in the very form and functioning of the earth. The great task that arises from our new understanding of the ecological evolving universe is to invent a human species whose structures of existence enable us and all beings in the community, both now and in the future, to enter the web of relationships in a mutually enhancing manner so that all might participate in the joy of life's fulfillments. This task certainly will occupy the great volume of human energy and human genius for the next few centuries at least. All our human structures require such a transformation, the structures of our psyches as well as the structures of our institutions. Only in such a way will we move from an intellectual understanding of our kinship with all beings to an embodied living of this kinship.

I have one final comment to make, and it concerns the difficulty of the task. It is a sobering fact that even though, in 1543, Copernicus discovered that the earth travels around the sun, we go about our day using a language that speaks of a "sunrise" and a "sunset" and thinking of the sun as a kind of hot yellow dot sailing over a fixed earth. So, if after four and a half centuries we have yet to embody this in our everyday consciousness, how long will it take for us to embody the Epic's insight into our kinship with all beings? Are we doomed to continue living as if we were disconnected from the earth, even though we know as surely as we know anything that this is an illusion? Will it require 500 years to change?

Without wanting to reduce the significance of the challenge we face, I do think a more hopeful assessment of our situation is possible. For though it is true that we have yet to assimilate even the first discoveries of the modern scientific venture, the simple fact of history is that we have never taken seriously the challenge of assimilating scientific truth into our structures of existence. We've invented reasons for freeing ourselves from taking science that seriously, such as the notorious interpretation worked out in a theological sense by Pierre Gassendi and others in the seventeenth century that regarded science as only instrumental knowledge. Or, in a later version, the deconstructionists' interpretation, always based on the most sophisticated French reasoning, that science is not really knowledge about the oceans and the phytoplankton and the galaxies so much as it is only another language game. No need to take seriously our discovery of genetic relatedness, of cosmic kinship, or of ecological interconnection and interpenetrability if science is just an instrumental language game. In these and other ways, the philosophical and theological elites of Western civilization have shielded themselves from the task of transformation that is called for in our time.

But still it will happen, the change will take place, powered forth by an ever-deepening awareness that our dysfunctional civilization has for its unconscious aim the ruin of the earth community. Life will awaken. The human will awaken. Especially the young. They will climb out of sleep one morning and as they greet the dawn they will know the life that pulses through them as blood and feelings and breath is the same life that pulses through the bear as blood and feelings and breath. They will know with every breath that it is the soil's mysteries of life that enable them to breathe, and it is the vitality of earth's oceans that sings in every soaring bird. Hydrogen atoms deep in the belly of the sun are given away as photons that become the final leap of a salmon over the falls, before hatching forth as fingerlings, and exactly that intricacy will be understood as the model for all economics.

Guided by the understanding of the Epic of Evolution, northern industrial humans will recognize that they are kin with all the humans of the southern hemisphere, and with every living being. They will recognize this kinship because they share the same language with the others beings of earth—the language of DNA; they will recognize their commonality because they come from the same tradition as these other beings—the 4 billion years of earth's living adventure. Just as a hominid a million years ago holding onto a smoldering branch was the first step toward a new structure of human existence, so too in our time, our entrance into the Epic of Evolution is a decisive step into the mysterious process of giving birth to a new form of human being. Out of these new structures of awareness humans will create programs and institutions that will be not a degradation but an evocation of a vibrant earth community.

5 Darwin and Darwinism in America: An Interview

Ronald L. Numbers *University of Wisconsin-Madison*

Editor's Note: Because of unforeseen circumstances, Ronald Numbers was unable to attend the Epic of Evolution Conference. However, he agreed to be interviewed on the topic of his presentation. The following is an edited transcript of that interview.

How would you describe Darwin's religious background and perspective?

Charles Darwin grew up in a religiously unconventional family that was very liberal Anglican. His grandfather was a deist. His father was a freethinker. So at home he was not exposed to a particularly orthodox environment. At the time he left to go on the voyage of the *Beagle* in the early 1830s, however, he did profess to believe in the Bible from cover to cover.

Darwin at the age of sixteen had been sent to Edinburgh, Scotland, to study medicine but after a couple of years left because he could not stand the sight of blood. His family then sent him to Cambridge for three years to get a bachelor's degree. Students did not major in particular subjects then, but Darwin intended to study for and take Holy Orders after completing his degree. He anticipated reading theology for an additional year. He initially had some concerns about swearing that he believed all of the teachings of the church, but eventually he decided that he could. But when the opportunity to sail on the *Beagle* to South America and the South Pacific came his way, he jumped at the opportunity to travel instead of reading theology.

Darwin's biological theories seem to have had very little impact on his religious thinking. Fairly late in life he recalled that disbelief had crept over him very slowly and that he had eventually abandoned Christianity. Some people have suggested that this movement came about as a result of abandoning creationism for evolutionism. But in recent years, largely through the work of the historian James Moore, we have learned that by far the most compelling reasons for his giving up Christianity were the conclusions he reached after suffering, during a three-year period, the death of his father and the death of his favorite daughter, ten-year-old Annie. His physician father had been a nonbeliever but a good man who took care of those around him. However, the church taught that, because he rejected orthodox Christianity, he would burn in everlasting hell. Darwin thought that this was a despicable view because it meant that not only his father, but his grandfather and later on his brother, who was also a nonbeliever, were eternally damned.

When Annie died, Darwin was taking care of her at a water-cure institution, because his wife, Emma, was about to deliver another baby. Annie was apparently the perfect child. When she passed away, he was so broken up that he was unable to attend the funeral; for years thereafter he would shed tears when he thought about her. The notion that an omnipotent, loving God, who could have spared Annie's life, failed to do so undermined Darwin's faith. Such moral issues rather than scientific ones led him to abandon his belief in Christianity.

Did Darwin understand his views to be anticreationist?

The question of what it meant to be a creationist in the nineteenth century is far more complex than it might seem at first, because there were various views of creationism. The term was not widely used to designate antievolutionary theories. In fact, although Darwin's primary goal in writing the *Origin of the Species* was to overthrow "the dogma of separate creations," he never spelled out which version of the dogma he was attacking. It could have been the view, widely associated with this eighteenth-century Swedish naturalist Carl Linnaeus, that there had been a unique creation at some time in the past in a particular location, from which all the plants and animals of the world had spread out to populate the earth. Or it could have been the view of his friend Charles Lyell, the Scottish geologist, who held that there had been any number of "foci" or "centres" of creation that appeared at different times and different places, as needed. Or Darwin could have been referring to a third view, associated with the Swiss-American naturalist Louis Agassiz, who suggested that, after extensive catastrophes, God had repopulated the earth in an instant. Thus a minute after one of the creations you might have seen whole families of human beings or large populations of rats, none of which would have been genetically related to one another. Darwin did not say which of these views of creation he was primarily aiming at, although virtually any notion of a special miraculous creation would have been anathema to him by this time.

How were Darwin's views received in America?

For the first few years after the appearance of the *Origin* in 1859, there was relatively little concern about Darwin's views. After all, fifteen years earlier a popular little book called *Vestiges of the Natural History of Creation*, published anonymously, had advocated evolutionary views; and the scientific community mostly ridiculed it. The religious community in America thought that maybe the same response would greet Darwin's notions. It was not until a scientific consensus in favor of evolution began developing in the early 1870s that Christian intellectuals in America realized that they had a problem on their hands, because the view of origins taught by Darwin was at significant variance with the view of origins described in the book of Genesis.

There was a spectrum of responses. A number of people, perhaps even the majority of those who knew about Darwin's work, claimed that it was so antithetical to the teachings of Christianity—to Christian ethics and to the plan of redemption—that it had to be dismissed. Such critics dismissed Darwinism as very bad science or, more frequently, as being too speculative to warrant the name of science. Others, such as the influential Harvard botanist Asa Gray, tried to baptize Darwin's theory by offering a theistic version of evolution. Darwin, for example, had not explained the origin of the variations on which natural selection works. So Gray helpfully suggested that Darwin attribute those to God's providence, which allowed God to channel evolution in particular directions. When Gray first read

Darwin's work, he wrote back to Darwin, saying, essentially, I like your ideas on the origin of species, but I do not see how natural selection can explain the origin of humans or of complex organs such as the eye. Darwin wrote back that he himself had spent sleepless nights worrying about how his theory could explain the eye but that he was willing to trust natural selection. Gray thought that a more plausible response was to attribute the appearance of complex organs and of humans to some sort of supernatural intervention. Although relatively few American scientists adopted Gray's particular spin on Darwinism, probably the majority of the evolutionists in the nineteenth century allowed for some theistic input.

At first Darwin's theory attracted very little reaction from the news media. At the time of the meeting of the American Association for the Advancement of Science in 1860, for instance, a writer for *The New York Times* commented negatively on the extent to which American scientists were avoiding any discussion of Darwin's new theory; he thought they were rather cowardly for doing so. For various reasons, including the American Civil War, Darwinism did not become a really hot topic until the 1870s.

Why then?

To the surprise of many Christians, the scientific community quickly joined Darwin's campaign to overthrow the dogma of separate creations. But though most American scientists became evolutionists—and some began describing evolution as a "fact"—very few of them attached the weight to the mechanism of natural selection that Darwin did. Nevertheless, it was clear that the *Origin of Species* had to be taken far more seriously than the *Vestiges of the Natural History of Creation*.

For a number of years Darwin's critics could hide behind the scientific authority of the Harvard zoologist Agassiz, the biggest name in American science and the most prominent anti-Darwinist in the United States. Although a creationist, for scientific and philosophical reasons, he rejected the biblical accounts of the Creation and the Flood—and despised efforts to reconcile science with the Bible. During the 1850s he had gained a fair amount of notoriety in religious circles for embracing the heretical notion that Adam and Eve were the ancestors of just one human race, not of all humanity. Religiously, Agassiz was at the best a nominal Unitarian.

Agassiz and Gray illustrate the difficulty of characterizing the opponents and proponents of Darwinism. The creationist Agassiz cared less about the Bible and orthodox Christianity than the evolutionist Gray, a Presbyterian who insisted on retaining supernatural interventions in the evolutionary process.

What was the response in the religious communities?

Although some liberal Christians accepted a theistic version of evolution, conservative Christians overwhelmingly repudiated the theory. The Princeton theologian Charles Hodge, perhaps the most influential Protestant scholar in the county, wrote a little book in the 1870s called *What Is Darwinism?*. His famous answer was "It is atheism." But Hodge was no knee-jerk fundamentalist. He accepted the fossil evidence for the antiquity of life on earth, and he even believed in the evolution of the solar system. However, unlike his fellow Presbyterian Gray, he concluded that Darwin ruled out any role for God in the process of evolution. Of course, he was right in that regard. (In the late 1860s Darwin had publicly rejected Gray's baptized version of his theory.)

A number of conservative Christians took potshots at Darwinism during the late nineteenth century and the early part of the twentieth century, but there was no organized crusade against evolution until after World War I, when several developments focused attention on evolution. One was its growing influence in the churches and schools of America. As more and more American children attended public high schools, they learned about evolution—and gleefully shared the news with their parents. Evolution also got caught up in the fundamentalist-modernist controversy. The fundamentalists, militant evangelical Christians, at first focused on the higher criticism of the Bible, which treated it as a historical document that needed to be understood in the context of the time in which it had been written. Increasingly, however, they turned their attention to evolution—in part because evolution was becoming more prominent in the cultural landscape of America, and because they saw evolution as the underlying idea behind the new approach to the Bible. The "higher critics" treated the Bible not as God's revealed word but as an ordinary book that had developed over time in response to particular social, cultural, and intellectual events.

World War I focused a lot of attention on the moral implications of Darwinism. Especially significant were reports coming out of the German POW camps that the German militarists had based their rationale for war on the evolutionary notion that might makes right, that only the fittest should survive. This moral teaching aroused both the scientific and religious communities in America. Scientists responded by trying to downplay the elements of conflict in the process of evolution and highlighting cooperation. The fundamentalists responded by trying to ban the teaching of evolution, particularly human evolution, from the public schools of America.

Was the Scopes trial, then, the direct result of this moral concern?

This was the world's most famous court trial at the time. It was the first trial broadcast on radio, over WGN in Chicago. But, in my opinion, the Scopes trial is one of the most misunderstood events in American history. Virtually all U.S. history textbooks get it wrong, partly because the authors have not taken the trouble to look at the pertinent documents and partly, I think, because of strong prejudice against fundamentalism. The trial occurred in the summer of 1925 in the small Tennessee town of Dayton. It came about as a result of a law passed earlier in the year by the Tennessee state legislature making it a crime to teach any theory of human origins contrary to the Bible or that linked humans to apes. The American Civil Liberties Union, an organization just getting off the ground in New York City at the time, heard about this law and placed notices in Tennessee newspapers soliciting a guinea pig to test this case. Some town fathers in Dayton, Tennessee, thought that it might be fun—and good for the local economy—to host a trial. So they asked a recently hired high school teacher, John Thomas Scopes, if he would be willing to test the law.

There was only one problem: Scopes had come down from the University of Kentucky a year earlier to teach algebra, physics, and chemistry, and to coach basketball and football, but not to teach biology. He recalled that the regular teacher of biology, the school principal, had been sick late in the year and that he, Scopes, had reviewed the students while filling in. He was pretty sure that he had at least mentioned evolution. So he agreed to be "arrested."

Most people's image of the Scopes trial comes from the play and subsequent movie, *Inherit the Wind,* where authorities walk into his classroom and arrest him and haul him off to jail, where he struggles with his love for the preacher's daughter and his devotion to evolution and science. But Scopes was "arrested" only as a formality; he never went to jail; the preacher's daughter was fictitious. The case was contrived from the very beginning. The part of the eight-day trial that attracted the most attention then, and that has attracted the most attention since, was the examination of William Jennings Bryan, who had come to Dayton to assist the prosecution, by Clarence Darrow, who was assisting the defense. Darrow was probably the biggest criminal lawyer in the country, and a prominent agnostic. Bryan was one of the best known politicians in the country. He had run three times, unsuccessfully, as the Democratic candidate for President of the United States. He had served as Secretary of State. He was an outspoken fundamentalist and opponent of Darwinism, especially of human evolution. In an unprecedented move the defense late in the trial called Bryan, a lawyer for the prosecution, to the stand as an expert on the Bible. According to various accounts Darrow either (1) got Bryan foolishly to defend a creation in 4004 B.C. on October 23 at 9:00 A.M. and then asked him, "Was that Eastern Standard Time or Mountain Standard Time?"; or (2) under intense examination he got Bryan to concede that the days of Genesis were not 24-hour periods but long geological ages, which resulted in loss of fundamentalist support for Bryan. Some authors have actually said that Darrow did both.

The truth is easy to determine because a published version of the stenographic transcript of the trial has been available since 1925. Like virtually all other fundamentalists at the time (at least among those who left written records of their views), Bryan readily accepted vast geological ages that revealed the development of life on earth. He believed that each "day" of the creation week represented a long geological age. As he freely told Darrow, he did not care if the creation week had spanned 600,000,000 years. Other fundamentalists favored a slightly different interpretation of Genesis (with a "gap" in time between the creation "in the beginning" and the much later Edenic creation), which also allowed the acceptance of all the evidence of historical geology. Only a tiny group of fundamentalists, mostly Seventh-Day Adventists, believed that life on earth was no older than about 6000 years, insisted on 24-hour days of creation, and attributed virtually all of the fossil-bearing rocks to activities during the one year of Noah's Flood. One of the most interesting developments in the cultural history of twentieth-century America, I think, has been how this tiny minority opinion among fundamentalists in the 1920s came by the 1980s and 1990s to co-opt the very label "creationism." But that's a very long story (told in my book *The Creationists*).[1]

Was Tennessee the only state with an antievolution law?

In the 1920s perhaps two dozen state legislatures debated antievolution laws. Only three passed them: first Tennessee, later Mississippi, and in 1928 Arkansas.

Oklahoma for a time banned textbooks teaching evolution, and Florida condemned the teaching evolution but did not make it a crime to teach it. So five states passed some kind of antievolution legislation. All of those states happened to be in the South, but support came from many different areas in the United States, and the leaders of the antievolution movement came largely from outside the South.

One state that almost certainly would have outlawed the teaching of evolution had people voted their true feelings was Minnesota. The founder of the World's Christian Fundamentals Association, the organization that brought Bryan to Dayton, was a Baptist pastor from Minneapolis, William Bell Riley. And lots of conservative Lutherans in the state did not like the theory of evolution. But because so many Lutherans were more concerned about government intrusion into education than about evolution, they voted against the antievolution bill despite their hatred of Darwinism.

Contrary to what is often claimed, the Scopes trial did not bring the antievolution movement to a screeching halt. Some magazines and newspapers made fun of Bryan and his views, but there was a lot of criticism of Darrow, too. In fact, because he had gone out of his way to offend Christians generally and the people of Dayton specifically (including the judge), the ACLU tried to drop him from the subsequent appeal to the Tennessee Supreme Court. Darrow did not want to leave the defense team, and Scopes wanted him to stay; so Darrow remained, but his presence was very controversial. At the end of the trial most people thought that the fundamentalists had won. And, of course, legally they had. But the sense of a fundamentalist victory went beyond the legal technicality. Even H. L. Mencken, the journalist from the *Baltimore Sun* who had come down for the trial and who had no respect at all for fundamentalists or antievolutionists, said in his last report from Dayton that the fundamentalists had emerged completely victorious.

It was not until the early 1930s that writers began reinterpreting the significance of the trial, making it appear to have been a total defeat for fundamentalism, at least in the eyes of the public. But that view was not widespread in the 1920s. In fact, there were more antievolution bills introduced in the state legislatures after the trial than before, roughly two to one.

What happened to the antievolution movement after the Scopes trial?

After about 1928 or 1929 the antievolutionists lost their place on the front pages of American newspapers, but they did not go away. Instead, they began organizing their own institutions and creating an infrastructure of their own. Around the country the fundamentalists began building Bible institutes, churches, and radio stations. They gave up trying to pass state laws banning the teaching of evolution in favor of working on local school boards, where they were often quite successful. Such activities did not attract much national attention; thus many critics concluded that these people had just gone away and that antievolutionism had disappeared. It was not until the 1960s, really, that creationism began attracting national attention once again.

I mentioned earlier that during the mid-1920s only a minority of fundamentalist Christians tried to condense all of the history of life on earth to about 6000

years, by invoking Noah's Flood. That view, partly because it was so closely identified with Seventh-Day Adventists, whom many fundamentalist dismissed as
"cultists" because they had an extrabiblical source of revelation, did not fare very
well. Very few other antievolutionists felt the need to abandon the day-age and
gap interpretations of Genesis for this distinctive young-earth view, which placed
so much emphasis on the work of the Flood. However, in 1961 two card-carrying
fundamentalists—a hydraulic engineer named Henry Morris and an Old Testament scholar named John C. Whitcomb, Jr.—brought out a book called *The Genesis Flood,* in which they took the Adventists' "flood geology" and presented it to a
wider conservative Protestant audience.

The activities of Morris and Whitcomb led in 1963 to the organization of the
Creation Research Society (CRS), an association devoted to the advocacy of flood
geology and a young earth, not to antievolutionism generally. Contrary to common perception, many of the people involved with the founding of this organization were qualified scientists, even biologists. Of the ten founding members of the
CRS, five had earned doctorates in biology from major universities, a sixth had a
Ph.D. in biochemistry from the University of California at Berkeley, a seventh
(Morris) had earned a Ph.D. from Minnesota, and at least one or two others had
master's degrees in biology. In contrast, no active antievolutionist in the 1920s
had possessed a doctorate in science. The proselytizing efforts of Morris, Whitcomb, and the members of the Creation Research Society among fundamentalist
Christians, and to a lesser extent among Pentecostals, proved very successful. By
the 1980s, if you said that you were a creationist, people just assumed that you
believed that everything started about 6000 to 10,000 years ago.

The antievolution movement got a big boost in the 1960s with the appearance
of a federally subsidized series of biology textbooks for high schools that brought
evolution back into the classroom. After the controversies surrounding the Scopes
trial, coverage of evolution in high school texts, already fairly limited, disappeared to almost zero. But as a result of the Russian success with *Sputnik* in 1957,
Americans panicked at the thought that they were now letting the Russians get
ahead of them in the space race. They attributed this failure to the poor scientific
education that American young people were receiving. To remedy this problem,
the federal government started throwing large amounts of money at science educators. A group called the Biological Sciences Curriculum Study received some of
this money to rewrite high school textbooks in biology. When these new texts became available in the 1960s, they once again brought parents and young people
face to face with evolution. It was this you might say "aggressive" move by evolutionists and biologists that prompted a backlash from creationists, who had
been organizing and coalescing around the very distinctive view of young-earth
creationism. As a consequence, during the 1970s many conservative Christians
came to promote "creation science" or "scientific creationism," a new name for
the old "Flood geology." They tried to sell it in the public schools as alternative
science: creation science versus evolution science. In 1968 the Supreme Court had
finally ruled that the old antievolution laws from the 1920s were unconstitutional;
so outlawing evolution was no longer a legal option for creationists. Instead, they
tried to push their way into the classroom with a "scientific" alternative.

Was this what led to Scopes II?

Several events have been labeled Scopes II by the press. Probably the one most worthy of that designation was the trial in the early 1980s in Little Rock, Arkansas. In the early 1980s a number of states had debated the wisdom of passing laws—so-called balanced treatment acts—that mandated that creation science be taught whenever evolution science was taught. Arkansas and Louisiana actually passed such laws, which were immediately challenged in the courts. The ACLU returned to the creation-evolution trenches.

The first trial occurred in Little Rock. At the end of the trial, which became a media event of sorts, the judge ruled that creation science was not science but religion, and thus violated the constitutional separation of church and state. One of the interesting sidelights to this legal affair was that it was not useful at all to argue that creation science was bad science, because it is not unconstitutional to teach bad science. To be effective, it was necessary to argue that creation science was not science at all. To make this argument, experts had to introduce arbitrary criteria demarcating science from nonscience.

There were substantial differences between the Arkansas trial and the Scopes trial. For example, during the Scopes trial the advocates for evolution had tried to show that evolution would do religion no harm, and they had actually argued in court that students should be exposed to both sides of the controversy. By the early 1980s, however, evolutionists had gained the upper hand to the extent that they now argued for teaching evolution alone and for, in effect, outlawing the teaching of creationism. This time it was the creationists who insisted on teaching both sides of the issue.

Where does intelligent-design theory fit in this history?

Intelligent design refers to the belief that the careful study of nature, especially at the microscopic level, reveals such complexity that only a "designer" could account for it. Although the advocates of this view rarely refer to God by name, it's clear that they identify the designer with God. The proponents of intelligent design have staked out a position somewhere between theistic evolution (the belief that God creates by means of evolution), on the one hand, and scientific creationism, on the other. As a matter of fact, the intelligent-design camp includes a few people who would probably regard themselves as theistic evolutionists, as well as a few who would regard themselves "young-earth creationists." The most distinctive feature of intelligent design is the insistence that a purely naturalistic theory of evolution cannot explain the world around us. To a person, its advocates are opposed to naturalistic evolution. Although creation scientists ordinarily like anyone who raises questions about naturalistic evolution, they have been rather critical of the intelligent-design people because the intelligent design advocates refuse to endorse their particular explanation of Genesis 1 or, for that matter, any interpretation of Genesis.

For decades creation scientists battled to show that the day-age and gap theories of Genesis let evolution in through the back door because either of these views allows for the time that biological evolution needs. If you collapse earth history down to about 6000 years, as they do, then there's no time for evolution.

The young-earth creationists keep pushing the intelligent design people to declare themselves on Genesis, while the intelligent-design camp wants to take a more scientific approach, without introducing divisive biblical opinions. This is exemplified by one of the leaders of the intelligent-design movement, a biochemist at Lehigh University, Michael Behe, who argues that he has discovered evidence in his laboratory of intelligent design. He thinks this discovery ranks right up there with the discoveries of Louis Pasteur, Isaac Newton, and the other great figures of the history of science. Other intelligent-design spokesmen, such as the Berkeley lawyer Philip Johnson, insist that the rules for doing science should be expanded to allow for nonnaturalistic (that is, supernaturalistic) explanations.

Theistic evolutionists tend to find the intelligent-design people to be too skeptical of naturalistic science to be comfortable with them. By and large, theistic evolutionists are happy to let naturalistic science explain the workings of nature—and then conclude that "This is the way that God operates." Unlike the intelligent-design theorists, they don't say "Oh, at this microscopic level you can see evidence of God actually working."

Does not all of the controversy surrounding evolution suggest that there is an inherent conflict between science and religion?

First, I should say that I do not believe that the image of ongoing warfare between science and religion accurately describes what has happened historically. Of course, there have been many battles—psychological, professional, disciplinary—involving scientific and religious claims. But rarely, if ever, have they simply pitted scientists against religionists. The battles have often erupted between scientists (remember, for example, Louis Agassiz and Asa Gray) or between members of the same church (Asa Gray and Charles Hodge were both Presbyterians). In some contexts you see groups struggling for cultural authority, with both sides appealing to science. Occasionally, you'll even find poignant evidence of struggles that go on in the individual minds of scientists or religionists, wrestling with the competing claims of science and religion. Although issues related to science and religion have generated a great deal of conflict and unrest, there has been no inevitable warfare between the two. And in many instances, science and religion have been mutually reinforcing.

NOTE

1. R. Numbers, *The Creationists* (New York: Knopf Publishing, 1992).

6 The Evolution of Life

Niles Eldredge *American Museum of Natural History*

The bare bones of the story of life's evolution on earth were known to Charles Darwin and his contemporaries; for even though paleontology was still in its infancy in the mid–nineteenth century, the outline for what we now realize has been the last half billion years of the history of complex animal and plant forms was already in place. What the early biologists and paleontologists did *not* know was anything about life's first 3 billion years, when all life was in the form, first, of microscopic bacteria and, somewhat later, more complex celled ("eukaryotic") microbes. And they did not have an accurate grasp of how old the earth and the life it supports was. But they did have a grasp of the relative chronology, the sequence of life forms, of the dominant animals and plants of the ancient seas and continents.

Science is a form of storytelling. We have, of course, our strict rules of evidence. So we can check on ourselves for the accuracy of our accounts. But accounts such as the following overview of the history of life are indeed stories. And the narrative that unfolds, while based on long-known facts, takes a very different form than it would have had another paleontologist (or even myself) been telling the tale, say, twenty-five years ago.

The history of paleontological narratives of life's evolution has been, for the most part, and up until very recently, depictions of a grand, gradual unfolding, as natural selection slowly and inexorably changed all species, making them, it was commonly said, ever better, ever more highly adapted, and ever more complex. That story agreed well with the prevailing genetics-based view of evolution, one that persists today in the writings of a school of thought I have labeled (admittedly unflatteringly) as "ultra-Darwinian." For example, British biologist Richard Dawkins, the very archetypal ultra-Darwinian, maintains that natural selection results from an endless competitive race among genes for representation in the next succeeding generation. Such a fundamental competitive genic race is both necessary and sufficient to explain life's evolutionary history—one that would be expected, in the main, to be slow, steady, and gradual—there being no reason, in the theory itself, to expect otherwise.

But that is not what the history of life looks like at all. Paleontologists now realize that little evolutionary change occurs at all unless something—meaning something *physical*—happens to destabilize ecosystems, drive many existing species to extinction, and thus spur on the evolution of new species as ecosystems are, in effect, reassembled, rebuilt, and eventually brought to stable equilibrium. This new emerging picture of evolution—its history and its internal mechanics— is radically different from the traditional image of evolution.

Paleontologists have long felt ill at ease with geneticists. In an amusing comment on this tension, one of my great intellectual heroes, and predecessor paleontologist at the American Museum of Natural History, George Gaylord Simpson, wrote (in 1944, *Tempo and Mode in Evolution*) that

> not long ago paleontologists felt that a geneticist was a person who shut himself in a room, pulled down the shades, watched small flies disporting themselves in milk bottles, and thought that he was studying nature. A pursuit so removed from the realities of life, they said, had no significance for the true biologist. On the other hand, the geneticists said that paleontology had no further contributions to make to biology, that its only point had been the completed demonstration of the truth of evolution, and that it was a subject too purely descriptive to merit the name "science." The paleontologist, they believed, is like a man who undertakes to study the principles of the internal combustion engine by standing on a street corner and watching the motor cars whiz by.[1]

Simpson's book was intended to bridge the formidable gap he so engagingly portrayed. He was only partially successful, as his central idea ("quantum evolution") was ridiculed by geneticists, and in any case greatly modified by Simpson himself in 1953 so as to bring his ideas into closer agreement with prevailing genetically based gradualistic evolutionary thinking.[2] But Simpson's book nonetheless left an indelible stamp on paleontological thinking on evolution: He taught us that recurrent patterns in the history of life have much to tell us about the nature of the evolutionary process itself.

That is what paleontologists have been doing intensively in the last twenty-five years or so: We have been scrutinizing repeated patterns in the history of life on all scales from the disruption and reestablishment of local ecosystems on up through cataclysmic events that have triggered global mass extinction events. I have concluded that there is a continuous spectrum between minor ecosystem disturbance and rebound (the ecological phenomenon known as "succession") on up through regional degradation of ecosystems and the consequent extinction of old and evolution of new species, and, further on up, to the truly global mass extinctions.[3] All such extinctions have been triggered by physical events (except the most recent one—the modern biodiversity crisis triggered by human degradation of the ecosystems of the planet), involving the die-off of entire groups of animals and plants and the consequent evolution of new, large-scale groups that, in effect, take their place. Natural selection indeed does lie at the heart of the evolutionary process but springs into action (in the sense of *directional* selection, effecting adaptive change) almost exclusively only after such physically disruptive events.

Thus, nothing much happens in evolution without such physical disruption and extinction as a necessary prelude. Now, at last, we can specify just how the evolution of life is tied in with the physical, nonliving side of the universe: the physical world of matter-in-motion regulates the evolution of genetic systems (species and larger groups, such as all mammals) via its effects on the structure and stability of ecosystems. The following narrative of the history of life highlights examples of these very points.

We now know that the earth was formed some 4.65 billion years ago. The oldest rocks are igneous and metamorphic and by their very nature have no fossil content. But it is indeed remarkable that the very oldest sedimentary rocks (the rocks that form from sedimentary particles such as sand, clay, or lime), the kind of rocks that *do* typically contain fossils, actually have minute bacterial fossils

(3.5 billion years) and/or chemical traces (perhaps 3.7 billion years) of life in them! That simply means that life is an intrinsic part of this planet!

Now, our knowledge of so-called Precambrian (3.5 to 0.54 billion years ago) life has grown by leaps and bounds in recent years, but the record is still sufficiently spotty that one must be cautious when looking for links between major evolutionary events, on the one hand, and physical events in the history of planet earth on the other. One very clever paleobiologist, Joe Kirschvink of Cal Tech, however, has suggested a tantalizing series of just such connections between the early history of earth and of life. For example, Kirschvink has discussed an event where the earth was subjected to a final mass bombardment of asteroids about 3.7 billion years ago—an event affecting the moon as well. Some geologists have speculated that significant amounts of water came to our planet during this event. There is also the possibility that life itself came in from someplace else—rather than evolving de novo here. Yet another possibility is that, had life already been present *prior* to this massive bombardment, it may well have been eradicated—the very first episode of mass extinction! *That* would mean that life evolved more than once on the planet and that would be extremely interesting insofar as debates over the mechanisms—and associated probabilities—of the origin of life are concerned. But, in this particular instance, the data are so scanty that all we can do, for the moment, is speculate on the impact (literally) that this bombardment may have had on the origin or extinction of living systems.

Life for its first billion or so years was just bacteria. Although most, of course, were microscopic rods, spirals, and balls, others grew to massive sizes as sediment-trapping colonial structures: the famous stromatolites, which are still forming today in such places as Australia's Shark's Bay. The next significant event was the evolution of the eukaryotic cell—cells that have true nuclei housing DNA, cut off from the rest of the cell's machinery by a double-layered wall. I think University of Massachusetts biologist Lynn Margulis is absolutely right when she says that the eukaryotic cell evolved as a fusion of different kinds of bacteria, a form of symbiosis that became evolutionarily permanent.

We have eukaryotic cells, as do all other animals—plus all plants, fungi, and such microorganisms as amoebae and flagellates. The oldest eukaryotic cells known with certainty are about 1.3 billion years old, but more recent, if less thoroughly convincing, evidence suggests that eukaryotes may go back as far as 2.2 billion years.

Enter, again, Joe Kirschvink, who, with his colleagues, has documented the rather astonishing conclusion that the earth was glaciated *almost completely*, not once, but twice, during the Precambrian.[4] His "snowball earth" scenario sees ice fields reaching all the way into the tropics the first time at 2.2 billion years ago. Once again, we see a coincidence between a major event in the history of life—and a major physical event affecting the entire planet. Cause and effect? We cannot be sure, but it may well prove to be the case that the origin and radiation of eukaryotic organisms was triggered by that massive glaciation event.

Kirschvink's second "snowball earth" happened between 800 and 600 million years ago—once again, just when the animal phyla began to diversify. The famous "Cambrian explosion," where arthropods, brachiopods and other major, wellskeletonized components of the marine invertebrate fauna seem to appear suddenly in the fossil record around 535 to 540 million years ago, itself seems to have been triggered by the rise of oxygen levels dissolved in seawater to sufficient concentrations to support the large bodies of multicelled organisms. But, then again, Kirschvink has published evidence that the entire crust of the earth may have rotated 90° just at the same time! We almost have too many major physical events to correlate with major evolutionary events half a billion years ago!

Although the correlations between earth and life historical events are certainly there throughout the Precambrian, it remains difficult to be equally certain that those physical events were actually driving the evolutionary process. Not so for the abundant, repetitive patterns of various scale that dominate the past 535 million years of life's history. Here, we can be far more precise in our correlations—and far more certain in specifying chains of events, with obvious cause-and-effect implications.

First, a disclaimer, an exception to the otherwise overwhelming generalization that all evolution is contingent upon major physical events in earth history. Organisms may invade entirely new terrains where there simply had been no life forms before them. The obvious example: the invasion of land by simple plants, quickly followed by the evolution of insects and other terrestrial arthropods. Exposed stretches of land were there all along, but it was not until the early-mid Paleozoic (not much more than 400 million years ago) that life managed to gain an evolutionary and ecological foothold on land.

For the most part, the fossil record of the entire last 535 million years is one of relative stability of ecosystems and evolutionary quiescence and great stability in species. The original example of the notion of "punctuated equilibria" (which I developed and published with Stephen Jay Gould in the early 1970s) involved a lineage of mid-Paleozoic (Devonian) trilobites. The main species of this lineage remained stable for some 6 to 7 million years; when new species in the lineage evolved, they did so very rapidly. It now turns out that the vast majority of the other species living cheek-by-jowl with these trilobites in those Devonian seas were also very stable. Looking at the overall history of life in the eastern and central United States, paleontologist Carl Brett (now at the University of Cincinnati) and his colleagues have documented some eight such stable successive faunas. Most of the species within each fauna remain stable throughout the 5- to 7-million-year interval; 70 to 85 percent are present throughout the interval; only 20 percent survive to the next succeeding fauna, the rest becoming extinct; the new fauna are a mix of survivors, plus immigrants from other regions, and new species that evolve in rapid bursts of evolution from their predecessors in the previous complex of ecosystems.

Nor is this pattern restricted to the Paleozoic. Yale paleontologist Elisabeth S. Vrba has found precisely the same sequence of events in the evolution of mammals and plants—including our own ancestors!—in the ecosystems of eastern and southern Africa. Once again, there is great stability of ecosystems with little or no evolution, interrupted abruptly by a major episode of extinction, and followed by bursts of evolution and migration as the new ecosystems take shape.

All such events are triggered by physical environmental change, most commonly global climate change. That certainly was the case in Africa 2.5 million years ago, when global temperatures dropped 10 to 15° C, changing the wet woodlands over to drier savannahs, touching off a mass exodus and dying off, and prompting the evolution of new species adapted to the drier, more open grasslands.

Less all-encompassing events punctuate the histories of regional ecosystems—triggering ecological succession, but not causing evolution unless a threshold is reached and many species are actually driven to extinction first. Thus these regional episodes, occurring at 5- to 7-million-year intervals in the marine environments of the Paleozoic—and seemingly with greater frequency in the climatically less-buffered terrestrial environments—are absolutely crucial to life's evolution. Without them, things would simply stay the same.

On the upper end of the scale, of course, are the global mass extinctions that have, with far less frequency but with much greater total impact, reshaped and reconfigured life on the planet. The five greatest mass extinction events of the past 500 million years occurred at the end of the Ordovician Period (440 million years ago); near the end of the Devonian Period (367 million years ago); the end of the Permian Period (245 million years ago); the end of the Triassic Period (208 million years ago); and the end of the Cretaceous Period (65 million years ago).

All were caused by physical environmental change that simply overwhelmed the majority of earth's species. The greatest of them all was the end of the Permian event, which so changed the complexion of life that geologists have used it to mark the end of the Paleozoic Era ("Ancient Life") and the beginning of the Mesozoic ("Middle Life"). Retired University of Chicago paleontologist David M. Raup once estimated that perhaps as many as 96 percent of the earth's species may have become extinct during this event. Think of it: All 10 million or more species on earth right now evolved from perhaps as little as 4 percent of the genetic information that managed to survive this extinction! Yet today we have at least as many species, and all the forms of ecological diversity, that existed prior to the event—a strong testimony to the evolutionary resiliency of life.

Although life springs back, as new species evolve to take the place of those fulfilling similar niches in former ecosystems, it is also true that the greater the extinction events, and the larger-scale the groups are that are driven to extinction, the more different those newly evolved groups will be from their predecessors. When corals became extinct at the end of the Paleozoic, we now understand that the modern corals that appeared to take their place (after a characteristic lag of some 7 or 8 million years) evolved from those Paleozoic corals' remote collateral kin: Modern corals are most closely related to naked sea anemones. It is now clear that "corals" were "invented" twice in evolutionary history. The disappearance of the Paleozoic corals triggered the evolution of hard, stony skeletons in the otherwise nonskeletonized anemones.

The most famous example of the effects of mass extinction on evolutionary history comes from the extinction event that is itself the most famous of all: the end of the Cretaceous event that saw the disappearance of terrestrial (meaning "nonbird") dinosaurs and a host of other species living in terrestrial and aqueous environments. Paleontologists have known for years that mammals and dinosaurs evolved at the same time, sometime in the Upper Triassic Period. For reasons no one pretends to understand, it was the dinosaurs and their close reptilian relatives that radiated into all the adaptive body forms to occupy a vast range of niches in Mesozoic ecosystems. Although extinction cut back the dinosaurs more than once during the Mesozoic, they, not the mammals, kept evolving new species and occupying the ecosystems—until, that is, the cometary impacts abruptly disrupted those Cretaceous ecosystems and finally drove every last remaining terrestrial dinosaur extinct. Then, and only then, did the mammals diversify, quickly evolving a great array of body forms and becoming the new tetrapod vertebrate occupants of the world's ecosystems.

It used to be assumed that mammals evolved and crowded out the dinosaurs by sheer physiological superiority. Indeed, the old movie *Godzilla vs. King Kong* (at least in its American version—Godzilla won in the Japanese edition!) saw the weaker King Kong ultimately vanquish Godzilla because he was smarter: The ape was brainier than the dumb reptile. Thus, our own evolution, as the brainiest of all mammals, was always seen as some pinnacle of evolutionary success and as an inevitability given natural selection honing adaptations as geological time slowly goes by.

Not so. We see now that the dinosaurs succumbed, not to superior mammals, but to cometary swarms that apparently knocked out the photosynthetic base of the food chain of all their ecosystems. Only after the dinosaurs were finally gone could mammals evolve into anything but primitive ratlike omnivores. The simple truth is, had those comets not struck the earth, the dinosaurs almost undoubtedly would still be here, mammals would not have undergone their own series of evolutionary diversifications, and we ourselves would not be here.

So much for inevitability in the evolution of life. We have a starkly different view of evolution now than we did twenty-five years ago. But I cannot close without mentioning the Sixth Extinction that we are now in. This time, it is humans that are acting as surrogates for global climate change or meteoritic impacts. But our effect on the earth's ecosystems and species—we are losing at least 30,000 species a year—is very much like that seen 65 million years ago when comets struck the earth, ecosystems collapsed, and dinosaurs and many other species became extinct.

I am often asked, in effect, "So what?" If evolution comes along and eventually "fixes" things and ecosystems rebound, why should we care? The answer is simple: We are still a part of this system—removed as we have felt ourselves to be after we developed agriculture beginning some 10,000 years ago. Our own future is still very much tied up to the future both of life and of the physical systems on this planet. Destructive as we are, we are simply too interesting, too novel an evolutionary experiment to just allow ourselves to perish. But to save ourselves, we must save our planet, or else we come to be just another casualty in the ages-old cycle of extinction and evolution.

NOTES

1. G. G. Simpson, *Tempo and Mode in Evolution* (New York: Columbia University Press, 1944).

2. G. G. Simpson, *The Major Features of Evolution* (New York: Columbia University Press, 1953).

3. See my *Pattern of Evolution*, 1999, W. H. Freeman and Co.

4. J. L. Kirschvink, "Late Proterozoic Low-Latitude Global Glaciation: The Snowball Earth," in J.W. Schopf, C. Klein, & D. Des Maris (eds.), *The Proterozoic Biosphere: A Multidisciplinary Study* (Cambridge, UK: Cambridge University Press, 1992), pp. 51–52.

7 The Mechanism of Evolution

Ursula Goodenough *Washington University–St. Louis*

It is helpful to begin by considering various kinds of evolution. Cosmic evolution—of the universe, the galaxy, and the planet earth—is grounded in the laws of physics: gravitation, atomic interactions, thermodynamics. The laws of physics were in no way violated as the next three kinds of evolution came to be. They were a given. But the next three kinds of evolution depend on, in addition to the laws of physics, the creation of instructions: instructions for making things, instructions that can be changed. It is as instructions change that we get new kinds of organisms and the process that we call biological and then cultural evolution.

Biological evolution occurs through the mechanism of variation and natural selection that was articulated by Darwin. But there are other kinds of evolution besides cosmic and biological. Language, it is proposed, evolves by means of the Baldwin effect[1] and the evolution of culture is, in many ways, Lamarckian.[2] Biological evolution, however, is about the processes that make instructions for making organisms.

The most important thing about life is the interactions of shapes with one another, and the shapes that are most important in life processes are the shapes of proteins. In order to get proteins that have particular shapes, the instructions for doing so are encoded as a sequence of nucleotides in molecules called DNA (deoxyribonucleic acid) and RNA (ribonucleic acid). Long strands of these nucleotides—ATGC (adenine, thymine, guanine, cytosine)—are called nucleic acids, and nucleic acids form the chromosomes in every cell in our bodies and in every organism. Specific segments of these long strands constitute the genes, and each gene codes for the sequence of amino acids in a particular protein. Because amino acids have different properties (some of them are "greasy," some of them have negative or positive charges), they associate with one another in specific ways such that the protein folds up into a particular, distinctive shape. So the various genes, each different in its coding sequence, produces different sequences of amino acids that give you proteins of different shapes (Figure 7.1).

Protein shapes are important because that is how things get done in life. Proteins, because they have particular shapes, literally fit together like a 3-D jigsaw puzzle (Figure 7.2). Given their shapes they join to form complexes of proteins, and these protein-protein interactions, in turn, have a lot to do with the way a living cell is structured.

Many proteins also have little areas in their shape, little pockets, that other smaller molecules can fit into. When these small molecules fit into such pockets, this greatly speeds up the rate of chemical reactions that can occur, chemical reactions that underlie such key life processes as photosynthesis and digestion. This process is known as catalyzing the chemical reaction. Proteins that carry out catalysis are known as enzymes.

Genes encode the shapes of proteins.

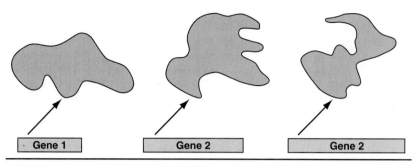

AATCGTAGTCGGATCGGTAGCAAATCGGGCTACGTAGCTATGGATCCCATCTC

FIGURE 7.1   Genes code for proteins with different shapes.

Finally, there is a very important class of protein called a receptor. One part of a receptor sticks out and interacts with the environment, picking up environmental cues. This interaction gives information to the cell, indicating what is out there in the environment and how the cell is to proceed.

The modern eukaryotic cell is formed and sustains itself by virtue of these basic features of proteins. Eukaryotic cells have a nucleus where the DNA is

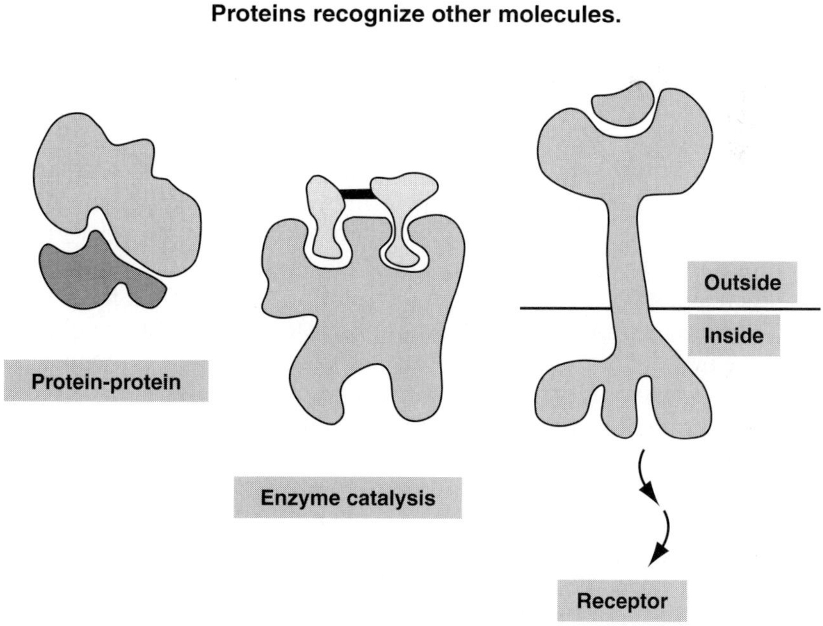

Proteins recognize other molecules.

Protein-protein

Enzyme catalysis

Outside

Inside

Receptor

FIGURE 7.2   Protein/protein interactions, enzymes, and receptors.

stored. Outside of the nucleus, in the cytoplasm, is where the protein is made and where enzymes are that catalyze the reactions that break down nutrients to provide energy for the cell. The membrane that encloses the cell is made of lipid and protein that is studded with receptors, poking out into the environment trying to sense what is out there and how to react.

But where does a complex system like this come from? Observation has shown that the universe is full of many of the kinds of small organic "building blocks" needed to form the components of a cell: methane, amino acids, and so forth. These molecules are created by chemical reactions that are driven by fluxes in stellar radiation. Most scientific hypotheses for the origin of life propose that these building blocks were brought to earth in cosmic dust. The formation of nucleotides poses more problematic chemistry, and much remains to be understood—indeed, scientific hypotheses for the origins of the first nucleic acids will likely never be "provable," but only "plausible." The following is such a plausible scenario.

The core concept in this scenario is that nucleotides formed in some ancient context on the earth, provisionally, some ancient puddle. Left to themselves over long periods of time, nucleotides would have the tendency to form long chains with one another, that is, nucleic acids. This process might well have been catalyzed by clays and other minerals in the puddle. But we do not have any life at this point. This is just chemistry in a puddle.

At some point, however, some nucleic acid not only existed as a sequence of nucleotides, but because of its particular sequence, curled up into a distinctive shape, much as proteins have later come to do, and acquired the capacity to catalyze its own replication. This is a process that has come to be called "self-replication." If one came back to this puddle 1000 years or 10,000 years later, one would discover that many of the original nucleic acids would still be there, but there would be many more copies of the self-replicating species (Figure 7.3). There is *positive natural selection* for self-replication.

But this is not enough for evolution. Self-replication is necessary. It is necessary to be able to make copies of molecules. But consider the original puddle. That puddle was already provisioned with everything needed to bring about self-replication. It was filled with preformed nucleotides. But what would happen when one kind of nucleotide in the puddle ran out? Then there would be a crisis: Not even the molecules with the capacity to self-replicate would be able to do so. Development in the puddle would freeze. At this point a second property emerges, the ability of life to acquire the raw materials it needs. It could make them, extracting energy from the sun to fuel the process. But in order to develop its own resources and to pass on this capacity to its progeny, it would be necessary to encode the instructions for these processes in its own DNA strand.

So in the end we have DNA strands not only encoding the ability to replicate themselves, but within the strand a gene that can code for an enzyme that can catalyze the formation of nucleotides from simpler carbon compounds. Another gene in the strand could be involved in contributing to the creation of photosynthetic processes. Yet another gene could code for a protein that begins the formation of a cell membrane. Once DNA strands are endowed with instructions for

Selection for replication

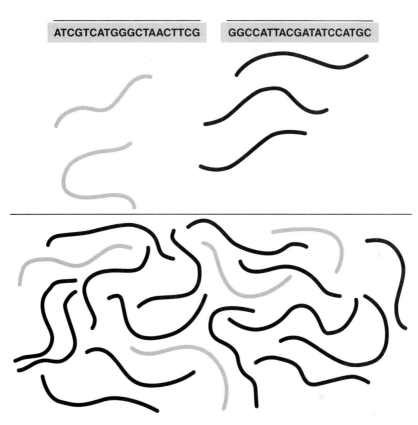

ATCGTCATGGGCTAACTTCG   GGCCATTACGATATCCATGC

FIGURE 7.3   *The differential impact of self-replication.*

their self-replication, those that have in addition the capacity to synthesize and harbor nucleotides within a membrane will have an advantage in replication over those that cannot. So the genes that allow for the formation of a cell membrane would be selected for and the first cells would appear.

If that were all there was to it, we would have something that could survive in the puddle. But one of the beautiful things about this planet is its enormous ecological diversity and its concomitant biological diversity. The fact that we have such diversity of life is a consequence of the fact that the DNA instructions are not static. They can undergo change, what is called a mutation.

Imagine two identical DNA molecules. During the course of its copying, there is an error. Instead of an A, a C appears in its place. Because of this change, there may be a difference of shape in the two long chains of amino acids that result from the instructions of these DNA molecules (Figure 7.4). That one amino acid difference can cause, for example, a pocket not to be there anymore; instead, a protuberance may stick out. There is a poignant modern example of this phenom-

Mutations often change the shape of proteins.

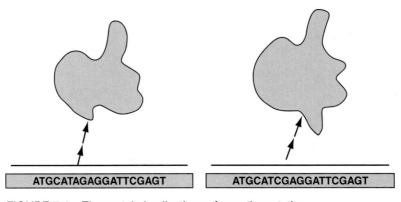

FIGURE 7.4   The protein implications of genetic mutation.

enon related to the hemoglobin protein. A single amino acid difference can result in a different shape for hemoglobin and hence for blood cells. This single difference is the cause of a disease called sickle cell anemia, but it also gives the person who has it an advantage in fighting the infectious disease malaria. Ironically, this one change has both positive and negative consequences for health.

Now, going back to our A → C mutation, imagine that this mutation occurs in one of two organisms (Figure 7.5). The consequences could be immediate. It could be that the mutation renders the organism unable to produce a protein essential for its existence. Therefore, the organism with the mutation is not going to survive and that is the end of it. On the other hand, it could be that the mutation produces a new protein that makes the organism better able to survive and reproduce in its environment. But what usually happens is neither of these alternatives. Instead, the mutant organism produces a protein that is a little better, or not quite as good as, the normal one. It is important to stress here that the external environment is not evaluating the new protein *per se* but rather the organism as a whole: natural selection "sees" traits that are the result of numerous protein activ-

Natural selection:
the environment evaluates

FIGURE 7.5   Organismic implications of genetic mutation.

ities. Thus, out new protein's influence is dependent on its interactions with existing proteins to produce a selectable phenotype.

A second kind of mutation has very important consequences as well. A chromosome is not just one gene after another. "Upstream" from each gene is a DNA sequence that does not code for a protein. Instead, this sequence is the "on-off switch" for the gene and is generically called the promoter (Figure 7.6). If a gene's promoter is in the "off" position, the gene is not being expressed and the associated protein is not being produced in the cell; in the "on" position, the gene is expressed and the protein is made.

Not only can mutations affect the genes themselves, but they can also affect the promoters. Mutations in gene promoters can affect not only *whether* the gene is expressed but also *when* it is expressed. As a multicellular creature develops it goes from a single-celled fertilized egg to a complex and differentiated multi-celled structure. If a gene whose promoter was set so that its protein is to be synthesized in one cell at the 4-cell stage, that protein would interact with all the other proteins in the other cells at that stage. But if there were a promoter mutation that delayed switching on of that gene until the 256-cell stage, then the protein from this one cell is going to encounter a completely different ensemble of proteins, a completely different cellular environment (Figure 7.7). As a consequence there would likely be a very different outcome in the embryo. It appears that a lot of animal and plant evolution has occurred as a result of this process, called heterochrony, where a shift in the timing of expression of genes has led to the transformation from one kind of organism to another.

So far, we have considered genetic changes due to mutations in genes and mutations in promoters. But this has been an account of how existing genes change or how their function is changed. We have yet to see how entirely new genes arise. Very occasionally, when genes are being copied, a mistake is made whereby the same gene is copied twice (Figure 7.8). The result is two identical genes right next to each other. If gene 1 is carrying out some essential function, it can keep on doing so. But that makes gene 2 a free agent. If it mutates, it can change in any

Regulation of gene expression.

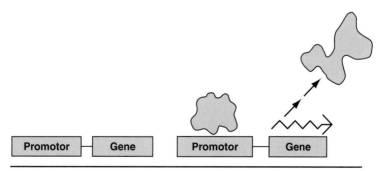

ATTCGCTAATGCTCCCTAGGTAGCCCGTTAGACTTAAAGGCTCTAGCTA

FIGURE 7.6   Promoter DNA.

Heterochrony

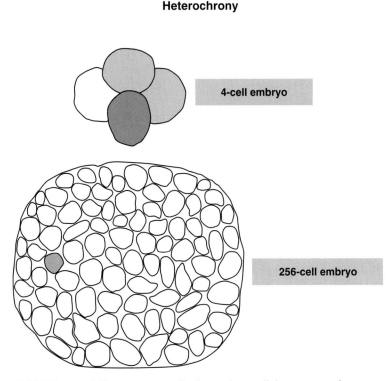

FIGURE 7.7   Different temporally dependent cellular contexts for gene expression.

number of ways without any impact on the function of gene 1. Of course, if the result of the mutation causes the production of proteins that are toxic, then the organism will be eliminated. But the new protein may instead have no immediate impact in which case the new gene may just drift through the lineage, available for the opportunity of a new function to emerge in the evolution of life.

Imagine how a new bacterium could develop. A lot of bacteria have appendages called flagella. They stick out from the bacterium and rotate like a propeller. They enable the bacterium to move. This is a very adaptive capacity to have because it allows the bacterium to move toward prey or away from toxic stimuli in the environment. Flagella have been the focus of considerable study, and it turns out that this propeller is structurally very complicated. About 20 different proteins are required to make this bacterial motor. In fact, in a modern bacterium, if you disrupt any of the genes that code for any one of the required proteins, the motor does not work anymore.

The question is, how can such a complex system evolve? How does it happen? No one knows, of course, but we can tell a story that illustrates the way that complex systems are thought to evolve as a general matter. It turns out that the basic

New genes by duplication.

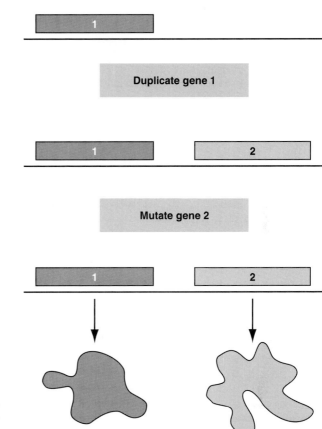

FIGURE 7.8   *Gene evo-
lution through duplication
and mutation.*

part of the motor is a channel [Figure 7.9(a)]. All cell membranes have lots of
channels that regulate which ions go in and out of the cell. This particular channel
is one that regulate hydrogen ions (protons) going in an out of the cell and at
what rate. This proton flux through the cell not only affects the ionic environment
but it is also a way that the cell gets energy. So hydrogen fluxing channels are
very important to the cell. Thus, there is a lot of selective advantage in having
channels that work efficiently.

Let us start with a primitive bacterium that possesses such channels but lacks a
flagellum. Imagine that there is a duplication in one of its genes and that a mutation occurs in the duplicate gene so that a new protein is produced. It turns out
that this new protein has a very good shape for binding to the side of the channel
and that, if it binds to the channel, the channel works more efficiently and pro-

Channel lets hydrogen ions into cell.

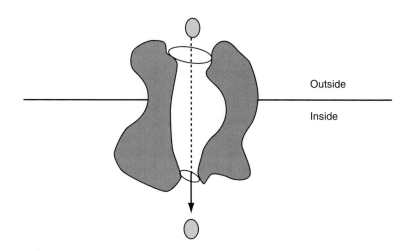

FIGURE 7.9(a)

duces more energy for the cell [Figure 7.9(b)]. In this scenario there will be selection for bacteria that have this second gene, and so over generations that gene will spread through the bacteria population.

However, it turns out, in our story, that when the protein binds to the ion channel, it also causes the channel to spin around in the membrane. This is an inciden-

New protein added:
channel works better (selected).
channel rotates (not selected).

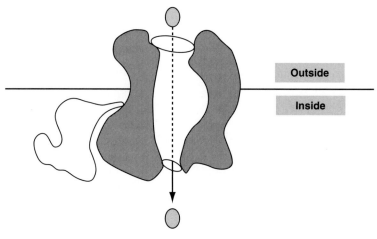

FIGURE 7.9(b)

tal effect. There is absolutely no selection for this new feature. What nature selects for is the channel that works better. But collaterally a new behavior has been added to the cell.

Now there is a second gene duplication and mutation [Figure 7.9(c)]. In this case the new gene is similar to an existing gene that codes for a long, fibrous protein that is used by the bacterium. However, the protein produced by this new gene, because of its mutation, has a pocket that effectively binds to the outside of the channel. Suddenly, because the channel is rotating, the bacterium now has a system that can propel it through in its environment, a flagellum. With the appearance of this new complex feature, there is now selection, not only for more efficiently working channels, but also for any new genes that might arise that would help this flagellum function better. Another mutation might produce a protein that better anchored the flagellum to the channel [Figure 7.9(d)]. Another mutation might improve rotation, now that rotation is something being selected for. In this manner it is possible to get complex traits through time, just by the

Add fibrous protein ⟶ rotating flagellum.

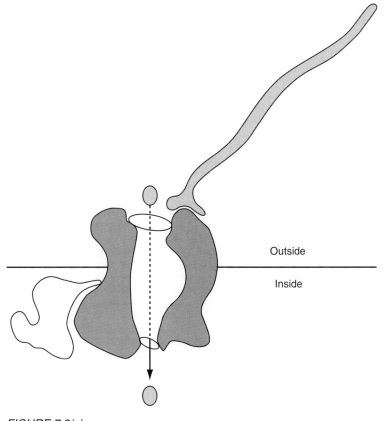

Outside

Inside

FIGURE 7.9(c)

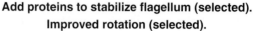

Add proteins to stabilize flagellum (selected).
Improved rotation (selected).

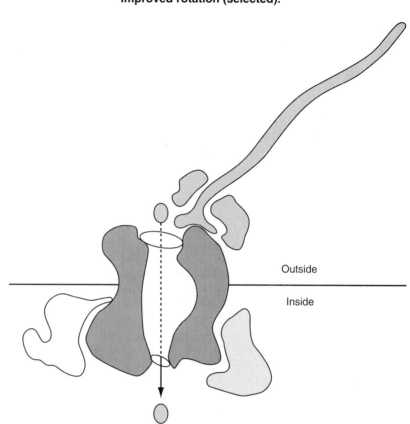

FIGURE 7.9(d)

accumulative acquisition of one new protein after another and natural selection for the resulting function or structure. As new genes are added to the structure, the genes encoding the preexisting structure are predicted to accumulate mutations that optimize the interactions of the old and the new. As a result, the biological machine becomes dependent on the interplay of all of these proteins such that, if one is removed, the whole can no longer function—that is, the machine has become irreducibly complex. But in no way does it follow that it was so "designed" at the outset. The irreducible complexity is the outcome of mutation and natural selection.

Another context for cell evolution is in relation to receptors. Receptors are the key proteins that enable an organism to navigate within its environment. There are all kinds of receptors, but it can be said generally that they all provide the cell with an immediate awareness of the environment. All receptors work basically the same way (Figure 7.10). A part of the protein sticks out from the cell and has a shape capable of recognizing something in the environment. There is a part of the

Awareness

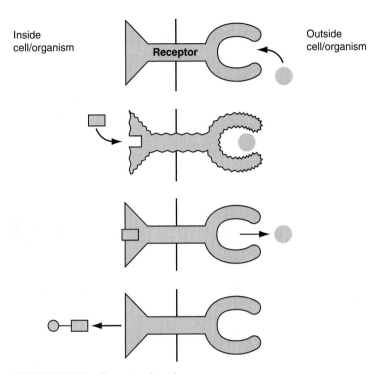

Inside
cell/organism

Receptor

Outside
cell/organism

FIGURE 7.10   Receptor function.

receptor that crosses the membrane. Then there is an element of the receptor on the inside of the cell. This is usually an enzyme.

Given this structure, the following process can occur. The portion of the receptor sticking out in the environment encounters a molecule that binds with it. Because of this binding, there is a change in the shape of the receptor protein that is transmitted along its length through the cell membrane to the inside of the cell, whereupon a cascade of biochemistry occurs that signals to the cell that the molecule is present in the environment.

An illustration of the evolution of receptors is known as *bricolage*, a French word that can be translated as "tinkering," making something from what is at hand, like a patchwork quilt (Figure 7.11). Not only can DNA in the chromosomes duplicate to make new genes, but pieces of DNA can "jump" around in the chromosomes and make new combinations that result in patchwork genes that produce new proteins.

As can be seen then, there are very different kinds of molecular mechanisms that can cause evolutionary change: There are mutations in the coding regions for proteins and mutations in the promoters that result in heterochrony; there is gene duplication that creates "rogue" genes that can then be sites for mutation and can

Bricolage

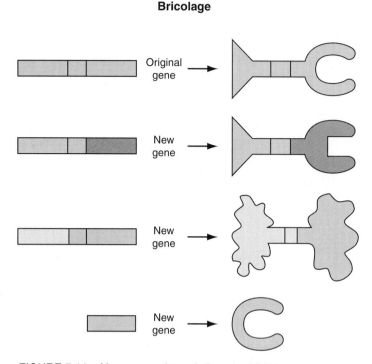

FIGURE 7.11   *New genes through "jumping" DNA.*

be selected for independently of the original gene; and there is bricolage, in which different genetic forms are used over and over again in different contexts.

We can now move from molecular evolution to evolutionary patterns. What happened between the original organism and modern organisms is not the kind of evolutionary picture that is often presented in textbooks, a picture where evolution goes from a simple cellular beginning to the present, ending with humans, while other species of organisms branch off to the side. In fact, evolutionary change has flowed through time more like a river into a delta. The genes that came into being in the original organisms are found today in all three branches of the evolutionary delta that formed shortly after life began. These three branches are the eubacteria, the eukaryotes (which is the branch in which humans eventually evolve), and a third group called the archaea. Some genes in all three of these branches encode proteins with the same basic structure and function. This allows us to conclude that these genes have all flowed through time from a common source. Along the way of the eukaryotic flow, some bacteria symbiotically entered into other organisms and became the mitochondria and the chloroplast of eukaryotic cells. This process of symbiotic integration is another way that biological complexity evolves.

Given this picture, it could be said that all the organisms that are alive today are equally old. Not "old" in the sense that their distinctive characteristics are equally old. Some functions and structures have arisen only recently. But they arose by the same kind of flowing process that has been at work from the beginning. In addition, all living creatures share the kinds of genes that are required for replication, for the production of proteins, and for transport across membranes. These genes are related across all species. So all living things are deeply interconnected in the deepest informational sense of that term.

Eukaryotic evolution entailed a long, slow process. Along the way, organisms branched off that gave rise to modern, single-celled life forms, many now parasites. Then, in the Cambrian period about 600 million years ago, there was a veritable "explosion" of new life forms. What can said about all of these eukaryotic lineages, what they all have in common with one another, is that they are all sexual in the Mendelian sense of the term. Whether the evolution of sexuality precipitated the Cambrian explosion or whether sexuality resulted from it is still undetermined. But without a doubt, the appearance of sexuality represented yet another remarkable way to get biological diversity.

In any kind of Mendelian sexual process there are two kinds of gamete cells involved (Figure 7.12). For convenience, we can call them sperm and egg cells. Each cell has its own set of genetic instructions, its genome. Such single-genome cells are called haploids. In sexual reproduction the sperm and egg cells fuse together and form a diploid cell. A diploid cell then contains two genomes, one contributed by each haploid cell. A cell with two genomes is one with the potential for many new biological characteristics. Genes have been brought from two different sources, and protein products from the two genomes are now interacting inside the diploid cell often in significantly new ways. The result of this process is, of course, lots of variation.

Then this diploid organism creates more haploid gametes by a process called meiosis, during which the two sets of genomic information are recombined in new ways. The result is that each haploid gamete is genetically distinct from its parent cells.

Sexual organisms have the ability to combine and recombine their genomes. But this process can only occur within a species. The genetic interactions associated with sexual reproduction must occur between organisms with similar genomes; otherwise the result is developmentally disastrous.[3] However, if this is the case, then how do new species arise?

The speciation process is one of the great biological mysteries. At the end of the process there is a new set of males and females that will only reproduce with one another and not with the species of their ancestor "mother" and "father." A new species is a new deck of genomes that can undergo its own shuffling. And these decks keep arising. But species are also going extinct. Because each species has a distinctive set of genes it is shuffling, the result is new opportunities for selective interaction with the environment. As a consequence, sexual organisms have populated most of the possible environmental niches on the planet.

Of the Post-Cambrian sexual organisms, some of the lineages have remained single celled. But the final core cellular innovation was the appearance of multicellularity (Figure 7.13). If we begin with the fertilized egg, the diploid zygote, it divides to form 2 cells, then 4 cells, then 8 cells, then 16, and so on and these cells

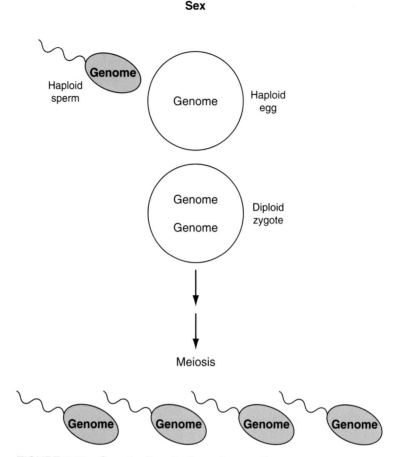

FIGURE 7.12 Genetic diversity through sexuality.

all remain associated with one another to form a single organism. As the cells divide they also begin to differentiate. Some of the genes turn on and some turn off (Figure 7.7). The result is a highly complex multicellular organism. In all such sexual organisms, as they develop, some of the cells differentiate as germline cells, cells that are going to give rise to the haploid gametes for producing the next generation. In the case of a female mammal, her germline cells become an ovary that will produce eggs containing the sets of her input genomes. The mammalian male develops sperm-producing testes. The genetic continuity of the species, the lineage, is transmitted through this germline. But as a consequence, a new dimension of life emerges. The multicellular organism is not required, as a whole, to be the unit of life that is passed forward to the next generation. The multicellular organism as a whole, what can be called the soma, can be selected for by virtue of its ability to function successfully in its environment. This selection will affect its ability to pass forward its gametes. But, because the soma does not itself have to go on into the next generation, it does not have to be immortal.

Multicellularity

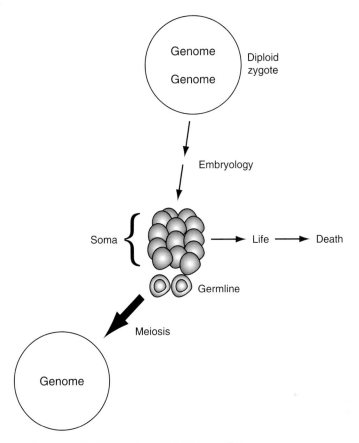

FIGURE 7.13   *Multicellularity and sexuality.*

It can die. This allows multicellular organisms to exhibit an extraordinarily wider range of form and behavior than single-celled organisms.

Multicellularity is manifest in three major groups: the green plants (with an enormous array of somas); the mushrooms (also exhibiting a wide range of somatic experimentation); and the animals. Animals not only exhibit a great diversity of body forms but, in addition, have evolved various multicellular reactive tissues, studded with awareness receptors, that allow the brain to process complex information from the environment. This information sensing and processing capacity has resulted in more complex patterns of behavior than found in the fungi or plants.

Although the general pattern of these lineages is relatively clear, the exact history of these lineages is still being reconstructed. For example, until recently the family tree containing humans was drawn such that humans branched off from the ape lineage about 15 millions years ago and then engaged in their own separate evolutionary development. Today it is becoming clearer that humans diverged from the lineage only about 5 million years ago. After the human lineage diverged, there was another divergence that distinguished between the chimpanzees and the bonobos. The brains of all our nearest primate relatives and their capacities for awareness are very well developed. On the other hand, their capacity for language is not well developed, and in nature they have not been observed engaging in symbolic forms of communication. But they do exhibit the neurological substrate that is also the foundation for the human brain.

Reviewing this remarkable history of species development and the biological mechanisms that make evolution possible, it is important to remember that at root the word *species* means "special." Each species is special and possesses distinctive capabilities that it applies especially well in its environmental context. Our species, *Homo sapiens,* has the remarkable capacity for language. It is this capacity, with others, that allows us to be scientists and artists, philosophers and theologians. As we consider the very unfortunate ways that we human beings are using our brains, to dominate, and all the other unfortunate things we are engaged in, let us not forget that we are also special. We do have these very wonderful things that we know how to do, including being aware of one another and our potential.

NOTES

1. In his 1896 article, "A New Factor in Evolution," which appeared in *The American Naturalist* 30 (June 1896): 441–451, 536–553, James Mark Baldwin proposed that learning can have an effect on the evolutionary process and abilities initially acquired by learning in one generation are replaced by genetically determined systems in later generations. Thereby, learned behavior becomes instinctual. See also Terrence W. Deacon, *The Symbolic Species* (New York: W. W. Norton & Company, 1997).

2. Jean-Baptiste Lamarck (1744–1829) proposed an evolutionary theory that characteristics acquired in one through behavior in one generation could be inherited by the future generation. Although this theory was rejected in favor of the Darwinian mechanism of random variation and natural selection, it does apply in the relation to culture, where the learnings of one generation are passed forward to future generations through various cultural systems.

3. If representatives of two species are able to produce viable offspring, the offspring is ordinarily sterile. Perhaps the most common example is the mule, which, although sterile itself, is the offspring of a horse and a donkey.

8 Neo-Darwinism in Theological Perspective

John F. Haught *Georgetown University*

My purpose here is to provide an introductory summary of some of the ways in which Darwinian and neo-Darwinian ideas have been received by theologians in the biblical, and particularly Christian, tradition. We shall see that what Daniel Dennett calls "Darwin's dangerous idea" (since it seems to him to render the whole discipline of theology superfluous) may in fact better be called "Darwin's gift to theology."[1]

It is important to note at the outset that Darwin is the author of two "dangerous ideas" and that the challenge he offers to theology may not be exactly the same in each case. The first idea is that all living beings share a common ancestry. All forms of life therefore are historically and organically interconnected, and this may seem to question the traditional sense of a sharp ontological discontinuity between humans and other kinds of life. But while awareness of the continuum of life is disturbing to some kinds of theology, to others it is a beautiful idea, confirming the biblical sense of the unity of creation and the interrelatedness of all members of the earth community. The theory of common descent is a troubling idea to some conservative Christians and to theologically underdeveloped interpretations of original sin. I shall not deal with these issues here, but instead focus on the second of Darwin's great ideas—namely, his explanation of *how* all the diverse forms of life have descended "with modification" from a common origin. This is his famous theory of natural selection.

From a theological point of view the theory of natural selection seems to be more challenging than the idea of common descent. According to this theory some organisms, by sheer chance, are better adapted to their environments than others. The better adapted obviously have a higher probability of surviving and producing offspring, and so nature "selects" the reproductively fit and eliminates all the others. Over a long period of time the natural selection of variations favorable to survival and reproduction brings about a wide diversity of species, including primates among whom the human species finds its biological classification. Today, the theory of natural selection has been widely embraced in the scientific community in the form of neo-Darwinism, a synthesis of Darwin's two revolutionary ideas with our more recently acquired knowledge of genetics.

What, then, is so theologically troubling about the theory? Three obvious features stand out. First, the variations that constitute the raw material for selection seem to be completely random, that is, undirected by any intelligent agency; this accidental or "contingent" aspect of evolution appears to suggest that the universe may not be governed by a divine providential intelligence after all. Second, the seemingly competitive struggle in which the weak (the reproductively unfit) suffer and eventually die out points to what Richard Dawkins calls "a pitilessly indifferent universe," one incompatible with a compassionate creator. Several years ago a tortured, formerly fundamentalist Christian clergyman who had recently become persuaded by the power of Darwinian explanations of life sent me a copy of a book he had just written. In page after page he sets forth the reasons for his newly acquired atheism. Here is but a brief sample:

> How could a loving God have planned a cruel system in which sensitive living creatures must either eat other sensitive living creatures or be eaten themselves, thereby causing untold suffering among these creatures? Would a benevolent God have created animals to devour others when he could have designed them all as vegetarians. What kind of deity would have designed the beaks which rip sensitive flesh? What God would intend every leaf, blade of grass, and drop of water to be a battleground in which living organisms pursue, capture, kill, and eat one another? What God would design creatures to prey upon one another and, at the same time, instill into such creatures a capacity for intense pain and suffering?[2]

We can see from this poignant and heartfelt outcry how difficult it is for some deeply sensitive people to embrace the Darwinian picture of nature.

In the third place, the disinterested way in which natural selection works—Daniel Dennett refers to it as "algorithmic"—suggests that we live in a remorselessly impersonal universe, hardly one rooted in the life of a personal deity.

What then are the responses theology can possibly make to such objections? I have found it convenient to organize these into three distinct types, which I shall call, respectively, *opposition, separatism,* and *engagement.* The first response (opposition) holds that Darwinian science and theology are irreconcilably opposed. The second (separatism) argues that science and religion deal with such totally different kinds of questions that they cannot logically conflict; and since evolutionary theory is supposed to be part of science, it is in principle not at all incompatible with theology. A third response (engagement) argues that theology cannot honestly remain innocently unaffected by science, and especially by neo-Darwinian biology. As it turns out, however, this third approach argues that neo-Darwinian evolutionary theory is not a danger but instead a great gift to theology, stimulating it to think in a fresh and vitalizing manner about the central claims of theistic faith while at the same time allowing theology to illuminate the natural world in which Darwinian evolution takes place. Let us examine each of these three responses more closely.

A. *Opposition.* Within the opposition camp there are several distinct groups, unanimous in their claim that theism and neo-Darwinian science are irreconcilable, but mutually antagonistic in their assessment of which of these two provides an ultimate explanation of the life world.

1. First, there are the "scientific skeptics," who argue that if we look very carefully at the Darwinian picture of life it will clearly render any realistic commitment to theism indefensible. Perhaps the most vocal of these skeptical voices today is the Oxford professor of the public understanding of science, Richard Dawkins. Dawkins states that after Darwin it is at last possible to be an "intellectually fulfilled atheist." Prior to Darwin, he admits, the exquisite adaptation of living beings to their environments could reasonably be accounted for by the hypothesis of divine "intelligent design." But Darwin's notion of natural

selection has now made the idea of a divine orderer completely superfluous as far as any substantive explanation of life is concerned. William Paley's famous divine watchmaker has been replaced by the "Blind Watchmaker," namely natural selection.[3]

Harvard paleontologist Steven Jay Gould would seem to agree, although he is not the outspoken critic of religion that Dawkins is. He even states at times that religion and science do not conflict (although in order to do so he first reduces "religion" to ethics). Nevertheless, throughout his career Gould has argued that it is not Darwin's science as such that makes it so difficult for people in the West to accept it. Rather, he says, it is the "philosophical message" that accompanies the theory. This message is that life has no direction, that there is no purpose to the universe, and that matter is "all there is."[4] Nowhere, at least to my knowledge, does Gould ever state that this "philosophical message" can in principle be disengaged from Darwin's scientific ideas. But if the ideology of materialism, with its inherent connotation of cosmic purposelessness, is indeed inseparable from the "science" of evolution, then Gould would also have to agree that theism is incompatible with neo-Darwinism. Theology can accommodate many different scientific ideas, but what it cannot get along with is a metaphysical materialism and the attendant claim that the cosmos is devoid of inherent meaning.

Believing with Dawkins and Gould that evolutionary science is most at home in a materialist intellectual setting, William Provine of Cornell University also asserts that the only outlook consistent with neo-Darwinian biology is a thoroughgoing atheism. Thus, if biologists continue to believe in God they must first "check their brains at the church house door."[5]

Skeptics such as the three just mentioned also find apparent support for their positions in Darwin's own gradual drift away from traditional theism as the result of long reflection on his discoveries. In his autobiography Darwin had written that "disbelief crept over me at a very slow rate, but was at last complete. The rate was so slow that I felt no distress, and have never since doubted for a single second that my conclusion was correct."[6] To some contemporary neo-Darwinians such "disbelief" seems to be the most tenable response to the question of God and evolutionary science.

2. Lying uncomfortably but nevertheless logically within the same king-sized bed (opposition) with the scientific skeptics are the so-called creationists. These are predominantly Christian theists who agree with Dawkins, Gould, and Provine that Darwinian evolution, if true, would logically rule out any plausibility to the idea of a purposeful universe created by God. They agree with atheistic evolutionists that neo-Darwinism is more than just an innocuous set of scientific ideas devoid of theological implications: Neo-Darwinism does carry a "philosophical message," namely, atheism. This conclusion follows from a very literalist reading of the biblical accounts of creation, according to which all the various species of living beings were created by the special action of God at the very beginning of life's history.

A vocal subcategory of this group are the so-called scientific creationists. They propose that even on purely scientific grounds the biblical creation stories are superior to Darwin's, which they consider in any case to be inadequately supported by empirical evidence. The lack of so-called transitional forms in the fossil record, for example, indicates the weakness of Darwin's gradualist theory, allowing logical room for the creationist theory of special creation by God.[7]

3. Finally, brief mention should be made here of another prominent partisan of the "opposition" approach, namely, Phillip Johnson, a Berkeley law professor and born-again Christian who views neo-Darwinism as a cultural weapon in modern materialist atheism's warfare against religion.[8] Johnson denies that he is a biblical literalist or a scientific creationist, and he admits the competency of science in areas other than that of neo-Darwinian biology. But he agrees with skeptics such as Provine, Gould, Dawkins, and Dennett that neo-Darwinism is so completely intertwined with the metaphysics of naturalism (the view that nature is all there is) that simply by accepting contemporary evolutionary biology one becomes locked into an inherently antitheistic position. Johnson is even grateful to the likes of Provine and Gould for their forthright admission that neo-Darwinism entails the radically secular ideology of scientific naturalism. Thus, he considers neo-Darwinism to be merely a subterfuge for atheistic materialism.

If this association is inescapable, then, of course, the many so-called theistic evolutionists, whom we shall mention later, are implicitly and illogically compromising theism with atheism. "Evolutionary theism" is, to Johnson, a contradiction in terms and proponents of evolutionary theology are enemies of genuine religious faith. It is interesting that Johnson has been eagerly adopted as an authoritative spokesperson by many political and religious conservatives today, who agree that neo-Darwinism is nothing more than an instrument employed by radical atheists to undermine traditional cultural and religious values.[9]

B. *Separatism.* A second species of theological response to the Darwinian challenge seeks to save both evolutionary science and theology by rigorously and consistently isolating them from any close contact with each other. In a more general sense separatism recognizes that science as such is self-consciously limited to dealing with questions about physical, or mechanical causes, whereas theology by definition is more concerned with questions about the *ultimate* explanation of things. And, since evolutionary theory is supposed to be purely scientific in nature, in principle it should pose no more threat to theology than do any other areas of science. Science by definition methodologically restricts itself to nontheistic explanations. So any apparent inferences from biology that the universe is either purposeful or Godless cannot possibly themselves be scientific since science is a way of knowing deliberately stripped of any sensors that could detect signals of purpose or divinity, even if these do exist. And so, because there can be no real competition between evolutionary science and religion, there can be no conflict between them either.

Because it seems so logically crisp and clean, the separatist approach appeals to many theologians and scientists. For them it allows the substance of theism to remain untouched by Darwin. But do not the randomness, struggle, and impersonality of the process refute theism, as the scientific skeptics have argued? A typically separatist response would go something like this:

1. Chance, randomness, accident (in genetic mutations and other contingencies of natural history, for example) do not imply a Godless universe but are simply

terms we all, including scientists, use to name events that are humanly and scientifically unintelligible, but which may make sense within God's wider vision and wisdom, to which we do not have adequate access.

2. The struggle and suffering in evolution, moreover, are consistent with the idea of a God who creates a world that supports life and builds character. If nature were in every sense benign and devoid of obstacles, after all, living beings would not be presented with the challenges essential to life's constant need to go beyond any given state, precisely in order to remain alive. The evolutionary terrain described by Darwinian science seems to provide as good a context for the nourishing of life and the building of soul in humans as we could possibly imagine.

3. Finally, the apparently impersonal law of natural selection is no more theologically problematic than is the law of gravitation. Gravity impersonally pulls toward earth both the strong and the weak, sometimes in a deadly way; yet, instead of ruling out a personal God, its relentless consistency can just as easily be interpreted as evidence of the noncapriciousness of the universe. Perhaps, then, we should view the invariant workings of natural selection no less leniently than we do other laws essential to nature's consistency and intelligibility.

By preventing any mixing or conflation of science with theology, the separatist approach avoids the antagonism that inevitably occurs when we confusedly allow religious texts to serve as sources of scientific information, or when scientists carelessly overlay their empirical data with materialist and other metaphysical assumptions. Whatever its own weaknesses may be—and the "engagement" position discussed later will point these out—the separatist approach provides an important critique of all three representatives of the "opposition" position (outlined previously) and their mutual agreement that there is an inevitable conflict between neo-Darwinism and theology. Separatists show very clearly that the creationists, scientific skeptics, and Phillip Johnson, all in their own ways, tolerate the conflation of science with belief, whether religious or materialistic. It is their conflation of science with ideology, and not any real conflict between science and religion, that lies at the root of the apparent sense of discord between theology and neo-Darwinism.

The scientific creationists, for example, unfortunately fuse science with religion by situating the biblical creation stories alongside of Darwinian evolutionary theory as a competing set of scientific ideas. This juxtaposition not only threatens the integrity of science; it also trivializes religion by placing it in the same mundane context as scientific discourse. The evolutionary materialists, however, are no less guilty of contaminating science with a priori metaphysical beliefs. For by unnecessarily conflating evolutionary science with materialist ideology, Dawkins, Gould, Provine, and Dennett transform neo-Darwinian science into an ideological alloy that is, as Johnson rightly points out, at odds with all versions of theism. To the separatists, however, this does not mean that the *science* of evolution conflicts with theism. Rather the source of conflict lies in the materialist ideological coating arbitrarily painted over the scientific picture by those scientists and philosophers who already have atheistic leanings.

At first it might seem that Phillip Johnson escapes the separatist critique since he too apparently wants to distinguish science from scientific naturalism. But in the end he too refuses to let scientists or theologians distinguish evolutionary ideas from the materialist ideological spin that a few well-known scientific skeptics superimpose on the data, and so he ironically ends up tolerating and promoting the very position he is trying to refute. According to the separatists there is absolutely no reason why evolutionary science cannot be methodologically naturalistic (as is all science) without being interpreted as also metaphysically naturalistic. From the separatist point of view Johnson merely adds to the appearance of conflict by dogmatically refusing to allow scientists and theologians to make such a distinction.

C. *Engagement.* Even though it has no objections to neo-Darwinian science, the separatist theological approach still holds evolution at arms length. It provides an essential moment of clarification, perhaps, but it does not give us an evolutionary theology. It tolerates evolution but does not celebrate it. A third family of theological responses to Darwin, on the other hand, after accepting the separatists' clear distinction of science from ideology, argues for the "engagement" of evolutionary science and theology. Darwin's supposedly "dangerous idea" is not to be held apart from our theological understanding but instead taken into the very center of contemporary reflection on the meaning of religious faith.

As it turns out, much theology has already been deeply influenced, and in some cases its whole character radically transformed, by contact with Darwinian science. Generally speaking, Darwin's impact on theology has taken two configurations. In the first instance, it has caused a noticeable shift in the character of "natural theology," the kind of theological reflection that looks for evidence of God in the natural world. And, in the second place, it has stimulated the emergence of what we may call "evolutionary theology," a reinterpretation of classic religious teachings in terms of evolutionary concepts. I shall say only a brief word about the first, and then go on to treat the second at more length.

1. *Darwin and natural theology.* Before Darwin, as even Dawkins agrees, the best explanation for the finely ordered structure and adaptive features of living organisms seemed to be that of divine "intelligent design," as William Paley expressed it in his familiar watchmaker analogy.[10] Paley argued that if you stumbled across a watch while walking through a patch of wild nature, upon opening it up you would undoubtedly conclude that it was the handiwork of an intelligent craftsperson. Analogously, the even more intricate design in nature points toward its creation by an intelligent designer whom theists readily identify with the Creator God of biblical religion. However, Darwin seemed to provide an adequate explanation of design in terms of natural selection of minute variations (now called mutations) over long periods of time. Given enough time—and now we realize that life originated as long as 3.8 billion years ago—the improbable design that we see in organisms can be accounted for in a purely naturalistic way. The story of life does not seem to require the special ad hoc interventions of a supernatural intelligence.

Incidentally, it is not only Darwinians such as Richard Dawkins who celebrate the demise of the design argument and natural theology. Many mainstream theologians, both liberal and conservative, want nothing to do with these either. They view natural theology as a futile and idolatrous attempt on the part of finite humans to grasp the Infinite and Incomprehensible in rational or scientific terms. Because natural theology inevitably diminishes the mystery of God by bringing it beneath the sway of our own limited rationality and sense of order, a good number of theologians—precisely for religious reasons—are grateful to Darwinians for killing it off.

However, while the evolutionary picture has been interpreted by some as the death-blow to all arguments for the existence of a designing Deity, natural theology still lives on after Darwin. It is important to note that much of this new natural theology is being done by scientists rather than theologians, but it is entirely appropriate to classify it as an important contemporary kind of theology. Nevertheless, instead of looking primarily at living organisms and their delicate adaptation as the primary evidence of God, natural theology today is more inclined to stand back and look with wider-angled lenses at the larger cosmic story of which Darwinian evolution is only one chapter.

For example, John Polkinghorne, a retired Cambridge University physicist and a practicing Anglican clergyman, argues that recent understanding of the physics of the early universe puts the whole question of evolution and natural theology in an entirely new perspective.[11] He insists that we cannot divorce our understanding of the fact of biological evolution from its larger cosmic context and the history of the universe as a whole. In the light of Big Bang cosmology, we not only have to account for life but also for the physical and cosmic conditions that made life possible in the first place. The new story of an evolving *universe* no longer allows us simply to take for granted the existence of carbon and other heavy elements essential for life. For the existence of these elements is itself "exquisitely dependent" on very finely tuned initial conditions and universal constants that became fixed during the first microseconds of the universe's birth. The rate of expansion of the universe, the force of gravity, the ratio of electron to proton mass, and innumerable other physical features had to be infinitesimally close to their established mathematical values or else the universe could never have produced hydrogen atoms, supernovae, carbon and other heavy elements essential to life.

Details of this fine-tuning can be found in many scientific works today, and so it is not necessary to discuss them any further here. In any case, Polkinghorne argues, there had to be an extremely high degree of "improbable order" even at the very beginning of time in order for life eventually to exist, to evolve into the various species, and to become conscious in us humans. Since such intricate and precise patterning was already present at the very beginning of cosmic history, its improbability could not have had the "time" to evolve by a process of gradual accidental changes in the manner required by the neo-Darwinian explanation of adaptive design in biological evolution. The initial order strongly suggests the work of a supremely intelligent creator. Consequently, there is room even after Darwin for a revived and revised natural theology focusing on design in nature.[12]

Of course, if you are truly addicted to the idea that our universe is a purely random, undirected, and unintelligible occurrence and that it *must* in no sense be the product of divine intelligence and wisdom, you may then imaginatively conjure up an endless series or proliferations of other "universes," most of them unsuited to life, so that perhaps purely by chance a life-biased set of initial conditions, such as we know to exist in this Big Bang universe, might eventually pop up. But to Polkinghorne, such unrestrained and purely ungrounded speculation is certainly less elegant and indeed no less metaphysical than the theological idea of intelligent design. Polkinghorne admits that his revised natural theology is not a "knock down" argument for God's existence, but he views it as strongly suggestive of the contemporary relevance of theistic explanation.[13]

2. *Evolutionary theology.* A second, and much more substantial form of theological engagement with neo-Darwinism is what I shall call evolutionary theology. Evolutionary theology claims that evolution, even in its neo-Darwinian presentation, is a most appropriate framework for thinking about God and God's relation to nature and humanity. However, it also agrees with Polkinghorne and others that biological evolution must be situated in the wider context of cosmic evolution. It would be artificial in the extreme to relate theology to neo-Darwinism without taking into account the entire physical universe that has sponsored the emergence of life and that has been a dynamic and creative process in its own right long before Darwinian evolution began around 3.8 billion years ago.

Evolutionary theology, unlike natural theology, does not search for definitive footprints of the divine in nature. It is not terribly concerned about intelligent design since such a notion seems entirely too stiff and lifeless to capture the dynamic and even disturbing way in which the God of biblical religion interacts with the world. Instead of trying to prove God's existence from nature, evolutionary theology seeks to show how our new awareness of cosmic and biological evolution can enhance and enrich traditional teachings about God and God's way of acting in the world. In other words, instead of viewing evolution simply as a challenge that deserves an apologetic response, theology today finds in both cosmic and biological aspects of the world process a truly consonant—perhaps even the best available—context in which to think about God and related theological ideas. We shall look very briefly here, for example, at how evolutionary science enhances theological understanding of creation and redemption, eschatology (that is, what we may hope for), revelation, divine love (or "grace"), and divine power.

a. Creation and redemption. Traditionally Christian theology spoke of three dimensions of God's creative activity: original creation (*creatio originalis*), ongoing or continuous creation (*creatio continua*), and new creation, or the fulfillment of creation (*creatio nova*). Prior to the scientific discoveries of cosmic and biological evolution, however, the latter two notions tended to be eclipsed by the first. *Creation* primarily meant something that God did in the beginning. Even today discussions between scientists and theologians about God and the Big Bang often assume that creation is only about chronological cosmic origins.[14] The fact of evolution, on the other hand, allows us to see more palpably than ever before that creation is not just an original but also a continuous and constantly new reality. In an evolving cosmos creation is still happening, no less in the present than "in the beginning." Every day is in a sense the "dawn of creation." The Big Bang is still unfolding. As Teilhard de Chardin put it, "incessantly even if imperceptibly, the world is constantly emerging a little farther above nothingness."[15]

Moreover, evolution has allowed theology to recognize that the notion of an originally and instantaneously completed creation is theologically unthinkable in any case.[16] If we could imagine it at all we would have to conclude that an initial creation, one already finished and perfected, would not be a creation truly distinct from its creator. Such a "world" would simply be the direct implementation of God's will and could in no meaningful sense be considered a world unto itself, nor could God conceivably transcend such a world. It would be a world without internal self-coherence, a world without a future, and, above all, a world devoid of life (since by definition living beings must continually transcend, or go beyond, themselves).

Additionally, if, as evolutionary science shows, this universe and its life story are still unfinished, then we cannot logically demand of them that they should here and now possess the status of finished perfection. But if the universe is not perfect, then this means it must now be imperfect. And if it is an imperfect world, then the appearance of evil (including the suffering and struggle depicted by Darwinian science) is possible—as the dark side of the world's ongoing creation.

For faith and theology, however, redemption is also something we may hope for in an unfinished universe, and evolution provides a most suitable framework for articulating the claim that God saves the world from suffering, loss, and evil. I shall discuss this prospect in the sections on eschatology and divine power, but here I would only note that the evolutionary picture has invited theology to situate the notion of redemption within the more fundamental context of a world still in the making. Redemption, thus construed, *is* essentially creation—technically *creatio nova*—the bringing about of something truly new and surprising in the face of all expectations to the contrary. According to this way of looking at things, the notion of sin would refer to our free human resistance to the ongoing creation and unification of the cosmos. And redemption or reconciliation, therefore, would mean more than the restoration of human community or union with God. It would mean realigning our lives and actions with the ongoing creative evolution of the universe.

There are ecological implications here also. The responsibility of "faithful stewardship" that God enjoins upon humanity would require more of us than simply preserving what has been present from the beginnings of creation. It would also imply our duty to shepherd the further evolution of the cosmos—in whatever limited way we can do so—toward the realization of humanly incalculable outcomes that may now be hiddenly present in nature as potential or promise. After all, when we look at things in the context of cosmic evolution it is not clear that the universe, simply by its arrival at the human phase of terrestrial evolution, has by any means fully exhausted its store of creative reserves.

b. Eschatology. Biblical faith is especially concerned with what we humans may hope for; that is, with what awaits us as our final destiny. This branch of theology is known as *eschatology* (from the Greek word *eschaton*, which means "last" or "final"). In an evolutionary context, however, our own human hope for redemption and final fulfillment must be situated within the wider context of the ongoing creation of the whole universe. The scientific epic of evolution invites us to extend our human hope outward and forward into the entire cosmos, thus retrieving an often lost theme in the biblical Wisdom literature, St. Paul, Irenaeus, and many other religious thinkers who also sought to bring the entire universe into the scheme of salvation.

Teilhard de Chardin often pointed out that as long as nature seemed static or eternal it had no future of its own. Human hope for what is truly new and fulfilling, therefore, could only take the form of withdrawing from the natural world in order to arrive, decisively after death, at an entirely different (supernatural) world situated "up above." But after Darwin and other recent scientific developments the cosmos began to be perceived as itself moving, slowly perhaps, but nonetheless moving. And so, the horizon of our expectations could begin to shift toward a future that includes the future of the universe and the entire sweep of its evolution. In this way evolutionary science has provided theology with a great opportunity to enlarge upon ancient religious intuitions—expressed so movingly by St. Paul—that the *entirety* of creation "groans" for an ultimate fulfillment. After Darwin theology may now speak more assuredly than ever of the inseparability of cosmic and human destiny.

Correspondingly, the sense of where the reality of God is to be "located" has also begun to shift from the One who abides vertically "up above" to the One who comes into the world from "up ahead," out of the realm of the future.[17] This God, as it turns out, actually corresponds—more closely than did our preevolutionary conceptions of the supernatural—with the God of the Bible, where God is the One who "goes before" the people leading them to liberty, who turns the eyes of faith toward the future and "who makes all things new" as depicted by Second Isaiah and the Book of Revelation. At the same time, the evolutionary portrait of life and the universe also permits a fresh understanding of the role of humans as co-creators with God in the building of the cosmic future.

c. Revelation. Evolution also helps theology understand more fully what is implied in the idea of revelation. Indeed, as Catholic theologian Karl Rahner has argued, reflection on the notion of revelation already anticipates an evolving cosmos.[18] Revelation is not fundamentally the communication of propositional information. Rather, revelation is at root the communication of *God's own being or selfhood* to the world. According to Rahner, the central content of Christian faith is that the infinite mystery of God gives itself away fully and without reservation to the world.[19] In simpler terms, the logical structure of revelation is that the infinite seeks to give itself away unreservedly to the finite world. But the fullness of a divine infinity cannot be received instantaneously by a finite cosmos. Such a reception could only take place incrementally or gradually. A finite world could "adapt" to an infinite source of love only by a process of ongoing self-opening and self-transcendence, the external manifestation of which would appear to science as cosmic and biological evolution. "Evolution" is the name we give to the empirically available aspects of the world's self-transcendence as it exposes itself to the divine infinity. The inner substance of what we refer to as the "epic of evolution," therefore, is the story of God's self-communication to the world and the world's response.

d. Grace. Reflection on evolution also helps theology illuminate the theme of divine love (or grace) and along with it the world's response to this grace. At the same time, a theology of grace may help us make some sense of the randomness, struggle, and natural selection that form the core of the Darwinian understanding of evolution.

The doctrine of grace claims that God loves the world and all of its various elements fully and unconditionally. By definition, however, love does not absorb or force itself on the beloved but instead longs for the other to remain and even become more and more other and differentiated. Along with its nurturing and compassionate attributes, love bears with it a posture of letting be in regard to the beloved other. Love, in other words, wills the independence of the other. Without such letting be of the beloved the dialogical intimacy essential to a loving relationship would be undermined from the very outset. Consequently, if the religious intuition is true that God loves the world with an unbounded love, then God's grace would also mean, in some sense, letting the world be itself. God's grace would refrain from forcefully stamping the divine will on the world, much less dissolving the world into God. Indeed, this love would even take the form of a self-withdrawal precisely as the condition for allowing the world to emerge on its own to the possible status of being capable of deep relationship with God.[20] Nicholas of Cusa's prayer to God was, "How could you give yourself to me unless you had first given me to myself?"[21] So likewise with the cosmos. Only a relatively independent universe could be intimate with God. Theologically understood, therefore, the epic of evolution is the story of the world's struggle—not always successful or linearly progressive—toward an emergent and expanding freedom in the presence of self-giving Grace.[22]

Evolution in all of its meandering, struggle, and temporally drawn out self-creativity—as described by the neo-Darwinian accounts—is perfectly consonant with this notion of divine grace understood as God's self-emptying letting be of the world. Indeed, if we reflect on things in the light of faith's assumptions about the selfless character of divine grace (impressed on Christians, for example, through the image of a crucified Goodness), we should *expect* to find a world riddled with contingency rather than one rigidified by necessity. Even St. Thomas Aquinas had argued that a world without chance or contingency would not be distinct from God. The world has to have aspects of nonnecessity or contingency in order to be a world at all: "It would be contrary to the nature of providence and to the perfection of the world," Aquinas said, "if nothing happened by chance."[23] Thus, the randomness and undirected features of evolution are not just apparent, as some of the separatists would argue. They are in fact essential features of any world created by a gracious God.

e. Divine power. That such a world can be finally redeemed from the evil and suffering that attend its evolution requires, of course, special theological attention to the notion of divine power. Of all the varieties of contemporary religious reflection on this doctrine of faith, I personally consider "process theology" to be the most responsive to our concerns about how God acts in a world wherein, according to neo-Darwinism, there is such a high degree of randomness and suffering as part of the contingent and "undirected" meandering of evolution. Process theology interprets the teachings of biblical religion about God's creative and redemptive action by using concepts formulated especially by the philosopher Alfred North Whitehead, who had made the fact of evolution central to his own metaphysics.[24] I cannot enter into an adequate discussion of process theology here but shall have to be content with a very brief summary of its understanding of God and God's relationship to an evolving universe.

Evolution, according to process theology, occurs in the first place only because God's power and action in relation to the world take the form of persuasive love rather than coercive force. In keeping with the notion of grace mentioned previously, divine love does not compel but persuades. But is persuasion an expression of power or, instead, a sign of weakness? Process theology responds that if power means "the capacity to influence," then a persuasive God is much more powerful than would be an imaginary deity who magically manipulated things to correspond immediately to the divine intentions. Such a coercive God—one that our immature religiosity often wishes for and the same one that scientific skeptics almost invariably have in mind when they assert that Darwin has destroyed theism—would not allow for the otherness, autonomy, and self-coherence essential for the world's being a world at all. Such a stingy and despotic deity, by refusing to permit any autonomy to the creation, would clearly be less influential in the final analysis than would a God who wills the independence of the world. A world allowed to become more and more autonomous, and eventually to arrive in its unforced and lengthy evolution at the status of human consciousness and freedom, has much more "being" or substance to it than any conceivable world determined in every respect by an outside "divine agency."

A coercive kind of divine power would be incompatible not only with human freedom but also with the prehuman spontaneity that allows the world to evolve into something other than its creator. Thus, process theology finds nothing religiously peculiar in the spontaneity manifested at the levels of quantum indeterminacy, or in the undirected mutations in life that we refer to as random, or in other contingencies in life's history, or in the capacity for free choice that emerges during the human phase of evolution. From the premises of theology we should logically anticipate, rather than be surprised, that God's creation is not coercively driven, that it is widely experimental, and that it unfolds over the course of a considerable amount of time. To those who object that process theology is hereby illegitimately redefining the idea of God's power in order contrivedly to fit neo-Darwinian theory, the reply is simply that no other conception of power has ever been consistent with the orthodox religious belief that God is infinite love. Neo-Darwinian evolution does not require that we abandon or modify the ancient biblical testimony to the unbounded generosity and compassion of God, only that we return to it more earnestly than ever.

Evolution occurs, according to process theology, also because God is the source not only of order but also of novelty. And it is the introduction of novelty into the world that makes evolution possible. For this reason the shared obsession by creationists, Phillip Johnson, and scientific skeptics with the idea of God as an intelligent designer is entirely too narrow for, and in great measure irrelevant to, a genuine engagement of theology with science on the issue of Darwinian evolution. The idea of nature as intelligent design shares with mechanistic biology the trait of abstracting from the concrete reality of *life*. As the ultimate source of novelty in evolution God is also the cause of instability and disorder and therefore of conditions essential to life. After all, there can be no process of ordering or reordering, such as life always exhibits, that does not also include aspects of instability or disorder. Thus it is simply inappropriate to think of God exclusively as source of order (a distortion shared by both natural theology and scientific skepticism). God is also the reason why there is disorder—and hence the possibility of life.

According to process theology, moreover, evolution occurs because God is more interested in adventure than in preserving the status quo. *Adventure* in Whiteheadian terms is the cosmic search for more and more intense versions of ordered novelty, another word for which is *beauty*. God's will, then, is the maximization of cosmic beauty, and the epic of evolution is the world's response to God's own longing that it strive toward ever richer ways of realizing aesthetic intensity. By offering new and relevant possibilities to the cosmos in every period of its becoming, God "acts" not only to sustain but also to create the world continually.

Finally, however, process theology also highlights the hope for redemption that perennially lies at the heart of human longing and comes to its most explicit expression in the world's religious traditions. But how can we think of redemption in a world of evolution and the perpetual becoming and perishing that go along with it? According to process theology, the answer is the same as that given in biblical and other traditions—namely, that God is infinitely *responsive* to the world as well as creative and nurturing of it. If evolution occurs because of the world's responsiveness to the persuasive power of God, this God is even more responsive to all that happens in the evolutionary process. Everything whatsoever that occurs in evolution—all the suffering and tragedy as well as the new life and intense beauty—is "saved" by being taken eternally into God's own feeling of the world in its totality. Even though all events and achievements in evolution are temporal and perishable, they may still abide permanently within the everlasting compassion of God. In God's own experience of the world all events can be redeemed from absolute perishing and receive an importance and meaning to which we humans have no unambiguous access, but in which religions encourage us to believe—always without clearly seeing. That we live in darkness on something of such ultimate moment is itself consistent with the fact that we live in an unfinished, imperfect universe—in other words, the only kind of universe consistent with the idea of an infinitely loving and active God.

NOTES

1. I have developed these ideas at greater length in "Darwin's Gift to Theology," in Francisco Ayala, Robert Russell, and William Stoeger, ed., *Evolutionary Biology and Divine Action* (Vatican Observatory and South Bend: University of Notre Dame Press, 1999).

2. J. Mattill, Jr., *The Seven Mighty Blows to Traditional Beliefs*, 2nd ed. (Gordo, AL: The Flatwoods Press, 1995), p. 32.

3. Richard Dawkins, *The Blind Watchmaker* (New York: W. W. Norton & Co., 1986), pp. 6ff.

4. Stephen Jay Gould, *Ever Since Darwin* (New York: W. W. Norton, 1977), pp. 12–13.

5. "Evolution and the Foundation of Ethics," in Steven L. Goldman, ed., *Science, Technology and Social Progress* (Bethlehem, PA: Lehigh University Press, 1989), p. 261.

6. Charles Darwin, *The Autobiography of Charles Darwin*, Nora Barlow, ed. (New York: W. W. Norton, 1993), pp. 85ff.

7. See, for example, Duane Gish, *Evolution: The Challenge of the Fossil Record* (El Cajon: Creation-Life Publishers, 1985).

8. See Phillip Johnson's book *Darwin on Trial* (Downers Grove, IL: Intervarsity Press: 1991).

9. The journal *First Things* is a good example.

10. William Paley, *Natural Theology* (New York: Boston, Gould and Lincoln, 1873).

11. John Polkinghorne, "Creation and the Structure of the Physical World," *Theology Today*, Vol. XLIV, no. 1 (April 1987): 53–68.

12. Ibid.

13. Ibid.

14. Stephen Hawking, *A Brief History of Time*, pp. 140–41. See also Paul Davies, *The Mind of God: The Scientific Basis for a Rational World* (New York: Simon & Schuster, 1992), p. 66.

15. Teilhard de Chardin, *The Prayer of the Universe*, pp. 120–21.

16. Teilhard de Chardin, *Christianity and Evolution*, trans. by Rene Hague (New York: Harcourt Brace & Co., 1969), p. 239.

17. See Ernst Bloch, *The Principle of Hope*, Vol. I, trans. Neville Plaice, Stephen Plaice, and Paul Knight (Oxford: Basil Blackwell, 1986). See also Jürgen Moltmann, *The Experiment Hope*, edited and translated by M. Douglas Meeks (Philadelphia: Fortress Press, 1975). The writings of Teilhard de Chardin, Wolfhart Pannenberg, and Karl Rahner also view God as essentially future.

18. See Karl Rahner, *Foundations of Christian Faith* (New York: Seabury Press, 1978), pp. 178–203.

19. Ibid.

20. However, this "self-withdrawal" must not be construed as an abandonment of the world such as we associate with the God of deism. Rather, God forgoes any annihilating "presence" to or compulsion of the world paradoxically in order to be nearer to it.

21. Cited by John J. O'Donnell, *Hans Urs Von Balthasar* (Collegeville: Liturgical Press, 1992), p. 73.

22. See Wolfhart Pannenberg, *Systematic Theology*, Vol. II, trans. by Geoffrey W. Bromiley (Grand Rapids: Eerdmans, 1994), pp. 127–36, where he writes, "Theologically, we may view the expansion of the universe as the Creator's means to the bringing forth of independent forms of creaturely reality" (p. 127). "Creaturely independence cannot exist without God or against him. It does not have to be won from God, for it is the goal of his creative work" (p. 135). For a perspective similar to Karl Rahner's and in part indebted to it, see also Elizabeth Johnson, "Does God Play Dice? Divine Providence and Chance," *Theological Studies* 57 (March 1996): 3–18.

23. *Summa Contra Gentiles*, III, chap 74. Cited by Christopher Mooney, *Theology and Scientific Knowledge* (Notre Dame, IN: University of Notre Dame Press, 1996), p. 162.

24. The philosophy of Charles Hartshorne has also been influential in shaping the ideas of many process theologians. A useful summary of process theology can be found in John B. Cobb and David Ray Griffin, *Process Theology: An Introductory Exposition* (Philadelphia: Westminster, 1976).

9 Innovation in Human Evolution[1]

Ian Tattersall *American Museum of Natural History*

The evidence for common ancestry among all living things is most compellingly found in the way in which the myriad attributes that organisms possess are distributed among them. We do not need a fossil record to persuade any but the most blinkered that common descent is the most parsimonious explanation indeed, the only testable explanation for the world's exuberant diversity of life. Nonetheless, it remains true that it is the fossil record alone that provides us with evidence for the actual historical events that culminated in the dazzling variety of living forms today. In this chapter I will look at one tiny part of that record—the part that documents our divergence from the common ancestor we shared with our closest living relatives, the great apes. I particularly want to look at the emergence of our own functionally unprecedented species, *Homo sapiens*.

The earliest evidence we have of creatures who were exclusively our ancestors and not those of apes as well comes from sites in Kenya and Ethiopia dating to the period between about 4.4 and 3.9 million years ago. The most convincing of these fossils have been allocated to the species *Australopithecus anamensis*, a form represented as yet only by a few fragments, which include a couple of fairly decent jaws and part of a shin bone. Despite a few detail differences the jaws and teeth look comfortingly similar to those of the next-in-line species, *Australopithecus afarensis*, known from sites in Ethiopia and Tanzania that date in the 3.8 to 3.0 million-year (myr) range. Tellingly, the shinbone shows unmistakable signs of uprightness in the part that contributes to the knee joint. Humans were up and walking on their hind legs by about 4.2 million years ago.

This is not something we can tell with any certainty from evidence so far reported for the earliest claimant of all to hominid (human-family) status: an equally fragmentary 4.4-myr-old form from Ethiopia that rejoices in the name of *Ardipithecus ramidus*. Much less like later hominids than *anamensis* is, the main importance of *ramidus* is to remind us that from the very beginning hominid history has been one of diversity and evolutionary experimentation: It represents at best a side branch on the human evolutionary tree. *Homo sapiens* is the exception, rather than the rule, in being the lone hominid on earth. This is something useful to keep in mind as we go through the human fossil record, since there is something inherently linear in any form of storytelling, and linearity, it turns out, is not a strong signal in human phylogeny.

Australopithecus afarensis is the first well-documented hominid known, including in its ranks such stars as "Lucy," who consists of much of a 3.2-myr-old skeleton, and the members of the "First Family," fragmentary bones of a group of at least 13 individuals who may have perished together about 3.4 myr ago. Beyond these Ethiopian fossils, it seems most likely that the famous 3.5-myr-old footprint trails of Laetoli, in Tanzania, were also made by members of this species, whose upright-walking behavior has thereby literally been fossilized. This unique insight into the locomotion of *A. afarensis* is confirmed by examination of the fossils themselves; but such scrutiny also reveals that these rather small-bodied creatures did not walk upright quite as we do. Descendants of tree-living ancestors, they retained a variety of features that would have helped them to exploit their ancestral habitat even as they moved more freely beyond it than ever before.

This have-it-both-ways adaptation made the early hominids neither as agile in the trees as apes are nor as efficient on the ground as we; but it served them well, remaining essentially unaltered for over 2 million years, even as new hominid species came and went. Over this period early hominids seem to have been largely confined to the forest fringes, where true forest grades into grassy woodland; and indeed, 4 million years ago true Serengeti-style savannas lay very far in the future, even as increased seasonality and climatic drying steadily shrank the African forests.

"Why bipedalism?" is a complicated and as yet incompletely resolved story for which there is no time here. However, it is important to note that, bipedalism aside, there is very little to indicate that the early hominids were functionally hominid in other respects. True, we see some typically hominid innovations very early on, such as both absolute and relative size reduction of the canine teeth and the elimination of the size differential between the sexes that is typical of the great apes. But these early hominids still had apelike cranial proportions, with large, projecting faces hafted on to small braincases (which housed brains little if any larger than those of apes, even if body size is factored in). And indeed, there is a strong tendency among paleoanthropologists today to refer to these ancestral early hominids as "bipedal apes."

In the period between 4 and 2 myr ago these creatures flourished widely in Africa, giving rise to several species in two major lineages that are often dubbed "robust" versus "gracile." The robust forms differentiated before about 2.6 myr ago. Typically they show huge cheek teeth (molars and premolars) in contrast to tiny front teeth (incisors and canines) and they are widely thought, in the absence of much direct evidence, to have specialized in exploiting the tough roots and tubers of the grasslands. The "gracile" forms, on the other hand, are believed to have hewed to a more opportunistic, omnivorous diet. Significantly, though, it is clear that each lineage made its own evolutionary experiments, each spinning off separate species or species groups in southern and eastern Africa (and presumably elsewhere in the continent, did we but have the fossil evidence to show it; the lone such fossil comes from Chad).

Presumably, it was one such experiment within the gracile lineage that gave rise to the first members of our own genus *Homo*. The earliest widely recognized species of *Homo*, *H. habilis* ("handy man"), was described in 1964 from Olduvai Gorge in Tanzania. The handful of fossils on which this new species was based was ascribed to our genus largely because it was plausibly associated with the crude stone tools found in the lowest layers of the Gorge and because there were indications of a brain vault a bit bigger than that typical for the early hominids. Since then the plot has thickened, and a variety of fragmentary "early *Homo*" fossils have been identified in eastern Africa in the period between about 2.5 and 2.0 myr ago, just as have several sites yielding early stone tools. We have yet to obtain a firm association between such tools and the hominid(s) who made them; more than one species may well have been involved. But right now it looks a fair bet that the first stone tool maker was physically of fairly archaic body build and possessed of a brain not a lot bigger than you might expect of an ape of his or her body size. And if so, we have here a good example of a theme we find consistently throughout the hominid record: Behavioral innovations do not tend to be associated with new kinds of humans. Which, if you think about it, makes considerable sense; for a new technology must be invented by an individual—who cannot differ too much from his or her own parents or offspring. Innovations arise within species, for there is no place else they can do so.

Still, whatever the first toolmaker looked like, the tools themselves mark a major cognitive leap among hominids. They allowed the exploitation of a new source of protein (animal carcasses) that had previously been largely off limits to tiny, defenseless foragers, who would have had to yield to most competitors for such resources. These early stone tools were crude—simple sharp flakes knocked off larger stone "cores"—but highly effective: Experimental archaeologists have butchered entire elephants using them. What's more, it takes considerable insight, well beyond what any ape has achieved, even with intensive coaching, to strike a cobble with another at precisely the angle necessary to detach a sharp flake. Further yet, we know that the earliest *Homo* anticipated needing the tools they would make, for we have evidence that they carried suitable stones around with them for long distances before making them into tools as needed. With the invention of stone tools, we have the first unequivocal evidence that hominids had moved cognitively well beyond the ape league, whatever they looked like.

At about 1.8 myr ago we find the first fossils of the earliest member of genus *Homo* to have a body size and build essentially comparable to our own—which makes us wonder whether it should not be with such creatures that we should really begin to recognize the genus *Homo*. Known as *Homo ergaster*, this new form is best represented by the miraculously complete "Turkana Boy" skeleton from northern Kenya. The remains of a 5-foot-3-inch youngster who died at the age of nine and would have topped 6 feet if he had lived to maturity, this skeleton tells us that the people who lived by Lake Turkana 1.6 myr ago were long limbed and slender—built, like the people of the area today, for life out in the hot and open savanna, far from the shelter of the forest. It seems that once this emancipation from the forest had been achieved, the way was open for ancient humans to indulge their wanderlust: New dates suggest that humans had not only exited Africa but had reached all the way to eastern Asia hard on the heels of achieving modern body form.

Still, while the Boy and his relatives had larger brains than any of their predecessors, these were still not a lot more than half the size of ours today. What's more, while the face of *Homo ergaster* was substantially reduced compared with those of *australopiths,* it still jutted out in front of the braincase and was equipped with pretty large teeth. There are incipient signs of the flexion of the cranial base that signals the presence of a vocal tract capable of producing the sounds associated with articulate speech, but speech and hence language are belied by the narrowness of the thoracic vertebral canal that carries the innervation of the thoracic musculature. The Boy apparently lacked our fine control of the musculature that produces the moving air column we modulate to generate speech.

For all the innovations borne by *Homo ergaster,* we have to wait over a quarter of a million years after its first appearance before we encounter the next technological innovation. The Boy and his kin made stone tools that were for the most part indistinguishable from those their predecessors had made for almost a million years, and it is not until about 1.5 myr ago that we begin to find a significantly new kind of tool. This is the "Acheulean" hand axe, an implement consciously and symmetrically fashioned on both sides to a deliberate shape. For the first time, toolmakers were making tools to a "mental template" held in their minds rather than simply going after an attribute: a cutting edge. Yet another cognitive advance; but we know little if anything about how this innovation affected the lifestyles of the toolmakers. These hominids presumably lived in small, mobile groups that moved consistently around a landscape shared with a variety of other hominid species. Most likely they gained the greater part of their sustenance from plant materials or scavenged animal carcasses; few archaeologists today would argue that they were accomplished hunters of anything other than small animals.

After about 1.4 myr ago the paleoanthropological focus shifts out of Africa, if only for reasons of geological sampling. We find the famous *Homo erectus* in eastern Asia perhaps as much as 1.8 myr ago (and perhaps as recently as 40 kyr[2] ago), and not long ago a new hominid species, *Homo antecessor,* was named from an 800-kyr-old site in Spain. Once humans had left Africa, new species were evidently spawned in different parts of the world, exactly as we might expect, though what was going on in Africa in this time period remains rather obscure. By about 600 kyr, however, we find in Africa evidence of a new hominid species, *Homo heidelbergensis,* at the site of Bodo, in Ethiopia; related fossils begin to show up in Europe after about 500 kyr ago. This new species boasted a brain well within the modern size range, though much below the *Homo sapiens* average (1100 to 1200 ml, versus approximately 1350 ml), and it possessed flexion of the basicranium to a degree that suggests the ability to produce the sounds of speech. Curiously, at the European sites there is, in early stages at least, a conspicuous absence of handaxe technology, stone tool kits remaining rather crude. Significantly, we find nothing in the way of symbolic artifacts associated with *Homo heidelbergensis;* but it is in the time range of this species, about 400 kyr ago, that we find the first evidence of simple structures and hearths, both significant technological advances. Again, though, we have to wait for some time, until approximately 300 to 200 kyr ago (dating is hazy) to find a significant innovation in stone toolmaking techniques.

This innovation was the "prepared-core" tool, whereby a stone core was carefully shaped until a single blow could detach a flake that required little modification into a finished tool. The overwhelming advantage of this technique was to provide a virtually continuous cutting edge around most of the periphery of the implement. Once more, where the prepared-core tool was invented, and by whom, remains uncertain; but what is undeniable is that the best-documented and probably the most accomplished practitioners of the technique were the

Neanderthals, *Homo neanderthalensis.* It seems likely that both the Neanderthals and our own *Homo sapiens* were ultimately derived from *Homo heidelbergensis* (or some species like it, but lacking the capacious sinus spaces in the skull that are such a striking feature of *Homo heidelbergensis*). The Neanderthals were an indigenous European and western Asian development from that ancestor, while *Homo sapiens* arose in Africa or nearby (even as *Homo erectus* ploughed its own evolutionary furrow in Asia).

The Neanderthals, abundantly known at sites from the Atlantic to Uzbekistan and from Wales to Gibraltar and the Levant, were hominids with brains as large as our own. Those brains were, however, housed in differently shaped skulls, with long, low braincases and faces that protruded in the midline and swept back toward the sides. These distinctive hominids emerged around 200 kyr ago and crafted stone tools beautifully but, as the French archaeologist Francois Bordes once remarked, "stupidly." By this he meant that the productions of the Neanderthals, skillful as they were (we would be hard put to match their craftsmanship) were rather monotonous, in the sense that there was a sameness to them over the whole vast expanse of time and space these people inhabited. This stands in stark contrast to the spirit of innovation and inventiveness that suffused the productions of the modern humans who entered Europe around 40 kyr ago, displacing the Neanderthals in the process.

The Neanderthals lived in a period of oscillating climates, sometimes extremely severe, and occupied a huge area as a homogeneous group. Exactly how sophisticated they were as hunters is not entirely clear, although many believe that in most places, at least, they probably only hunted smallish mammals, scavenging the remains of larger ones. In most cases their living places seem to have been rather haphazardly organized, unlike those of modern people. It's been suggested that, like their predecessors, Neanderthals were "foragers," opportunistically availing themselves of food sources they encountered while roaming fairly randomly around the landscape. This contrasts with modern hunters and gatherers, who are (or were) "collectors," carefully monitoring the resources around them and planning their exploitation.

One Neanderthal propensity that may bespeak a profound humanity is the burial of the dead—something that was practiced at least occasionally, and simply. Burial might, of course, have been no more than a convenient way of disposing of a particularly unpleasant form of clutter, and the Neanderthal preference for placing the corpse in a flexed posture might have resulted simply from the desire to dig the smallest pit. But it is hard to avoid the impression that the act of burial conveys some form of empathy with the deceased. Whether it implies more than that is less certain. Spiritual awareness in all early modern human societies has been marked by the inclusion of grave goods with the deceased: objects that might be useful in the afterlife. Nothing of this kind is found in Neanderthal graves, in which any found objects are invariably things that could well have been kicked in accidentally.

In one intriguing case, though, at Iraq's Shanidar cave, a Neanderthal grave was found to be unusually rich in the pollen of spring flowers. Perhaps the deceased was laid to rest on a bed of flowers, but there are other ways in which the pollen could have found its way into the grave. More suggestive at Shanidar was the skeleton of an aged individual who had suffered, maybe since birth, from a withered arm. This individual must have enjoyed the consistent support of his group over his long lifetime, for he could not have survived on his own. This observation, surely, carries echoes of humanity.

In the Levant we find evidence for anatomically modern people—people with high vaulted skulls with small faces tucked underneath rather than jutting forward—at almost 100 kyr ago. At the same time, however, we find Neanderthal remains at a mere 40 kyr ago. *Homo neanderthalensis* and *Homo sapiens* thus shared this region in some way for at least 60 kyr. How they did so is uncertain, although very interestingly the two species shared a virtually identical stoneworking technology. Functionally, at least, we have little reason to suspect any cognitive difference between them in this period. It is surely significant, though, that the last recorded Neanderthal occurrence in this region comes only a few millennia after the appearance of an "Upper Paleolithic" stoneworking technology similar to that brought with them by the earliest *Homo sapiens* who invaded Europe at about 40 kyr ago. These latter are the Cro-Magnons, the people who in not much more than ten millennia entirely eliminated the Neanderthals from the vast area they had inhabited—whether by conflict or by competition is not known. These invading moderns brought with them (from where exactly is not known) abundant evidence of the entire cognitive panoply that characterizes humans worldwide today. Not only did these new people make tools—in a dazzling variety—out of new materials such as bone and antler, in addition to stone, but from the very beginning they showed abundant evidence of symbolic behaviors.

The record of the Cro-Magnons is truly extraordinary. Over 30,000 years ago they had begun to leave extraordinary art on the walls of caves. Bone flutes of complex sound capabilities announce the advent of music. Markings on bone plaques clearly represent systems of notation, perhaps even lunar calendars. Some of the most beautifully observed and crafted sculptures ever made date from this time. Technology became more complex; by 26 kyr bone needles announce the advent of tailoring, and at this same time ceramic technology was invented, figurines being baked in simple but remarkably effective kilns. Hunting became more complex, and fish and bird bones show up for the first time in food refuse. The list of Cro-Magnon achievements could go on and on, but the point is already evident: These people were us, possessed of a sensibility totally unprecedented in human history. As we have seen, innovation in human evolution, technological as well as anatomical, had previously been sporadic, and it is fair to say that, perhaps with a couple of exceptions, new kinds of hominids had just done what their predecessors did, if a little bit better. With the emergence of behaviorally modern *Homo sapiens*, however, a totally unprecedented entity was on the scene. *Homo sapiens* is not simply an extrapolation of earlier trends.

So what happened? This issue was the cause of the deepest disagreement that ever fissured the relationship between Charles Darwin and Alfred Russel Wallace. Darwin firmly believed that natural selection was the unambiguous explanation of human consciousness, while Wallace simply could not see how this could be so. It seems to me that both men were right, in different ways. Our peculiar consciousness is the product of our brains, which are in turn the product of a long evolutionary history. But the properties of the modern human brain are evidently emergent, the result of a chance coincidence of acquisitions. Clearly, while natural selection plays an essential role in the evolutionary process, it is not a creative force: It has to act on variations that come into existence spontaneously. Nothing arises for anything, and natural selection can only work on variations presented to it. We must thus conclude that the immediate ancestor of modern humans possessed a brain that had, for whatever reason, evolved to a point where a single change or genetically related group of changes was sufficient to create a structure with an entirely new potential.

But this is probably not the whole story. Recall that the earliest humans who looked exactly like us behaved, as far as can be told, pretty much like Neanderthals—for upward of 50 kyr. These humans had brains that were externally like our own but that evidently did not function in the way that the Cro-Magnons did in later times. Again, what happened? Did the earliest anatomically modern and the earliest behaviorally modern humans represent separate but skeletally identical species, the latter eventually replacing the former? This scenario seems inherently improbable, since any such dramatic worldwide replacement would have had to have taken place in a very short window of time; and there is in any event no direct evidence for it. The only evident alternative is that the unique human capacity was born with anatomically modern *Homo sapiens* and lay fallow, as it were, until unleashed by some unknown cultural stimulus. This innovation would then have been able to spread by cultural contact among populations that already possessed the latent ability to acquire it; no wholesale replacement would have been necessary.

What might that stimulus have been? Like many others, I am almost sure that it was the invention of language, and we must bear in mind that by the time *Homo sapiens* evolved, the peripheral equipment that allows articulate speech had already been around for several hundred thousand years (having evolved initially for other purposes entirely). The archaeological record is but a dim record of the full panoply of behaviors of any early hominid, but if it shows us anything at all it is the starkness of the contrast between the torrential outpouring of symbolic behaviors by the Cro-Magnons and the essentially symbol-free behaviors of their predecessors. The fundamental innovation that we see with the Cro-Magnons is that of symbolic thought, with which language is virtually synonymous. Like thought, language involves forming and manipulating symbols in the mind, and our capacity for symbolic reasoning is virtually inconceivable in its absence. Imagination and creativity are part of the same process, for only once we create mental symbols can we combine them in new ways and ask "What if?". Intuitive reasoning can, of course, take one a long way; and indeed, we can probably look on the considerable achievements of the Neanderthals as the ultimate example of what intuition can do; but it is symbolic thought that above all differentiates us from them, and from every other hominid, indeed every organism, that has ever existed.

In the next chapter, Professor Deacon will present a much more informed discussion than I ever could of the cognitive aspects of our evolution. But nobody who has ever studied the hominid fossil record can fail to note that the emergence of the human capacity was a recent, and emergent, happening. Much as paleo-anthropologists like to think of our evolution as a linear process, a gradual progress from primitiveness to perfection, this conceptual hold-over from the past is clearly in error. We are not the result of constant fine-tuning over the eons, any more than we are the summit of creation. For all of our remarkable and recently acquired cognitive uniquenesses (which is why we are alone in the world today), we are the lone surviving evolutionary experiment among many.

NOTE

1. Parts of this chapter are based on the following publication:

    Tattersall, "The Origin of the Human Capacity," *68th James Arthur Lecture on the Evolution of* *the Human Brain* (New York: American Museum of Natural History 1988), 27 pp.

2. Kyr equals thousand-years.

10 The Evolutionary Spirit: Brains, Language, and the Human Difference

Terrence W. Deacon   *University of California—Berkley*

INTRODUCTION

We are experiencing the last of a series of revolutions that began with Copernicus. From the date that Copernicus suggested that the then current understanding of the movement of planets and stars was in error and that the earth was not the center of the universe, discoveries of science have progressively eroded each aspect of a once intuitively satisfying self-centered worldview. At the hands of science, we humans have been demoted from the status of demigods in a world designed with us in mind, to the that of molecular machines that are cousins to the great apes and merely cast adrift on an unremarkable grain of sand located somewhere in a vast seashore of a universe. Not only are we chemical machines, but we were designed by accident, so to speak, in that random walk of macromolecular statistics called biological evolution.

Scientists have elevated this assault on anthropocentrism to the status of a general rule of thumb, sometimes called the *mediocrity principle.* It codifies the working assumption that there is not any aspect of the universe designed *for* us, or designed *with respect to* us, or designed at all, and it presumes that we may not even be particularly special in the broad scheme of things. We are typical products of chemical evolution that might at least in general terms have been expected on planets harboring life, with no privileged status. This is the ultimate denial of human self-importance, a sort of reverse anthropocentrism. And now, even the last vestige of any illusion of cosmic distinction is rapidly being dispelled. The last straw is that we are realizing that this principle even applies to our own subjective experiences. Not only is life just a typical product of blind chemical mechanism, but so it appears is our experience of consciousness!

It should not be surprising that the scientific ideas that contributed most to this sense of self-unimportance (i.e., cosmology and evolutionary biology) were not greeted with open arms by religious belief systems, at least not in the West, and contain many claims still found unacceptable in certain religious circles. If the origin of human beings in the scheme of things is fully explainable in terms of chance and blindly mechanistic forces, then any belief system founded on ultimate purpose, whether for the cosmos or an individual life, is thrown into doubt.

The cosmic mediocrity principle nevertheless has a complementary corollary, often called the *anthropic principle.* It states that the laws of physics that describe the universe that we observe must also be consistent with the production of organisms like ourselves, capable of such reflections, for the obvious reason that we are here, reflecting on them. In cosmic terms, we could not have come into existence in a universe with even modestly different physical laws. These must be so arranged so that stars persist in their burning for tens of billions of years, nuclear reactions within stars produce stable heavy nuclei, and the density of interstellar matter allows planetary systems to form and persist long enough to support biological evolution for billions of years, and so on. Other conditions and laws are conceivable, other sorts of universes are not impossible in principle, but only a universe with laws very much like this one would have produced beings that could perceive and interpret its regularities. The fact that we are here, thinking about what it all means, demonstrates that both we and the universe reflect some very specific initial conditions. In addition, because we possess an ability to comprehend the world around us, certain other things about the conditions of our existence must follow. We must have a certain level of complexity and flexibility, and we must have a means of representing the abstract properties this world exhibits. In other words, it could appear as though the universe was set up so that I would eventually appear, right on schedule, on a rocky planet, near the rim of a middle age galaxy, some few star life cycles since the Big Bang, and a handful of a billion years since this particular planetary system formed. Many have hit on this mysterious cosmic coincidence to redeem the role of grand intelligent design, even in a world that is otherwise blindly mechanistic, since in a perfectly determined world it still allows for each event and creature in it to have been prefigured in this grand design. There is, however, one personal metaphysical price to be paid for believing in such a clockwork universe—we too turn out to be clockworks—an issue I will return to shortly.

The significance of cosmic mediocrity and anthropic specialness collide in the study of human evolution. Humans were not always on the earth, and our species was not always as it appears today.

Evolutionary thinking tends to emphasize the mediocrity via focusing on the connectedness of humans to other species. The commonality of DNA to all cellular life, 99 percent similarity in gene sequences between chimpanzees and humans, the scant 5 to 6 million years of separate evolution from a common African ape ancestor, the many grades of intelligence of other species, the similarity of human and primate brains, and so on—all these attest to the fact that we are just one among numerous other species on the earth, evolved under the influence of biological forces that are not fundamentally unique to us, only different in emphasis and intensity from those that have shaped other species.

In contrast, however, many philosophers, psychologists, and linguists emphasize anthropic specialness. The most commonly cited uniquely human feature is language. Human culture and human consciousness are difficult to make sense of except in the light of language and its unprecedented powers of reference and expressiveness. The distinctiveness and dizzying complexity of human languages and the diversity and richness of human cultures seems more than just an elaboration of non-human counterparts. Even many scholars who have otherwise not had difficulty accepting Darwinian accounts of organic evolution have balked when it comes to applying this to human minds and language. Famously, Alfred Russell Wallace, the co-discoverer of natural selection with Charles Darwin, argued that the origins of the human mind could not be explained by this theory and that only a sort of intelligent (e.g., divine) intervention could explain our unique mentality. Ideas of human discontinuity from other species have, as a result, fostered the suspicion that evolutionary continuity would turn out to be a false hope and that a key "missing link" would mark an unbridgable leap from ape to human.

The study of human paleontology has now traced the origins of our species, through dozens of intermediate fossil forms within our own ancestral lineage, the hominids. Nevertheless, there are still ancestral forms unaccounted for in the fossil record. Specifically, we lack fossils from the period where a common ancestor of both chimpanzee and human lineages would have existed. So it could still be claimed that there is a critical missing link. Although the record is incomplete at the beginning, it is well represented at the transition from apelike to humanlike forms. The apelike forms, grouped into the genus *Australopithecus,* predate the humanlike forms, grouped in the genus *Homo,* but still exhibit clear continuities with *Homo.* This transition took place over a half-million-year period and exhibits features that show this transition to be associated with significant cognitive changes: an increase in brain size and the introduction of stone tools.

I argue that these changes were related to the first subtle beginnings of symbolic, crudely languagelike communication (a still hotly contended question). Whenever this form of communicating began to play a role in the evolution of *Homo,* it marked the entry into something we would recognize as humanness. Language-aided thought offered a sort of software revolution that allowed a brain only slightly modified from ape patterns to operate with unparalleled efficiency and do things that would literally be unthinkable without.

This linking of humanness to language is not new. Descartes, for example, argued that the human/animal and mind/mechanism distinction were linked, and they remain so for many thinkers. People have considered the symbolic abilities reflected in language to be quintessentially part of the definition of the human species, demarcating the rational/nonrational distinction. To know when this transition occurred, what conditions initiated and drove it, and what changes in the brain correlated with it are essential pieces to the puzzle that also resides at the heart of each of the world's great spiritual traditions as well. The mystery of humanness, the mystery of the origins of rationality, and the mystery of language are not one and the same, but they are clearly part of one story.

A story that purports to explain the genesis of humanness has spiritual implications. To understand what these implications are, however, requires that we understand what happened.

BEGINNINGS OF HUMANNESS

Let's begin with a rough timetable. The major placental mammal groups diverged from a common ancestor following the demise of the dinosaurs about 65 million years ago. The primates as a group date back to just after this initial divergence of mammal groups. The ancestors of monkeys and apes separated from the rest of the primates less than half that long ago. Our anatomical characteristics and our genes show us to be one branch of the African apes, which today only include two chimpanzee species and the gorillas, besides ourselves. According to genetic comparisons, hominids (our distinct lineage) diverged from the common ancestral lineage of all these living African apes just prior to 5 million years ago and probably no more than 7 million years ago. These inferences from molecular biology correspond well with the now remarkably rich fossil record of remains from hundreds of individuals from over a dozen related hominid species dating back to more than 4 million years before the present.

All members of our once diverse lineage, the hominids, are distinguished from other African apes by their adaptations to bipedal (walking) locomotion. All exhibit a shallow bowl-shaped pelvis, vertical backs, extended legs, flattened less-manipulable feet, and many other features that today are only found in humans. One lineage among the hominids also developed large brains, manufactured stone tools, and communicated with the rudiments of language. It is from this lineage that modern humans arose and ultimately came to be its last surviving representative. These changes of brain and behavior did not happen all at once, and they didn't appear until long after hominids were good bipeds, so almost certainly it was not walking that alone made the difference, even if it did perhaps set the stage. The transition to these features characterizing humanness began about two and a half million years ago—roughly halfway from the point at which the hominid lineage as a whole diverged from the common ancestor we share with the chimps and gorillas.

Because the entire range of identified hominid species has become extinct save one—anatomically modern *Homo sapiens*—it is tempting to view them all in the context of the one survivor. We tend to see ourselves as either the best, the pinnacle of hominid evolution, or as the prime exemplar with respect to which the others must be ranked on a scale of descending humanness. This turns out to be a dangerous source of misconceptions because evolution is neither linear nor progressive. This is particularly the case with respect to our brains, our cognitive abilities, and our communication. We are an extreme and idiosyncratic case. So long as we avoid implicit progressivism, avoid thinking of our current state as the end product of some inevitable gradual improvement of mental functions, and recognize our adaptation as a rather singular, extreme, and unprecedented variant, we may be able to use the rich anatomical and developmental evidence available in living comparative anatomy to help understand the brains and behavioral abilities of our now fossilized ancestors.

The transition to *Homo* between 2.5 and 1.8 million years ago is identified by paleontologists with four major changes: the first appearance of stone tools (sharpened choppers), the first significant enlargement of the brain beyond ape proportions (in both absolute and relative size), a reduction in the robusticity of the teeth and jaws (indicating a major change in diet), and a reduction of sexual dimorphism (which likely signals a shift away from a highly polygynous social structure). This period is also marked by a drying climate, an expansion of the savanna, and an increase in the populations of hoofed animals that survived there.

This transition was characterized by variety in adaptations and not some ladder-like progression.

The earliest unambiguous stone tools date to about 2.5 million years ago, from a region in Ethiopia called Gona. These tools represent an elementary stone technology that flourished for nearly a million years and is collectively called the Oldowan tool industry. These tools were crudely fashioned by a few stone-on-stone strokes and were not particularly dependent on any specific kind of rock. They may have been made only as needed, near butchery sites, although there is some evidence that stones were transported from separate sites as well. The earliest fossil specimens of *Homo* do not date quite as far back as these first stone tools, so manufacture of these tools actually preceded the anatomical changes that define the genus *Homo*. Since the use of stone tools allowed their users to enter into an unprecedented ecological niche on the savanna, that of meat eating, this behavior could have played a role in producing the anatomical changes of this transition by virtue of an effect on both the dietary and social context of the species. In this way tool use may have helped to precipitate the subsequent evolution of brain and body that characterizes *Homo*. The details will probably become clearer as more fossil and archeological evidence is unearthed for this period in Africa.

The complementary patterns of adaptation to a stone tool–mediated lifestyle were united into a single pattern in a single species by approximately 1.6 to 1.8 million years ago. This species, *Homo erectus,* has a further enlarged brain, reduced molars, and less robust jaws. This species also exhibited unprecedented geographic range for a primate species. Current (still debated) estimates suggest that *erectus* populations migrated out of Africa and out to the southern extent of Indonesia as early as 1.8 million years ago—essentially as early as the species can be reliably dated anywhere.

During the recent 700 to 350 thousand years, *Homo erectus*'s anatomy appears to grade into archaic and then modern patterns, characteristic of *Homo sapiens*. Brain size increase is one of the major features used to delineate *Homo sapiens* from *Homo erectus*. The archaic *Homo sapiens* brain size average was around 1500 grams (it is 1330 in modern humans). The stone tools used by *sapiens* populations were significantly more complex and diverse than those of *erectus*. Both the Neanderthals of western Europe and more anatomically modern forms exhibited similar brain sizes and used similar tools and may even have coexisted in Europe and the middle east for tens of thousands of years; but eventually, about 30,000 years ago, the last Neanderthals disappeared from Europe and only one form of human was left on the earth. Just before and continuing after this transition, tools and other indications of culture began to become more complex. This period, known as the Upper Paleolithic, provides the first unambiguous "hard" evidence that humans are engaging in symbolic cultural activities.

But the evidence for the initial origin of symbolic culture is not easy to interpret. Although stone tool technologies and the associated social adaptations that enabled our distant pre-*sapiens* ancestors to colonize much of the old world have been present for over 2 million years, direct evidence for the production of external symbols in the form of carvings, body decorations, and cave paintings is minimal except for the last 20 to 50 thousand years. These earliest forms of "art" are mostly restricted to Europe and were associated with an elaboration and diversification of tools as well. But this is long after the origins of anatomically modern *Homo sapiens* and long since many modern lineages became genetically and (presumably) culturally distinct, so it is probably misleading to suggest that this unusual preservation of symbolic artifacts represents the first of its kind. The antecedents to this were apparently more perishable or were expressed only in behaviors, as are language and ritual. The evidence must be sought elsewhere: in the brain.

In summary, the fossil record suggests that the shift from apelike to humanlike patterns of mental and social adaptation began with the discovery of stone tools and the shift in feeding adaptation that it enabled. The shift to this socioecological strategy correlated with a constellation of interdependent changes in brain and body. Selection for differences in brain functions to support this lifestyle have thus been operating for over 2 million years. Two million years of sustained directional selection could have produced significant changes in many features of neural structure and function. This suggests that the differences between human brains and other ape brains should provide important clues to nature and origins of uniquely human mentality.

HUMAN BRAIN SIZE

For over a century, the size of the human brain has been considered a key factor in explaining human cognitive differences. Human brains are among the largest brains to ever have evolved, but there are a few species with larger brains. Elephants, large dolphins, and whales all have larger brains; and yet, despite this they do not appear to exhibit intellectual capacities that exceed humans. This fact was recognized by nineteenth-century anatomists and led them to conclude that relative size, with respect to the body, and not absolute size was more relevant, and humans have a much larger ratio of brain to body size (roughly 2 percent by weight) than these other larger brain species (only a small fraction of a percent for elephants and whales). The basic idea was that a major fraction of neural processing must be occupied with simply operating the various organ systems of the body, including sensory input and motor output systems. Consequently, although an elephant might have a larger brain, much more of it should be taken up with these basic somatic functions so that less of it would be available for higher cognition.

Some version of this brain proportion story is likely relevant, but it turns out to be much more complex than this suggests. One obvious hint that some important step in logic is missing from this argument derives from the fact that mice and other small mammals actually have brain/body ratios that can be much greater than the human ratio (up to 4 percent of body size). Moreover, these smaller brains are far more densely packed with neurons and connections. But for over a century brain evolution theorists have considered a slightly modified version of this story. In 1891 a biologist named Otto Snell discovered that when plotted in logarithmic coordinates (which renders simple growth curves linear) the brain and body sizes of mammals tended to fall along a line of roughly two-thirds slope (i.e., brain size scales to the square and body size to the cube power). Many have tried to explain this linearity as related to surface to volume scaling or metabolic scaling (which is actually near the three-quarters power relationship) among other possibilities. This mathematical regularity of brain and body sizes has captured the imaginations of generations of researchers and theorists ever since. It offers an intuitively appealing placement of human brain size as well. Compared to other species, human brain size is more positively divergent from the average trend than any other. This deviation is referred to as encephalization. The fact that human encephalization exceeded that of all other species has consequently been taken as the relevant correlate to explain human intellectual superiority.

Human encephalization cannot, however, be the whole story. It may even be a misleading fact in some respects. It turns out that the most encephalized nonprimates are very small breeds of dogs, like chihuahuas, and the most encephalized humans on the planet are dwarves. Chihuahuas and very small-bodied humans are not vastly more intelligent than normal dogs or normal humans, respectively. In defense of encephalization theory we might argue that these are examples where encephalization is produced by reduction of the growth of the body and not expansion of the brain. But why should this matter? Apparently, *how* encephalization is achieved is a critical factor (or, more specifically, when and how it develops during embryonic growth).

Humans are not dwarfed apes. Hominid brain size increased faster than body size in the last 2 million years of our evolution, and during that same time body size remained roughly the same. Also, unlike dwarfism, human growth does not follow a pattern that is indicative of early normal cranial and postcranial growth followed by slowed postcranial growth later in childhood, as occurs in dwarfism. The human encephalization is a consequence of brain growth that is more characteristic of a much larger species whereas body growth is typical for an ape of our size. In other words, it is as though the fetal brain from a 1000-pound ape species has been transplanted into the fetal body of a chimpanzee size ape. Although both are growing as one might predict from these two "donors," their patterns of growth are out of synch with respect to one another.

Could the shift to this pattern have affected cognition?

HOW BRAIN EVOLUTION DEPENDS ON DEVELOPMENT

The wiring of neural circuits is influenced by the relationship between how and when brain/body proportion develops and its timing. This is because the wiring of any given region of the brain is not completely determined by the genes expressed in the cells of that region but also depends to an important degree on contextual information arriving into that region from the rest of the brain, the body, and even from the outside world.

There are tens of billions of neurons in a human brain each connected to hundreds or even thousands of others, but there are only about 30,000 coding genes in the human genome. Moreover, it appears that about the same number of genes is used to build mouse brains as is used to build human brains. Clearly not all the information for building this complex network is encoded in genes. Much of it must come from somewhere else. The source of this missing information is in a sense nowhere and everywhere in the organism and its environment. This is because the information essentially *evolves* in the course of the developmental process itself. Well, it does not evolve in the usual way. The process is similar to Darwinian natural selection, but it involves the survival of the fittest cells in the developing body (rather than survival of the fittest lineages of organisms in an ecosystem), as different cells find themselves in a kind of competition and selection process. The components of the brain *adapt* to the body during development and, like their counterparts in phylogenetic evolution, create new forms and complex organizations anew, by internalizing certain aspects of the surrounding context.

We might say that a developing mammalian neural system adapts to the body it finds itself in, much as species adapt to a surrounding ecosystem—by utilizing overproduction, unspecified variation, competition, selective elimination, and perpetuation of only a fraction of the original variants. There are two levels of this process that are crucial to matching the central nervous system to the needs of an unprespecified body. The first involves the initial overproduction of neurons that are later selectively culled away by "programmed" cell death (also called apoptosis). The second involves a related overproduction and underspecification of connections between neurons and a subsequently pruning of these connections. The competition appears to be mediated by neural signaling processes themselves, in a way that enhances the survival chances of cells and connections that are carrying signals that are "in tune" with the signals around them. Both processes are highly reminiscent of Darwinian selection and are variants of related competitive processes that are also used elsewhere in the developing embryonic body to specify form and function.

The importance of neuronal overproduction and culling was first demonstrated by investigations of motor neuron development in the spinal cord. Early in fetal development, far more motor neurons are produced than will persist into maturity. All grow their output connections (axons) into the periphery, guided by relatively generic signals to a predefined class of target muscles. Once in the periphery, these axons compete for connection to individual muscle fibers, which ultimately will allow only terminals from one motor neuron to develop mature neuromuscular junctions. In the ensuing competition for muscle contacts, a large fraction of motor neurons fail to maintain any contacts and eventually get eliminated due to the lack of essential growth factors provided by these connections. Elimination of the unconnected cells results in a precise matching of muscle and motor neuron populations, post hoc.

This is relevant for the evolution of nervous systems because it allows variations of neural and muscular systems to occur almost irrespective of each other and yet guarantees coordination of function. Thus, novel adaptive responses, produced by mutations that shift the distribution of muscle masses within the body, would not require any corresponding neural mutations to match, and vice versa.

It is now evident that developmental cell death and a parallel culling of connections throughout the developing nervous system in a similar competitive-cooperative process plays an analogous role in matching neural populations throughout the developing brain. This contributes more than just a matching and population sculpting function. It is a major factor in neural network pattern formation as well. Axonal overproduction and pruning of connections has been shown to play critical roles in circuit patterning all levels of brain development and in the delineation of major subdivisions of cortical and subcortical structures. For example, severing the optic tract early in development causes axons from other sensory systems to innervate the now novelly available targets. This can alter the patterning and connectivity of the structures that would normally have subserved visual processing, with the result that many visual areas of the brain (e.g., the visual cortex) will now subserve nonvisual functions.

The effect of this Darwinian developmental logic on pattern formation is perhaps most vividly demonstrated by the neural adaptation for binocular visual perception. Crucial to both primate and carnivore vision is the ability to see depth by integrating information about binocular disparity (i.e., the difference in angle of gaze to the same object from each eye). The perceptual experience of depth is computed "online" in the visual cortex of these mammals by virtue of complex overlapping interdigitated projection maps arriving from each eye. This composite map is like what would result from putting two copies of a map through a paper shredder and then realigning the strips interdigitated with each other to form a single map with the portions from each eye in alternating strips. The extent of overlap of the maps and their interdigiation depends on the relative convergence of the eyes in the head. So the composite binocular map differs for different species, ranging from essentially no overlap in many rodent brains to nearly complete overlap in primate and human brains.

Given the complexity of this map structure and the precision with which it must be formed in order to function, it would seem to be a candidate for genetically prespecified organization. However, blocking visual signals from one eye during a critical period during early development can cause the entire map to become dedicated to one eye, thus undermining depth perception. So, beginning with a weak topographic pattern, the competition between connections utilizes the synchrony or dissynchrony of input signals from the two eyes, viewing their only slightly different images, to generate the composite binocular map.

One remarkable example of the power of this mechanism to generate pattern is provided by a study in which an additional (third) eye was implanted into the head of an embryonic frog, between its existing eyes.[1] During development it was found that this extranumery eye, because it conveyed information that was partially redundant with information from the closest normal eye, also produced a pattern of interdigitated eye-specific stripes in the frog brain. Normal frogs have essentially no normal binocular overlap and no phylogenetic history (so far as we know) of binocularity. The stripe pattern emerged de novo.

HOW BRAIN GROWTH AFFECTED CONNECTIONS

Putting these two pieces of the puzzle together, we can now see why the pattern of human brain growth with respect to the body matters, in terms of its functional organization. Dwarf creatures' brains and bodies grow pretty normally with respect to each other during the fetal period when brain circuits are forming and only begin to significantly diverge from normal proportions later in development, so the disproportion does not affect neural wiring. But human brains and bodies diverge from the typical plan fairly early in life. The brain grows for longer and is at a comparatively more immature state at corresponding stages with respect to body growth. As a result, the competitive processes that carve up the brain into interconnected regions and the patterns of their connections are altered in comparison to either a chimpanzee brain or the hypothetical 1000-pound ape species' brain.

So bigger isn't just bigger, it's different. For example, far less of the brain is used for direct input and output functions of the body than would be expected in the brain of a 1000-pound ape, with its larger eyes, skin surface, and retinas. This means that areas not directly connected to such peripheral structures will tend to comprise a much larger fraction of the whole. It also means that projections out from the central nervous system to peripheral structures like the hands and vocal tract will be more extensive than in chimpanzee bodies. Both central cognitive functions and control of the periphery have thus been altered, with significant consequences specifically for functions relevant to language.

First, consider human vocal abilities. Alone among land mammals we humans have the capacity to learn to produce a vast repertoire of vocal sounds. Although vocal mimicry and learning play a significant role in the communication of many bird species and a few dolphin and whale species, other mammals have relatively fixed vocal repertoires inherited from birth and relatively unmodifiable in form and correlation with arousal state. This appears to be a reflection of the way that vocal muscle systems are represented in the central nervous system. The muscles of the larynx are part of the visceral motor system. Most visceral muscles systems, such as heart, lungs, and digestive organs, need to run automatically and with minimal interference from conscious volitional processes. Both oral and vocal tract muscle systems serve double duty, for eating and breathing besides vocalization. Because these functions are to a large extent mutually exclusive and the costs of confusing them are great (e.g., choking), they tend to be controlled by highly stereotypic motor programs.

Vocalizations in nonhuman primates follow this logic and tend to be highly stereotypical. They are apparently controlled from structures deep in the midbrain and brainstem and regulated by emotional centers of the limbic system deep within the forebrain. Unlike speech, such vocalizations (including human laughter and crying) are not controlled from the motor areas of the cerebral cortex (the convoluted surface of the forebrain), where most skilled volitional movement is regulated. This explains why efforts to train monkeys and apes to produce learned vocalizations, other than from their fixed repertoires, have failed. In fact, even extensive damage to the motor cortical areas that control the mouth and oral tract in monkeys fails to block their typical "calls" even though it completely paralyzes the mouth. In contrast, in humans, damage to the motor mouth area of the cortex, even if confined to the left side alone, can produce profound mutism.

The Darwinian-like processes of brain development coupled with extended growth of the forebrain might contribute to this difference. Early in development in many mammals, projections descending from the neurons of the cortex send off collateral branches that initially reach into these visceral and oral control centers of the midbrain and brainstem but are quickly eliminated by competition from other systems. In monkeys, whose brains are larger with respect to these subcortical targets, fewer of these connections appear to be eliminated, though connections to areas controlling the larynx are eliminated. Although direct evidence is missing, it seems likely that the larger human forebrain has allowed these once transient cortical connections to the laryngeal motor nucleus to persist into adulthood. The result is that, like our hand and finger control, we have independent control of the individual muscle movements underlying vocalization and can recombine them with individual tongue and mouth movements to produce the syllabic units essential for speech.

Another major difference relevant to language and also to some of our most distinguishing aspects of cognition is our capacity to understand the symbolic relationships of language. Although much more difficult to explain than the evolution of vocal articulation, there are interesting hints about the basis of this uniquely human capacity in the proportions of forebrain regions that play a major role in these functions. Specifically, the relative expansion of the part of the frontal lobes called the prefrontal cortex may be the critical factor. This region is vital to cognitive tasks that involve holding information in mind while examining alternative behavioral opportunities and contingencies. Some have referred to these processes as "working memory" or "executive function."

Although the use of symbolically encoded knowledge provides unprecedented augmentation of cognition and communication, symbolic representation systems are difficult to acquire. This is because symbolic information is not actually present in the stimuli or even in the correlations between stimuli that a learner has available to him. To understand that something is an abstract symbol for something else—not just a correlated mark (i.e., an index)—one must understand how the relationships between symbols corresponds to relationships that hold between objects to which they refer. This higher-order correspondence is not evident in any one instance but must be "guessed" from patterns that emerge from many uses of many symbols. So it is necessary to hold a considerable number of alternative possible relationship patterns in one's mind at one time in order to figure out which pattern provides the relevant pattern to constitute the symbolic reference system. Discovering a symbolic relationship is thus a bit like breaking a code. This requires considerable working memory support and a facility at switching among alternative hypotheses as new information becomes available.

The relative exaggeration of the size of that part of the human brain that is essential for handling these sorts of information processing demands was likely one of the crucial adaptations enabling humans to surmount this threshold that keeps so many other species out of the symbolic processing game.

The logic of this embryology also provides evidence for a pretty good guess as to the evolutionary time course of the development of these abilities. Both shifts in proportions and connections follow from the shift in the large-scale difference in brain growth and postcranial growth that distinguishes us from other primates. We can therefore use the crude brain/body proportions available from the fossil record to estimate when these changes began and how rapidly they progressed. Since the first shift away from ape brain/body proportions began over 2 million years ago and continued until only a few hundred thousand years ago, it is reasonable to assume that both vocal and symbolic abilities were also both improving in our ancestors over this time. This suggests a gradual transition to full humanness, not some momentary discontinuous transformation. Modern human language and thought may only go back a hundred thousand or less years, but the roots of humanness are apparently much older.

But what initiated and drove this process? Although it is pretty hopeless to speculate on the details of what went on 2 million years ago, or even a hundred thousand years ago, the general nature of the process can be sketched with somewhat better hope for accuracy. There are good reasons to suggest that these changes in the brain were both cause and consequence of human symbolic communication and rudimentary speech. In other words, the language and human brain origins story is a typical chicken and egg story. Each formed the context in which the other evolved and in turn changed the conditions affecting the evolution of the other. They co-evolved a bit like beaver dam building and pond living adaptations probably co-evolved. This seems likely because these changes seem both unusual and too coincidentally relevant to language function to be merely a chance association. Language abilities are too good and too odd (with respect to other species) to be evolutionary afterthoughts. They must be the result of extensive evolutionary "preparations."

This evolutionary interdependency is probably a paradigm example of what is often called the "Baldwin effect" (after James Mark Baldwin, who first outlined this kind of evolutionary dynamic in 1896).[2] This occurs when a learned behavior becomes essential for the survival of future generations and thereby creates new niche conditions imposing novel selection pressures on them. The use of stone tools, for example, must have had this effect on the reduction of teeth evident in early *Homo*. Symbolic communication is also a sort of tool, a social tool, and it would have generated at least as much of a restructuring of the hominid lifestyle as did stone tools (in fact, as I argue in *The Symbolic Species*, they were probably mutually interdependent adaptive innovations).[3] The gradual evolutionary changes in brain/body proportions and the correlated changes in brain organization supporting speech and symbolic learning were thus likely an adaptive response to the novel demands imposed by using an initially very simple languagelike communication system. In this sense, then, we may have been created in the image of "the word," or rather its demands. The word made flesh.

HUMANNESS EMERGING

Although we are still a ways from agreement on these details—on the order of events, the essential changes in the brain, the age, and nature of early symbolic and vocal communication—it seems pretty clear that a co-evolutionary account, much like this one, best describes the transition from an upright ape to a person able to think and communicate in symbols. The ability to master this unprecedented cognitive trick is correlated with *some* difference that distinguishes human from ape brains. This difference evolved within the last 2 million years. To explain this will demystify much of human uniqueness. Does it make us any less unique or make this mental difference any less incredible to know that it has an identifiable neurological basis and an evolutionary origin?

NOTES

1. M. I. Law and M., Constantine-Paton, "Anatomy and Physiology of Experimentally Produced Striped Tecta," *Journal of Neuroscience* 1 (1981): 741–759.

2. For example, J. M. Baldwin, "Consciousness and Evolution," *Psychological Review* 3 (1896): 300–309.

3. T. W. Deacon, *The Symbolic Species* (New York: W. W. Norton & Company, 1997).

11 Theological Perspectives on Being Human

Nancey Murphy *Fuller Theological Seminary*

INTRODUCTION

What are human beings made of? I know: bones, muscle, fat—all those things you study in biology class. But is that all? Most Christians, throughout most of their history, have believed that there is another part, generally called the soul. This second part has been considered important—it is often thought of as that which is saved for eternal life. It is also thought to account for the capacity, in this life, to be in a relationship with God.

Other religions have similar concepts. The doctrine of reincarnation in Eastern religions presupposes the existence of an immortal soul that lives a number of lives in a series of different bodies.

Increasingly, though, our culture is developing an understanding of the human person that sees us as purely physical. Contributions to this newer view come from sciences such as biology—the theory of evolution already pointed many in this direction over 100 years ago. Philosophers are increasingly arguing such a view. The most dramatic evidence now comes from the neurosciences. As Terrence Deacon's chapter has made clear, it seems to be the brain that does most, if not all, of what was once attributed to the mind or soul.

So we are heading for a major conflict between science and religion, right? Wrong. My goal in this chapter is to convince you that there is another option. I will argue that a physicalist account of the human person is compatible with Christian teaching; in fact, more compatible with original Christian teaching than dualism.

Note that I can only speak for one tradition, my own Christian tradition. With some adjustments what I say will be relevant to Jewish thought. I regret that I cannot deal with issues as they arise in other world religions.

My chapter will have four parts: First, I will say a few words about the historical background that makes it appear that a conflict is brewing here between neuroscience and Christianity; second, I will take a brief look at the Bible to consider what it does, and does not, have to say on this issue; third, I will comment on one major theological problem (what about life after death, if there is no soul); and, finally, I will reflect on human distinctiveness in light of both science and Christian teaching.

HOW HISTORY HAS SET US UP FOR CONFLICT

First, we do have to recognize the fact, which I mentioned at the beginning, that most Christians, throughout most of their history, have held some form of body-soul dualism. This has been the case at least from the fifth through the nineteenth centuries. This view has had repercussions throughout Christian theology, but it shows up most clearly in the expectation, held by theologians and ordinary believers alike, that humans "come apart" at death. The soul departs to be with God; the body molders in the grave until the Resurrection of the dead, at which time body and soul are to be reunited.

This fact about the mainstream of Christian thought would be enough to raise the specter of conflict, but one particular strategy for reconciling Christianity with Darwin's theories has made things worse for some. It has sometimes been said that it is okay to believe that the human body evolved from lower life forms, so long as one maintains that the soul did not, and, in fact, the soul is often said to be a special creation of God.

Pope John Paul II, in a recent address to the Pontifical Academy of Science, presented the views of one of his predecessors. He said,

> Pius XII stressed this essential point: if the human body takes its origin from pre-existent living matter, the spiritual soul is immediately created by God. . . . Consequently, [he says,] theories of evolution which . . . consider the mind as emerging from the forces of living matter . . . are incompatible with the truth about man.[1]

Many Evangelical Protestants have made this same move. Anyone who has adopted this strategy to reconcile scientific and theological accounts of human origins ought to be very nervous about the developments reflected in Deacon's paper.

To show you why, I need to insert here a note about terminology. Contemporary scientists and philosophers talk about the mind and its relation to the brain. Religious folk generally talk about the soul. In my introduction, I was supposing that these are the same. As a matter of fact, although we have two different words in English, they both translate a single word in Latin, *anima*.

Now, I suspect that if you ask contemporary believers just what the soul is, they will not have a very definite reply. Therefore, it is helpful to look back at earlier writers in the Christian tradition who did have a definite idea. My favorite is Thomas Aquinas. He produced a list of the higher capacities or faculties of the soul that closely match what contemporary cognitive scientists and philosophers would describe as mental capacities or operations. Thomas's list includes the five senses, four internal senses (memory; imagination; judgment, and the *sensus communis*, i.e., the ability to collate data from the five exterior senses), as well as emotion, intellect, and will.

It is enlightening to look at contemporary neuroscience and see just how many of these capacities, which Thomas attributed to the soul, are now studied by neurobiologists. Most significant, in my view, are localization studies—that is, research indicating not only that the brain is involved in specific mental operations, but that very specific regions correlate with very specific cognitive abilities.[2]

Localization studies used to be limited to correlating regions of brain damage with cognitive deficits after the patient had died. A variety of new scanning techniques now make it possible to locate damaged regions while the patient is alive and even to locate regions of activity (in undamaged brains) while assorted mental tasks are being performed. Here is a sample of the results.

Vision depends on the transmission of signals from the retina to the visual cortex. Smell involves transmitting signals from six kinds of receptors to the olfactory lobes. Thomas's interior sense, called the *sensus communis,* the ability to synthesize input from the various external senses, is now studied by neuroscientists as "the binding problem."

Memory has been much researched. Long-term memory is conceived of as the result of patterns of connections within the neural network. Short-term memory is believed to be enabled by a system of "recurrent pathways," such that information is processed, then recycled and fed into the process again. The hippocampus is known to be involved in converting short-term to long-term memory.

Language abilities are associated with two regions of the neocortex, called Broca's area and Wernicke's area. Recall of words is even more precisely located: Different regions seem to be involved for verbs, proper names, common nouns, and even for color terms.

The parietal lobes are involved in memory of faces. The ability to recognize other people's emotions can be lost as a result of brain damage, although there does not seem to be a specific region responsible for this capacity.

Antonio Damasio has recently reported on victims of localized brain damage whose injuries or illnesses have resulted in the specific loss of moral character. That is, their intellectual capacities remain unaffected, but they are unable to act in accord with what reason tells them.[3] This is a particularly important finding, from a theological point of view. For Thomas, it was the will, the ability to be attracted to the good, that accounted for human ability to be in relationship with God.

Note that none of this research disproves mind-body or body-soul dualism. One can still argue that it is the nonmaterial mind (or soul) that is responsible for these functions, and that for some reason they are simply well correlated with brain activity. However, it is clear that the burden of proof has shifted to the dualists to explain why we need to postulate an additional entity, the mind, when accounts in terms of brain activity are becoming increasingly more powerful.

WHAT THE BIBLE SAYS (AND DOES NOT SAY) ABOUT THE PERSON

The issue at hand has been an important one in biblical studies in this century. By the middle of the century there was considerable agreement among Christian scholars on the importance of distinguishing in theology between the original Hebraic views and later Greek, or Hellenistic, views. One instance of such a difference was a contrast between Greek dualism and a Hebraic conception of the person that is much more holistic and physicalistic.

Scholars no longer draw the distinctions so sharply between Greek and Hebrew thought, but nonetheless there remains a near consensus that the Hebrew scriptures do not promote dualism.

Now, if this is true, how could people have been so mistaken for so long (for over 14 centuries)?

One answer is translation. Early Christians' access to the Hebrew Bible was primarily through a Greek translation, called the *Septuagint.* It was very easy to impose Hellenistic ideas on Hebrew texts simply by the choice of translations.

To illustrate, let me show you a few familiar lines from the Psalms, King James Version:

Psalm 16:10: For thou wilt not leave my soul in Hell.

Psalm 25:20: O keep my soul, and deliver me; let me not be ashamed. . . .

Psalm 26:9: Gather not my soul with sinners.

Psalm 49:14-15: [They that trust in their wealth] like sheep they are laid in the grave; death shall feed on them . . . but God will redeem my soul from the power of the grave: for he shall receive me.

These passages fit nicely with a view that, while the body may decay in the grave, God saves souls. It sounds exactly like body-soul dualism.

However, there are a lot of other references to the soul in the Hebrew scriptures that don't fit this dualist picture at all:

Psalm 7:1–2: O Lord my God in thee do I put my trust: save me from all them that persecute me. . . . Lest he tear my soul like a lion, rending it in pieces.

Psalm 22:20: Deliver my soul from the sword.

Psalm 35:7: . . . without cause have they hid for me their net in a pit, which without cause they have digged for my soul.

So this does not sound right. Souls are not capable of being torn or stabbed. And it is bodies that people throw in pits. Even stranger,

Leviticus 7:18: And if any of the flesh of the sacrifice of his peace offering be eaten at all on the third day, it shall not be accepted . . . it shall be an abomination, and the soul that eateth of it shall bear his iniquity.

Souls eating meat? What is going on here?

Well, it is widely agreed now that the Hebrew word translated "soul" in all these cases—*nephesh*—did not really mean what later Christians have meant by *soul.* In most of these cases, it is simply a way of referring to the whole living person. Here is how a more recent version of the Bible translates some of these same passages:

Psalm 16:10: (KJV) For thou wilt not leave my soul in hell;

(NIV) because you will not abandon me to the grave.

Psalm 25:20: (KJV) O keep my soul, and deliver me; let me not be ashamed;

(NIV) Guard my life and rescue me; let me not be put to shame.

Finally,

Leviticus 7:18: (KJV) the soul that eateth of it shall bear his iniquity;

(NIV) the person who eats of it will be held responsible.

So the Hebrew word *nephesh* is translated as person, life, or just used as a way for a person to refer to him or herself. It is also used of animals, and here it is best translated as "living being." Those who have seen body-soul dualism in the Old Testament, including many earlier translators, have been reading it back into the texts, not getting it out of the texts.

The next question is, What does the New Testament teach about body-soul dualism versus physicalism?

This is a more difficult question, but the best answer is, Nothing! Let me explain.

There are a number of issues on which the Bible has clear teachings. There are other things that the Bible says in order to put forward those teachings. For example, when Isaiah says that God will gather Israel and Judah from the four corners of the earth (Isaiah 11:12), he does not mean to teach that the earth has four corners. That is a conception of geography and geology that he simply assumed in making his prophecy.

I believe that the New Testament has a lot to teach about what it means to be human but does not mean to teach specific details about how many parts we are made of: body and soul; body, soul and spirit; or just one.

Just as in our own day, there were in New Testament times a variety of ideas about the make-up of the person. The various New Testament authors used different ideas in order to make clear their teachings on other matters. So if we try to go through the New Testament to see what it teaches on this subject, we will end up frustrated and confused.

One good way to get at New Testament teaching on what it means to be human is to look at the stories in the gospels of the healing Jesus did. We can see that they portray a concept of health that has much in common with contemporary views of holistic medicine. Typically Jesus does not merely heal bodies. In addition, or at the same time, he reestablishes the person's connections with community. For example, the lepers that Jesus healed would have been excluded from normal society because of purity rules. He also reestablishes the person's harmony with the cosmos, if we take demons to be emblems of evil cosmic powers.

Most important, he establishes or reestablishes the person's relationship with God—seen in the fact that forgiveness of sins is associated with healing.

So my conclusion is that a holistic, physicalist account of the person drawn from contemporary science is not at all incompatible with the picture we see of the nature of human persons in the Bible.

WHAT ABOUT LIFE AFTER DEATH?

Here is where the difference between physicalism and dualism will have a big impact. It is one thing to read scholars' commentaries in the library; it is quite another to talk about these things at a funeral. I mentioned that one of the clearest places dualism has had an impact is on what Christians think happens at death. This was brought home to me personally this past summer when Mother and I went for the first time to my father's grave. "He's not really here," she said. "Oh, yes he is," I thought. Fortunately, I kept my thoughts to myself.

I recognize the comfort it brings to imagine that loved ones are not really dead, but just "gone." However, I stand with the majority of contemporary scholars in saying that such a view is not part of original Christian teaching about life after death. The original view was that the whole person dies, but the whole person will later (at the end of history) be raised from death. The model for this death and resurrection, of course, is that of Jesus. Paul writes to the Church at Corinth that, "If Christ has not been raised, your faith is futile . . . [and] those who have died in Christ have perished. . . . But in fact Christ has been raised from the dead, the first fruits of those who have died" (1 Corinthians 15:17–20).

In our day it is difficult to talk about resurrection. This has to do with the question how there could ever be historical evidence for such a strange thing. If we find resurrection unimaginable, that is just about right, because we cannot have any clear idea of something beyond the life of this present age. We get only a variety of suggestive pictures in Scripture.

The problem was difficult in Paul's day, too, but for different reasons. The idea of resurrection of the body was already available at the time in some Jewish circles, so this was a conceivable prospect for the Jews, but simply disbelieved by many. However, it must have appeared positively ridiculous to many of the Gentile Christians, whose exposure to Greek philosophies and other Mediterranean religions had led them to believe that they already had a soul destined for immortality and that the religious quest was to liberate the soul from the encumbrances of the body. Why, then, should one hope to have the body restored after the liberation that comes with death?

We can see that there are two different accounts of life after death available in Western philosophies and religions: One is the (more common) notion that humans possess an immortal soul, which will survive death; the other is the (now strange) expectation that the entire person will be raised, or re-created, at the end of history. Many Christians have worked out a hybrid in which the soul survives in an intermediate state, awaiting the return of its body at the end. I am claiming that the original Christian view was simply death followed by bodily resurrection. On this view, nothing of value is lost if one adopts a physicalist account of the person, and such an account appears to be closer to original Christian teaching.

HUMAN DISTINCTIVENESS

I turn now to my final topic. This is a reply to the question, if humans are, as evolutionists tell us, closely related to other animals, and if, as contemporary neuroscience suggests, we have no immortal soul distinguishing us from animals, then what makes us distinctively human?

The way to put this question is not in terms of special parts, but, as Ian Tattersall did, in terms of special capacities.

Let me go back to the Pope's address to the Pontifical Academy of Sciences. The present Pope speaks not of the creation of the soul, as did Pius XII, but of "the moment of transition to the spiritual." Science cannot determine this point, he says, but it can determine at the experimental level a series of valuable signs indicating what is specific to the human being. In addition, philosophical analysis can reflect on what is distinctively human. The Pope lists metaphysical knowledge, self-awareness and self-reflection, moral conscience, freedom, aesthetic experience, and religious experience. But only theology, he says, can bring out the ultimate meaning of these characteristics according to the creator's plans.

What, then, are the capacities that are most distinctive of our humanness? What does it look like to reflect scientifically on this question, and what does it look like to reflect theologically on this question?

A number of scientists study the higher primates and from these studies we could construct lists of things we can do and they cannot. As it turns out, most of the differences are matters of degree rather than the presence and total absence of certain characteristics. However, what may be small differences in basic capacities interact to produce huge differences in final outcome.

For example, apes can be taught rudimentary forms of language. There is debate over the question of whether chimpanzees possess self-awareness (one of the distinctives listed by the Pope). Do chimps recognize themselves in a mirror? Perhaps it depends on what we mean: Chimps do *recognize* themselves; but do they recognize *themselves?*

Higher animals have emotions, but ours are more finely modulated. Animals can be angry but cannot experience righteous indignation.

So here are some features that are associated with our sense of what it means to be human, and animals share rudimentary forms of them. What matters is the way these enhanced capacities interact in human life. For example, put together our clear sense of self with finely tuned emotions and subtle linguistic abilities and we have immensely different capacities for interpersonal relationships.

What does theology have to say about human distinctiveness? Here the question is not so much what it is that makes us different from animals, although differences have to be presupposed. Here the question is rather what it is about us that is important to God. I will emphasize two factors: first is our capacity for morality; second is our capacity for relationships, with God as well as with other humans. I mentioned earlier that I believe this emphasis on proper relationships to be central to New Testament teaching on what it means to be human.

The point I wish to emphasize here is that scientific results do not interpret themselves. That is, we need, in addition to all that science can tell us about ourselves, a religious point of view in order to know the significance of the scientific findings. This is what I take the Pope to be saying when he says that only theology brings out the ultimate meaning of these characteristics according to the creator's plans.

Morality has become a hot topic for debate among sociobiologists. Some claim that genetics can explain human morality, and the arguments go something like this: Human morality has parallels in the animal world, and even among insects. The parallel is that they all exhibit altruism, meaning that the individual sacrifices itself for the good of the group.

This can be explained in animal behavior because group survival is generally survival of kin, and kinship survival means survival of one's genes. Evolution favors whatever is good for the survival of one's genes. Hence, human morality can be seen, also, as a product of genetics.

Recent arguments are much more nuanced than this, but however sophisticated, there is something wrong at the core of such an account. First, a philosophical analysis. One of the most prominent philosophers of the modern period was Immanuel Kant. According to Kant, to be moral is to do one's duty. This means that if you are doing only what you are genetically programmed to do, or even acting on what you are predisposed to find enjoyable, what you are doing does not count as moral behavior at all. Being moral is not just doing good; it involves, essentially, doing good for the right motive. The right motive has to be that you recognize it as a duty. Already we see an essential difference between what a human is doing when engaging in a moral action and anything an animal or insect could be doing.

Now let us move to a theological level of analysis. We can ask the further question: Where do moral duties come from? Kant tried to show that we could know our duty on the basis of pure reason, but the traditional theological answer is that duties come from God. That is, morality for Christians, and I think for Jews and Muslims as well, is, at its heart, obedience.

Here we take a further step away from equating human morality with animal altruism. The theological interpretation of morality is theocentric. One does what one does because it is obligatory, and it is obligatory because it fits with God's purposes for human life. To sacrifice oneself for others, on this account, is as different as it could possibly be from doing it because it is genetically programmed. The motive is entirely different.

Let us look at the content of morality as well as its motive. On the surface it may appear that the sociobiologist has it just right: Self-sacrifice is central to Christian morality.

But look more closely. The sociobiologists' account depends on similarity of genes in the group for which one sacrifices; that is, they must be family, kin. Christian morality is in some ways strangely antifamily. Jesus says, "I have come to set a man against his father, and a daughter against her mother . . . and one's foes will be members of one's own household" (Matthew 10:35–36).

The emphasis in Christianity is, rather, on loving the stranger (and this is a part of Jewish morality as well). For Christians the one for whom one is to sacrifice is, most particularly, the enemy. Later New Testament teaching focused on reconciliation of Jews and Gentiles—whom no one at the time could have considered to be physically related. So Christian morality is different not only in motive but in content from kin-preserving altruism.

My point in addressing this issue: I want to maintain that science studies the whole of human life—there is no metaphysically distinct part of us that is immune from scientific investigation. However, science gives us an incomplete account of human life, an account that can only be put into perspective by a religious point of view. Science can say, in this, this, and this way we humans are like the animals, and in that way and that way we are different. But then the question is, So what? Birds sacrifice themselves for the group; humans sacrifice themselves for the group. So what? That is, which similarities matter and why? Which differences matter, and why? Only a worldview that can talk about ultimate issues can answer this question.

I am arguing against reductionism. I want to distinguish between reductionist and nonreductionist accounts of the human person. Reductive physicalism says that humans are physical organisms, and *nothing but* that, and, in addition (and this is the reductionistic part), everything about us can be explained in naturalistic terms: not only morality but even religious behavior. Religious experience, the reductionist says, is merely a neural event; religions themselves can be explained sociologically as human inventions for promoting social cohesion.

Nonreductive physicalism, on the other hand, grants that we are biological organisms but emphasizes that our neurological complexity and the history of cultural development have together resulted in the capacity for genuine moral reasoning, including the ability to recognize an objective obligation to obey the voice of the creator.

I come to my second instance of human distinctiveness, the ability to be in relationship with God, the ability to have religious experience, in fact, the ability to hear the voice of God.

I said at the beginning that one reason religious believers might object to discarding the notion of a soul is that the soul has often been thought of as that which gives humans the ability to relate to God. Medieval mystics spoke of withdrawing from the world of the senses, entering into the soul, wherein they experienced God's presence. How could one conceive of experiencing God if there is no soul?

I just came across an account of experiencing God, in fact an account of hearing God speak, in a book by Nicholas Wolterstorff, a philosopher at Yale, titled *Divine Discourse.* Let me quote a passage to you:

> Let me present part of the narration of some experiences which recently befell an acquaintance of mine who is a well-established member of the faculty of one of the other Eastern seaboard universities. . . . I shall call her "Virginia" . . . and call [her pastor] "Byron." Perhaps I should add, [says Wolterstorff] that though Virginia is . . . a Christian, she neither is nor was what anyone would classify as an Evangelical. It's worth saying that because Evangelicals have the reputation of believing that God speaks to them rather more often, and rather more trivially, than most of us think God would bother with.
>
> So here is Virginia's own account:
>
> On February 12, 1987, while folding laundry I suddenly knew with certain knowledge that Byron was supposed to leave St. Paul's Church. There was no external voice, but there was a brightening in the room at the moment of revelation. The experience was so overwhelming that I called my husband and invited him to come home for lunch. . . . I needed to reassure myself of reality. Later that afternoon . . . I found myself sobbing. I knew the knowledge I have been given was not me, and I knew it was correct. As the day progressed, it became clear to me that there were seven insistent statements that I needed to tell Byron. . . . I was awe-struck and terrified. . . .
>
> The next morning, when I went to see Byron. . . . I told him the seven statements: "Your work is done here. You have accomplished what you were sent to do. You are still young. There are great things in store for you. Do not be afraid. God will take care of you. I will help with the transition." This message was not a surprise to Byron. He had already come to that conclusion prior to our conversation.[4]

Virginia goes on to tell about the ways her message was confirmed in the days to come. There was a second message to be delivered to a meeting at church, which was well received as just the thing that needed saying. Byron did get a call to another church. In addition, after visiting a psychologist to reassure herself she was not crazy, Virginia's own spirituality deepened.

What I want you to notice is how ordinary this experience was—not ordinary in the sense that people regularly report getting messages from God, but in the sense that it used or depended on nothing but ordinary cognitive abilities that we all have. A set of ideas came into her mind. She had a variety of feelings—a feeling of certitude, a feeling of awe. I submit that for such an experience, nothing is needed beyond the ordinary neural equipment that we all possess.

What makes this a religious experience is that it was attributed to God. The question is, then, If it was so ordinary (in the sense I have specified), how could one know it was from God? Wolterstorff takes up this question, pointing out that the circumstances in which it happened, the consequences, and the confirmation by the community all pointed in that direction.

I would add that this sort of judgment well reflects the regular criteria that Christians have used all along to distinguish between their own fancies and the voice of God. This is called, in some circles, spiritual discernment.[5] This form of judgment is, of course, less reliable than judgments about the natural world. For example, the right kind of consequences can assure us one way or the other whether we were seeing a mirage or a real oasis. Things are never so clear with religious experience, but they are often as clear as we need them to be.

I am claiming that religious experiences are not to be distinguished from others by the fact that they occur in the recipient's soul (however one might recognize that!) but rather by the circumstances, by the patterns into which they fit, by the way a judgment to the effect that God was at work stands up to further evidence in the course of one's life and that of one's community.

CONCLUSION

I began by raising the question whether Christians are headed for conflict with science, especially because of recent developments in brain science. I pointed out that in fact it has been a mistake to think that the Hebrew Scriptures offer a dualist account of the person. We have been misled by the way early Christians translated the Hebrew texts. The next question was what the New Testament has to say, and I claimed that the New Testament writers are actually pretty silent about this issue. However, it is clear that the New Testament holds out the hope, not of everlasting survival of an immaterial soul, but rather the hope for the resurrection or re-creation of the entire (physical) person.

However, while commending physicalist accounts of the person, I cautioned against reductionistic versions of physicalism. Reductionism involves the claim that the natural sciences can provide an exhaustive account of what it means to be human. I looked at two features that Christian theology makes central to an account of human distinctiveness, morality and religious experience. In the first case I wanted to show that we need a theological interpretation to make sense of the similarities and differences between ourselves and the animals. In the second case I wanted to show the sufficiency of our physical equipment to account for the phenomena of religious experience, but again to claim that a theological interpretation is necessary. It is only a theological perspective, knowledge of the regular patterns of God's action, that allows one to make a distinction between genuine religious experience and its counterfeits.

I want to end by emphasizing the value of scientific interpretations for balancing and correcting theological accounts. The physicalist account of the person can call Christians back to truths about both their origin and their destiny that have been obscured. We are earth creatures; in Hebrew *Adam* is created from *adamah* (earth). Phyllis Trible has suggested a parallel play on words in English: We are humans created from humus.

Our future is the Kingdom of God—not a Platonic heaven of solitary contemplation, but a future state for which the best metaphor is a banquet, a wedding feast. We take our bodiliness with us to our final destiny. Eating and laughing and touching and dancing are not evils to be left behind.[6]

NOTES

1. Pope John Paul II, Message to the Pontifical Academy of Science, "L'Osservatore Romano," 44 October 30, 1996.

2. For a very readable and engaging overview, see Paul Churchland, *The Engine of Reason, the Seat of the Soul. A Philosophical Journey into the Brain* (Cambridge, MA: MIT Press, 1995).

3. Antonio R. Damasio, *Descartes' Error: Emotion, Reason, and the Human Brain* (New York: Putnams's Sons, 1994).

4. Nicholas Wolterstorff, *Divine Discourse: Philosophical Reflections on the Claim that God Speaks* (Cambridge: Cambridge University Press, 1995), pp. 274–275.

5. See Nancey Murphy, *Theology in the Age of Scientific Reasoning* (Ithaca, NY: Cornell University Press, 1990), Chapter 5.

6. For a more detailed account of the issues in this chapter, see Nancey Murphy, Warren Brown, and H. Newton Malony, eds., *Whatever Happened to the Soul? Scientific and Theological Portraits of Human Nature* (Minneapolis: Fortress Press, 1998).

12 Cultural Evolution and Biology: The Biocultural Evolution of Nutriculture

Solomon H. Katz *University of Pennsylvania*

OVERVIEW

At the macro level of the history of the human species, there is a relatively wide agreement that a cultural evolutionary process underlies the enormous biological and social success of contemporary humanity. There is also an emerging consensus that (1) culture is the cumulative product of learned and shared experiences; (2) the capacity for culture has a biological basis emanating from the biological capacities of our cerebral cortex to abstract, innovate, discover, and communicate these cumulative products and thoughts and experiences of past and contemporary culture(s); and (3) human individuals and societies use culture to adapt more effectively to their physical and psychosocial environments.

Given this wide emerging agreement about the properties and function of culture, there are still few, if any, theories to date that account for any significant aspects of this evolutionary process at the macro level or significant details at the micro level. Thus, very little of the variation, natural origins, development, and adaptive significance of the differences within and among cultures can be explained and comprehensively accounted for by any contemporary theory of cultural evolution.

Some of the major reasons for this lack of significant theoretical paradigms are probably due to two factors. The first factor is that the nature of the interactions is very complex and involves incompletely understood variables in the model. For example, the functions of the chief organ of culture, the human cerebral cortex, and its relations to the rest of the human central nervous system are only now coming to be understood. A second factor is historic and stems from a remarkable reticence by contemporary scholars to directly deal with the advancement of theory and models available in the late twentieth century. Since the first problem involves contemporary scientific knowledge and the second, the history of ideas, this chapter will address the historical issues first. The chapter will then provide a brief overview of the concept of cultural evolution and develop the concept of "nutriculture" as a means of generating hypotheses concerning the interface of nutrition and food as a paradigm for generating significant models and testable hypotheses about what I have called the *biocultural evolutionary process*.[1]

INTRODUCTION

Cultural evolution attempts to explain and account for the natural origins, development, and overall variation of culture as the most important species-specific adaptive resource humans have. At the end of the twentieth century it is widely agreed by many social scientists that we humans function within societies, are the social products of our cultures, are "free" to innovate within them, and can effect significant changes of all kinds to our lives. Thus, it is reasoned that cultural changes and differences must be the products of free will processes that are independent of our biology and, therefore, the explanation of culture is best found in history and the social sciences rather than the natural sciences. Historically, this philosophical position can be traced back to the Renaissance, when the shift first emerged in the understanding of human nature from a static fixed place to one that gives us freedom to be independently willful and responsible for making our own decisions about all aspects of our lives.[2] Humans were not subject to the laws of nature like other animals; we had the free will to decide for ourselves. This fifteenth-century reconfiguration of the place of humanity in the world is key to understanding the philosophical controversies and the later developments of theories of cultural evolution.

However, if we ask biologists at the end of the twentieth century interested in the biological bases of human nature, they widely agree that humans are a species like all others and that we have evolved some critically important capacities that have given rise to our ability to have cultures that solve problems that we are biologically incapable of effectively solving on our own. Our cultures provide the knowledge and integration that enable our societies to feed, clothe, and shelter us. Cultures also regulate our fertility, care for us when we are sick, raise our children, socialize the next generations, and provide meaning for our past, present, and future as we traverse our life course. If culture provides all of these necessities that our bodies do not provide so well on their own, what is culture and how did it get that way?

Remarkably the answer to these two rather simple questions has led to some very complicated answers. Hundreds of anthropologists have studied culture over the last century, and they have produced several hundred definitions of *culture*. However, the diversity of their ideas about the definition of *culture* also reveals some of the underlying controversy about how culture got that way, since the answer to the question of what it is implies how it changes, and this issue, in turn, confronts the concept of cultural evolution. While most everyone in anthropology agrees about some of the concrete elements of what culture does, many throughout the twentieth century have had problems with the explanations of how it came to be. This is so because how "culture came to be" implies where it might be going and such a predictive implication does not fit with the indeterminacy inherent to free will and the lack of determinism that such evolutionary ideas espouse.

To delve further in the problems of the concept of cultural evolution in the twentieth century, it is useful to examine the previous history of the concept.[3] Cultural evolution has had several parallel roots in the eighteenth and nineteenth centuries. Briefly, with the development of Newtonian physics that gave rise to mechanistic explanations of the world, there were numerous and successful attempts to borrow this logic and apply it to other developing scientific fields. For example, geology benefited enormously from the mechanistic logic when applied to the enormous expansion of the time dimension of rock formation, which included fossils. Likewise, geology, in turn, enormously benefited biology as evident in the work of Darwin and Wallace, who incorporated the ideas of fossils and the origins of species into a grand model of evolution based on natural selection. Since the model of evolution accounted for all species, including humans, there were immediate controversies generated with a biological, rather than a religious, explanation of human origins. Another source of controversy stemmed from borrowing a ladder like approach (the "Great Chain of Being" as Owen Lovejoy called it) in which all of life was ranked on the ladder in order of importance with humans at the top. Human civilizations were ranked at the very top of the ladder, and it is not surprising that the European scholars ethnocentrically ranked their Western European civilization on the top rung.[4]

The combination of this hierarchical ranking and biological evolutionary theory, as first promoted by those who tried to interpret Darwin, led to attempts to explain the evolutionary basis of societies. By the last quarter of the nineteenth century, a number of scientists were trying to build models of human social evolution. Herbert Spencer, the English philosopher, proposed the concept of the "superorganic" in which he could derive stages of evolution in the behavior of societies, which evolved and progressed in a trajectory up the ladder. Other anthropologists of the time, like Morgan and Tylor, emphasized the concept of culture as a generalization gleaned from ethnographic studies that also followed stages of development from primitive to complex civilizations. However, coincident with this philosophical and scientific theorizing about cultural evolution, there was an infusion of sociopolitical and economic opportunism that took advantage of the Darwinian model as a justification to establish exploitative colonies throughout the world.

The ensuing controversy about "dog eat dog" and *laissez faire* politics and economics associated with Social Darwinism gave rise in the early twentieth century to its rejection. As Social Darwinism was being condemned, the philosopher G. E. Moore redeveloped David Hume's work on the naturalistic fallacy and expanded it to promote the idea that whatever "is" learned in science had nothing to do what one "ought" to do in making moral decisions. What one ought to do was best left to the moral philosophers and theologians and was not, nor could it ever be, the provenance of the evolutionary sciences or, for that matter, any other science.[5]

In anthropology, the American movement under the leadership of Franz Boas and the continuing influence of Ruth Benedict and Margaret Mead criticized the idea of cultural evolution as over generalizations with insufficient data. In response, they advocated and went about empirically establishing the facts about the unique cultural history and geography of small ethnographically manageable, and in some cases rapidly disappearing, societies throughout the Americas and the world. As the data from these empirical studies grew larger, the concept of cultural relativism became established, which in essence said that cultural evolution had no place because there were no regularities of substance beyond the boundaries of the culture of a particular society.

THE LAST 50 YEARS

By the latter half of the twentieth century two new directions emerged for the concept of cultural evolution that was beleaguered by the cultural relativists. First, the empirical collection of data, such as in the Human Relations Area Files, begun by George Peter Murdock, and the enormous data collected by archaeologists characterizing the material past of the great civilizations produced a sufficient corpus of data to raise the evolutionary questions once more. Universals were a key element of these generalizations. For example, there were cross-cultural regularities of energy use and irrigation for agriculture of state societies in the studies of the functional significance of kinship conducted by Marshall Sahlins. This helped to spur a kind of consensus among anthropologists like Leslie White, Julian Haynes Steward, and Elman Rogers Service that cultural evolution did not involve anything so simple as stages of development but rather must be the product of processes involving a wide range of variation in styles and individual history that overall lead to some species wide cultural evolutionary generalizations. Initially, White's ideas on the progression of energy use and Steward's ideas on ecology and environment were seen as competing explanations of cultural evolution. But it became clear to many at that time that both provided critical insights on the phenomenon of interest. Another approach to this problem of cultural evolution was to measure the effects of large newly emerging variables on the evolutionary outcomes. In this instance Ester Boserup developed a concept that the demographic shift to large population sizes was so significant that demographic variables must play critical roles in the evolution of society just as the concepts of energy utilization elaborated by White and Steward.

Universals remained an important element of these cultural generalizations and since culture was a product of the "mind," it reestablished this concept that tracked back to Lewis H. Morgan and then to A. Irving Halowell and to Eugène Dubois. In the newer synthesis of the study of the "mind," a thorough analysis of culture and personality was incorporated into psychological anthropology. Anthony F. C. Wallace was the first to link the powerful revitalization movements with the universals of mental health, seeing cultures undergoing rapid change as response to a loss of a sense of integrity. The detailed psychological analysis of the universal appeal of the charismatic leader in times of cultural crisis became an important and enduring contribution of this work that has yet to be incorporated into cultural evolutionary theory.[6] Other trends involving the broad generalizations necessary for a cultural evolutionary theory are Roy A. Rappaport's and Robert Netting's contributions to cultural ecology, which represent sophisticated analyses of ecological concepts first elaborated by Steward. Also, the extensive work of Marvin Harris on cultural materialism as a scientific theory has continued to play a critical role in the dialog necessary to develop any comprehensive models of cultural evolution.

Nevertheless, the scope of knowledge necessary to create comprehensive models of cultural evolution has become so daunting that developing macro models sparked Clifford Geertz to question the "megalomania" of anyone even attempting to embark on grand theoretical enterprises of this kind. In this intellectual climate, with the fall from grace of Marxism, there has been a renewal of social criticism of the lack of "scientific" objectivity on the part of social scientists studying humans. This postmodernist critique is an outgrowth of the history and sociology of science, which called into question the "scientific pursuit of the truth," seeing the "truth" as only a relatively attainable goal. Thus, so much of the last decade of work in cultural anthropology has been so consumed with the postmodernist debate about the validity of even asking the question about cultural evolution and the continued subtext concerning free will and determinism that little progress from within the field of anthropology has been made on this issue.

While there are clear indications that this debate in cultural anthropology is slowly shifting back to this important problem, the gains outside of cultural anthropology from biology, the neurosciences, and the cognitive sciences and the emerging fields of sociobiology, behavioral ecology, and memetics have continued to accumulate and a major consensus concerning the parameters that can be considered as a part of the cultural evolutionary paradigm are emerging. However, if anthropology is going to participate more widely in the development of these emerging models, there is a need by these fields to overcome their serious philosophical criticisms of cultural evolution. There is a real need to develop a science of humanity built on evolutionary theory that does not diminish the dignity of the individuals or societies and populations from which they have originated. In this regard one of the challenges of the twenty-first century is to overcome this long standing tradition of philosophical challenges and to make new commitments to the development of scientific approaches that do not diminish the traditional peoples who are the subjects, objects, and products of the research.

THE LAST 30 YEARS

Other influential concepts emerging in the early 1970s came as a result of the developing field of information science. In part, the field, defined as information theory by Claude Shannon, developed into a field of study that Norbert Weiner called cybernetics, and then was incorporated as information science and used by Marvin Minsky and others to develop the conceptual basis for the contemporary design of computers. The ideas and models of information theory crossfertilized many other fields of scientific study. Francois Jacob and Jacques Monod used information theory in the early 1960s to name analogously a species of RNA molecules that carries the genetic information from the DNA of a cell to the ribosomes that create the proteins that exactly reflect the information coded in the four bases in the DNA. They called it "messenger" RNA.[7] Since then DNA and RNA have become known as informational macromolecules. In the social sciences Ross Ashby's work on informational feedback systems of the central nervous system became the basis for numerous works in the social sciences, including mine in anthropology, James Grier Miller's in psychology, Walter Frederick Buckley's in political science, and Ervin Laszlo in systems theory.[8]

Both sociobiology and memetics focus on units of analysis that have not been widely used before. For sociobiology the individual phenotype is no longer the point natural selection as it was for Darwin, nor is it the population as it is for the contemporary synthetic theory of evolution. Instead the locus of control that Edward O. Wilson's sociobiology attempts to focus on is the gene and how genes control the behavior of the individual and the population. By combining inclusive fitness models, optimization theory, and game theory computations into an evolutionary stable strategy, sociobiologists can compute the advantages of one gene at a time. However, it is as if the single gene controls the individual, independently of all other genes. Granted that for experimental purposes, it is legitimate and significant science to hold the rest of the genes constant to determine a single gene's effects. The possibility that this approach at the core of sociobiology can ever yield the broad explanations that the theory promises, however, seems remote. Over the past decade, however, the field of behavioral ecology has emerged and is integrating a broader ecological perspective into the basic sociobiological paradigm.

Richard Dawkins likens the *meme* to a self-spreading or even "infectious" learned cultural item stored in the brain as an idea, thought, belief, or attitude. As with sociobiology, the focus is on the unit. But in the case of the meme the unit is never well defined; nor is the mind/cerebral cortex with its myriad of differential functions that receives, processes, invents, contains, and transmits the meme ever characterized. These are serious deficiencies that reflect the fact that not all memes are treated equally in the mind. We respond with substantial differences to different memes at different times in our lives. For example, telling me about a sweet food after I just ate one produces a vastly different response than telling me about one while I am still very hungry. Or telling me about the sweet taste when I am very young will probably produce a very different response than when I am an adult. There are state differences, and, because I may not detect and experience a particular taste the same way as my neighbor, there are also trait differences. Then there are differences of age, sex, disease state, previous experience, and so forth. These variations in how memes are received, processed, stored, invented, and the transmitted are only the first order of any model that can help us understand the process. In summary, even if we accept the more reasonable premise that memes have some intrinsic attraction as a heuristic device that may help us derive some deeper understanding of cultural evolutionary processes, a more formalized theory remains to be developed.[9]

Several other important approaches to information transfer and cultural evolution have also been developed. These include the models developed by Cavalli Sforza and Frederick Bodmer, which attempt to use models derived from population genetics to infer how the process of cultural transmission occurs. While in some narrower cases this concept does provide a useful model, it nevertheless begs questions about the degree to which cultural transmission follows the same or even similar degrees of uniformity that underlie the inheritance of genes from each parent. William Durham has provided other sets of insights about these cultural evolutionary processes. He has tracked the concept of cultural evolution and suggests that cultural selection, somewhat like natural selection, has been a major factor (but not the only one) in cultural evolution. Specifically, he has identified five different kinds of relationships between the biological and cultural realms and, even though the relationships are complex, the result is ultimately an evolutionary process between the biological and cultural dimensions.

Another approach is embodied in the questions of dynamic tension that result when the cultural evolution of a population is at cross purposes with the needs of the individual. By focusing on these key issues, these approaches help to explain the answers to major questions about the evolutionary process that underlies the evolution of culture when it does not appear to favor the biological survival of the individual. Such is the case with altruism in which self-sacrificial behavior is socially programmed to replace the individual need to survive. Since, on the face of it, altruistic behavior is counterintuitive to the survival of the individual, its study has raised a number of important issues. William Hamilton first determined that self-sacrificial behavior can be demonstrated to have survival value at the genetic level if we consider that offspring and siblings are closely related to the altruistically behaving relative. As Robert Trivers has demonstrated, and Edward O. Wilson has amplified, this type of altruism applies to the order Hymenoptera (ants, termites, and bees) that clearly have elaborate social systems characterized by self-sacrificial behaviors and extensive cooperation. Charles Lumsden and Wilson later turned their attention on human behavior using this important starting point and concluded that cooperation and altruism in human societies of unrelated individuals cannot be explained genetically. However, writing much earlier Donald Campbell pointed out that this phenomenon of cooperation and nonfamilial altruism is accounted for by the evolution of moral norms that help to regulate human behaviors. Likewise, I have attempted to demonstrate how this concept of altruism can be extended into an understanding of the evolutionary origins of religion and religious behavior where the belief in higher god(s) serves to create a quasi-familial relationship among members of the same religion. Such a process serves the social advantages of the society by extending cooperation and altruism culturally and behaviorally much further than strictly genetic model of sociobiology does. While these models offer sources of new insight about some of the specifics of important underlying generalities, they do not necessarily provide the kind of comprehensive models that are needed to account for the vast variation in human cultures that can be observed.

Daniel Sperber, a psychologist, has also criticized the gene model of information transfer as inadequate for cultural transmission because human communications operate on an inferential basis of utterances and other behaviors, such as gestures, that are crudely replicated yet mean more or less the same thing to each individual. Therefore, to use a model that depends on exact replication as in the case of genes misses the point of the type of communication process that occurs in humans. He advocates an epidemiological model in which information spreads like a contagious disease through a culture. While this approach is similar to that of Dawkins, Sperber and others also recognize that memetics as a field would like to move into cultural dynamics with the same precision that geneticists use. However, in fact, the theory of cultural evolution is much more like the chromosomes that Gregor Mendel first experimented with in the last century and later clarified by E. B. Ford and others (including Sewall Wright, Ronald A. Fisher, J. B. S. Haldane, and Theodosius Dobzhansky, to name a few) in the earlier part of the twentieth century. In this case large segments of the information are linked in complexes that are transmitted very early in life and become differentiated with the processes of learning and socialization. Hence, this approach places emphasis on the functioning characteristics of the chief of organ of culture, the information processing and limitations of the human cerebral cortical structures.

The problem with these approaches is that they exist at too high a theoretical level to adduce the parameters and units of cultural evolution. There is no explicit reason for the evolution of culture to follow the same rules as genetic evolution. Although the human brain, which is the principal source of culture, is genetically evolved, and therefore subject to all of the rules of evolutionary genetics as an organic system within an individual (e.g., the requirement of reproduction), it is not likely that many of the other rules of human cognitive processes follow genetic principals. Instead, a much more profitable approach would be to determine the structures and functions of the human central nervous system that gives rise to culture and model the limits and facilitation that this system provides. Thus, this model demands a neurobiology of culture, such as found in the promising work of Eugene D'Aquili and Andrew Newberg, and by Terrence Deacon, as a critical element of the new approach.

To develop new approaches we need to be able to integrate the enormous mounting evidence about human cultural behavior. This includes the fact that, while the potential for culture exists at birth, the culture is not there until there is an experiential unfolding of phenotype of the individual through the exposure, experience, learning, and discovery that characterizes all human development. In other words, if culture were largely withheld from the next generation, by and large that culture would cease to exist as such because so much of it is learned. This is not to say, however, that anything can be learned. Instead while there are vast areas that humans are very facile at learning, there are many other areas in relation to which human learning capacities are inadequate. So culture does not occur independently of the human central nervous system capacities. Instead cultural capacity is the interactive product of many highly regulated and genetically controlled sequences of child brain development that require environmental interaction to unfold and mature. One does not happen without the other. Unlike most organ systems of the human body, the human central nervous system is relatively "wide" open to learning all that our forbears already discovered was doable and learnable. We are good at speech and language, as the work of David Armstrong and others shows; in fact so good that every culture has a language. But none of us is born with a language, only the capacity to speak words and the grammatical capacity for structuring these words as emergent "agreed upons" providing a means for communicating abstractions about ourselves and our world.

From the perspective of using information theory as a means of modeling cultural evolution, it is evident that a profitable approach to understanding the phenomenon is to analyze how the capacity for processing cultural information develops. Since this does not happen quickly, because it is dependent on a biological process, all societies of the world spend a great deal of effort inculcating the necessary information from one generation to the next. This transfer of knowledge and experience from one generation to the next is limited by several factors, including (1) the rules of inclusive fitness through which the information is part of the evolutionary process by which parents interested in the survival of their offspring transfer cultural traditions from one generation to the next; and (2) the process of child development the world over that has become differentiated in more complex societies and institutionalized in all societies in the form of rituals and traditions, such as puberty and other initiation rites and various passage rites. These cultural acts are widely practiced and are the result of both the universality of the developmental processes of maturation of children and the universality of the integration of this knowledge into the fabric of every society the world over.

BIOCULTURAL EVOLUTION

I have used two heuristic models as the basis for these analyses, which were developed in the late 1960s. The first model is an ecosystems model that helps focus attention on the interactions of the biological, cultural, ecological, and demographic variables on human behavior through time. Most of this biocultural interaction is made possible by the evolved structural and functional capacities of the higher cortical central nervous system (CNS) of humans. This biocultural evolutionary interface is expressed in the exchange of verbal and nonverbal behaviors among the members of the society.[10]

Another way of conceptualizing this biocultural interface is to use the same units to describe both systems and to integrate them into a single evolutionary model. This alternative approach analyses the interactions of the "genetic information pool" of a population with its "cultural information pool." The interaction between these two information pools is made possible by the unique processing and behavioral capacities of the human brain. I named the information that was outside of the two principal pools as extrasomatic information that exists when the cultural information is no longer stored only in the collective central nervous systems of individuals.[11]

In this biocultural evolutionary model the biological mechanisms of evolution are continuously shifting the genetic information pool of the population and the cultural traditions, practices, knowledge, and "wisdom" of a society form a cultural information pool that complements and supplements the biological information pool over time in the particular ecosystem. The heuristic value of this model of information pool interaction and exchange is that it helps to generate useful propositions by focusing on mechanisms of reception, processing, storage, transmission, and change within both the biological and the sociocultural realms, and it particularly addresses their evolutionary integration through time.

This heuristic model of information flow and evolution also helps focus attention on several principles.

1. Every human population creates, perpetuates, and participates in an information system that evolves through time in an attempt to maintain a dynamic equilibrium among the ecological, sociocultural, biological, and demographic variables within the human ecosystem.

2. The greater the cultural information pool grows in its complementary and supplementary relation to the genetic information pool, the greater the combined system becomes independent from biological limitations.

3. The cultural information pool can grow at the processing speed of the collective minds of the society within the limits of the established culture to change, whereas the biological information pool (at least before widespread genetic engineering) is subject to the rules of evolutionary change. Under these conditions it is likely that cultural information will far outweigh biological information as a means of achieving adaptability and survival.

4. Complex systems like a biocultural system have to build in many self-correcting feedback mechanisms to remain stable. It is well known that such systems can be unstable as complexity increases. A good example of this increasing complexity is the extrasomatic information pool now being shared on the Internet that is growing faster and is more adaptive than any other medium of information exchange.

5. There are several primary interactions that are at the core of the biocultural information exchange. These include among others food, sex, shelter, and health. Food is one of the principal variables in the maintenance of this equilibrium between biology and culture and information and survival. Because we are completely dependent biologically on our nutrient intake, food ascends to a primary level of biological and cultural significance in the human life cycle and provides a highly significant means of establishing the empirical data on which to base the development of more sophisticated models of biocultural evolution.

Ideally the models we develop need to inform us about the key questions to ask about the dynamics of cultural information. At this stage, we can ask how they help us identify heuristically how the systems work and how cultural information is different from genetic information. A more complete theory of the human cultural evolutionary process will require a much better formulation of the many essential questions that such a model will need to answer. In this way the model can be tested with real scenarios, and once having the broad heuristic formulation validated, hypotheses, which are statistically testable, can be developed to account for the evolutionary outcomes predicted by the model.

Although we know currently that there is a cultural evolutionary process and it involves the development and operation of the human cerebral cortex, we know little about the units of cultural evolution and about the relationships between and among the units and how they evolve in the first place. In addition, there is a serious lack of empirical data to test any of the existing models. Much of the endeavor remains a theoretical exercise rather than a developing discipline. This is not entirely the case and there are important and notable exceptions. The important work of Peter J. Richerson and Robert Boyd and also the work of Leda Cosmides and John Tooby hold considerable promise of delivering new models and particularly some empirical data with which to test these models. Nevertheless, examples of successful application of these cultural evolutionary models have been relatively sparse. While they hold the promise of new advances in the future, there may be other approaches that could be more revealing at this stage of disciplinary development.

The approach that I advocate operates at several levels. First, there is the assumption that no widely accepted formal working models of cultural evolution exist; because, in part, the cultural behaviors need to be more closely tied to their biological significance. Hence, I have focused many empirical studies on the relationships between the biologically evolved capacities of the human species and the culturally evolved factors that complement and supplement biological adaptations to human dietary problems. The importance of this area of nutrition and diet is critical to the survival of every human population every day of the year. As such, food practices provide an ideal means for establishing empirical data to develop and test more sophisticated models of biocultural evolution.

Second, using this approach gives a highly researched data base on nutrients in order to assess the evolution of cultural practices that address various problems such as nutritional balance, availability of critical nutrients, and the toxic effects of foods. For example, a society may survive because of the accumulation of information that codes for survival under extreme nutritional conditions. Just as there are genes that are only expressed in extremes, there may be cultural behaviors that are transmitted from one generation to the next but are only expressed when the society runs out of food.

Third, the goal of this empirical work would be to fill out the heuristic models with sufficient detail in order to provide the basis for testing other hypotheses that would be generated from the more complete models of cultural evolutionary processes. Such a dual level heuristic model-building and empirical-testing approach may also become useful in the reanalysis of some of the previously discussed approaches as they continue to develop. It is likely that some kind of convergent synthesis may occur between these heuristic biocultural evolutionary models I am suggesting and the more formal theoretical models that have been developed during the last 20 years.

AGRICULTURE AND NUTRICULTURE

Biologically, human nutrition is a well-understood science in which "nutritional universals" in the form of essential components, without which we cannot survive and/or reproduce, have been defined for the human diet. Specific nutrients such as essential fatty acids, amino acids, vitamins, carbohydrates, and minerals as well as other trace components all fit in this universal pattern of human needs. There is also a range of nutrients associated variations in the biology of digestion and metabolism that significantly differentiates one population from the next. Moreover, foods contain a variety of pharmacologically and psychopharmacologically active compounds that alter and account for a wide diversity of biological and behavioral variations throughout the world. These "nutritional universals" provide a powerful measure to evaluate the constant evolutionary processes that have been especially pronounced since the development of agriculture, which provided the resource base for the rise of the great civilizations over the last 10,000 years.

Specifically, since the neolithic era agricultural practices have continuously improved the productivity of crops and this intensification has led to an increased dependence on fewer of them. However, this dependence, in turn produces a nutritional problem. Since no single plant can satisfy human "nutritional universals," nor can any small group of them supply these nutritional needs. When a small number of plants is depended on, this tends to enhance the naturally occurring toxic and antinutritional secondary compounds that the plants carry as part of their natural defenses against predation. Thus, a high dependence on a few plants produces a classic evolutionary bottleneck in which the increased dependence on fewer crops increases the nutritional liabilities that each crop retains and limits the success of the agricultural strategy.[12]

If we analyze what happened over this period of time, it is evident that the behavioral response to this evolutionary bottleneck was to innovate ways and means of eliminating the disadvantages through the evolution of cuisine traditions that overcame these limitations.[13] In other organisms this would have only been possible through the processes of genetic evolutionary adaptation. However, in humans it is evident in the many societies dependent on a diversity of major food crops throughout the world, there was a cultural evolution of cuisine techniques that transformed the raw products to the "cooked" state. Recently, I called this process "nutriculture" to reflect its tight reciprocal step-by-step evolutionary connection to agriculture. In essence agriculture is not possible without nutriculture. A process of evolving food technology had to mirror reciprocally the success of each step of increased dependence on major crops that underlies the agricultural process. Nutriculture evolved to keep up with the restrictions in dietary variation that dependence on fewer crops required. This evolutionary process became highly adapted to overcoming the nutritional limitations and toxic constituents of the plants ecologically exploited for their high productivity. Since the processes of nutriculture involve a very tight integration of cultural adaptations with these biologically based nutritional needs, I suggested that this evolutionary process that involves both biology and culture be called biocultural evolution.[14]

EMPIRICAL STUDIES OF MAIZE

What we eat is largely dictated by cultural traditions, but the degree to which a diet satisfies basic nutritional needs largely depends on human biology. This obvious interface between biology and culture has encouraged the development of a new approach or "paradigm" that analyzes and interprets biological and cultural adaptability as continuously interacting phenomena throughout human evolution. Given the extensive data already developed in the nutritional, bio-chemical, ethnobotanical, and pharmacological literature, however, a more pow-erful strategy for developing biocultural evolutionary theory might be to screen the extensive emerging scientific research and literature in related fields for the generation of testable hypotheses about the related social and behavioral prac-tices essential to the consumption of critically limited foods.

In conducting these empirical studies we are continuously focusing on ques-tions that help further explicate the biocultural evolutionary model. For example, we address how food traditions are transmitted from one generation to the next. What are the biocultural processes that underlie this transfer? How is new knowl-edge about the foods discovered and evolved? What are the factors that facilitate the necessary learning and transfer the knowledge between generations? How important are these factors? Can populations survive without them? Domesti-cated plants comprise over 90 percent of the caloric content of the diets of the world's living populations. The plants we have analyzed for purposes of devel-oping the model of biocultural evolution have included maize, barley, wheat, sorghum, rice, bitter manioc, potatoes, fava beans, soybeans, kidney beans, and lima beans as well as various spices, garlic, and xanthine-based drinks.

For heuristic purposes this paper will only deal with our work on maize, first begun in 1972.[15] Maize ideally fits with this paradigm for several reasons. Maize is a highly productive crop that formed the agricultural basis for the growth and maintenance of the great Mesoamerican civilizations. Modern maize also played an important part in the development of the American agricultural research sys-tem. In the 1920s, studies of the nutritional properties of corn led to the scientific discovery that maize diets were strongly associated with the occurrence of pella-gra, a condition that results from a dietary deficiency of niacin. An interesting question can therefore be raised about this "nutritional universal": How did the prehistoric Native American civilizations survive on a diet that historically pro-duced pellagra in the rest of the populations of the world?

After a careful analysis of the nutritional literature, a testable hypothesis was generated that took advantage of some important findings regarding the amino acid profile and niacin content of maize. Corn (maize) contains very low levels of the essential amino acid lysine, and it also has several characteristics that increase the risk of pellagra among those who consume large quantities. The niacin in maize (when used as a staple) is not nutritionally available; it is indigestibly bound to a protein complex. Maize is also very deficient in tryptophan, which can be partially converted to niacin (trytophan is also the precursor of serotonin). Fur-ther, the ratio of leucine to isoleucine in maize inhibits the conversion of other sources of dietary tryptophan to niacin.

It has been demonstrated, however, that treatment of maize with an alkali counters these disadvantages. It frees the indigestibly bound niacin and thus makes the niacin that is present nutritionally available. Alkali treatment also im-proves the digestibility of the lysine in maize severalfold and likewise improves the digestibility of tryptophan. In addition, the ratio of leucine to isoleucine is made favorable for the conversion of tryptophan to niacin. These laboratory findings provide the basis for generating testable hypotheses about the significance of alkali use in traditional cuisines in the preparation or transformation of maize into foods.

The extensive anthropological literature on traditional Native American culinary practices provides considerable data for hypothesis testing. We analyzed these practices for a large sample of those populations we could locate who resided in areas where it was ecologically possible to grow maize. We proposed that a significant association would exist between the culinary practices that used alkali and the degree of production and consumption of maize. The results of this analysis demonstrated a highly significant association between the use of alkali in maize processing and the degree of production and consumption of maize. In fact, alkali was used universally in those societies that were rated as high consumers and producers of maize. In other words, it appeared as if the only culinary practice that supported the high exploitation characteristic of the great Mesoamerican civilizations was the use of a step involving the alkalization of maize. The maize was usually heated with an alkali made from lime (or shells), wood ashes, or lye.

Subsequent studies have shown that the introduction of maize to Europe and the rest of the Old World, made possible initially by Columbus, was not accompanied by the introduction of Native American cuisine. As a result, the intensive consumption of this very productive crop was accompanied by massive outbreaks of pellagra. In Europe, corn was initially processed with the methods traditionally used for other cereals. In fact, it was not until the second decade of this century, and only after a great deal of medical controversy, that the nutritional source of pellagra was identified.[16]

In Africa, where maize is still widely consumed, significant associations are also found between the degree of maize production and the presence of pellagra. Although there is no evidence of the use of alkali processing, it is important to point out that in most African populations maize is used to make beer. Since the niacin content of beer is greatly enriched by the yeast used in the fermentation process, it is likely that beer consumers largely avert pellagra. Children and childbearing women, who traditionally do not consume the beer, may be at greater risk. However, elsewhere in the contemporary world, where neither alkali processing nor fermentation is practiced, pellagra is known to occur. In India, the introduction and integration of appropriate alkali-processing technologies into the local food traditions is one possible option for dealing with this important nutritional problem.

BIOCULTURAL EVOLUTION AT THE MICRO LEVEL

At a theoretical level, it is clear that alkali processing enhances the nutritional value of maize, but how these culinary practices evolved in the first place is still an open question. Accordingly, we began to work over the last 15 years with the Hopi Indian population of Arizona in an attempt to understand the origin and evolution of their blue corn tradition. Hopi blue corn is a highly selected, purebred maize cultivar. Its dark blue/black color comes from a high concentration of a naturally occurring anthocyanin dye. This dye changes from pink to blue, like litmus paper, as the medium goes from acid to alkaline.

In the desert ecosystem of the Hopi, where water is very scarce and the productivity of maize could be very marginal in drought years, we hypothesized that the evolution of a pH indicator to enable the optimal concentration of alkali to be added to the corn would be highly advantageous. Since the Hopi practices surrounding the use of blue corn are well documented, we are attempting to determine whether the pH of the blue color that the Hopi women are traditionally trying to achieve in the mixing bowl matches the pH necessary to alkalinize the maize and free the niacin. If this is the case, then this tradition would provide a number of insights into the broader question of how these culinary practices related to alkali use could have evolved.

The data suggest that the practice does fit the kinds of hypotheses generated by the heuristic biocultural evolutionary model. Specifically, the traditions of making the corn product are highly overdetermined. The making of piki bread is the most important food technique a woman traditionally learned before she was allowed to marry. Ground blue corn is mixed with water and ashes to produce a thin paste of the appropriate consistency for cooking. In addition, the color achieved in the preparation of the food appears to be very closely related to the color associated with the pH necessary to free the indigestibly bound niacin.

Moreover, unlike the Mayan technique of making a tortilla with excessive amounts of alkali, which must then be washed off (along with a significant portion of the nutrient value), this technique has clearly evolved in the midst of scarcity. The Hopi technique liberates the niacin, but none of the nutrient value of the maize is lost; the corn is alkalinized and then completely consumed. There are probably further sex related enhancements to this process since Barrett Brenton has reported that women are approximately 2.5 times more sensitive to developing pellagra than men and therefore they are the ones in greatest control of making this product (this also raises the intriguing question about the role of women in food preparation and the degree to which the differentiation of male female labor in food preparation is associated with greater sensitivity to deficiencies and other toxic compounds).[17] Thus, in this important case, it appears as if the tradition evolved to enable the use of a visual endpoint as the means of optimally alkalinizing the maize and enhancing the nutritional value without losing any of the original products. Since this visual endpoint is crucial for the effective outcome, it is not surprising to find at the cultural level a very rich tradition among the Hopi of symbolic associations with the use and consumption of this food in the traditional diet. Thus, although not fully confirmed, the hypothesis about the significance of the blue corn tradition has very strong support.[18]

NUTRICULTURE AND BIOCULTURAL EVOLUTION

The data from the empirical studies suggest several directions for further development of a more formal data-driven model of biocultural evolution. Given the critical importance of this step there is a need to investigate more thoroughly how the various alkali innovations occurred. One possible hypothesis is that new discoveries become firmly implanted in the cultural repertoire during periods of crisis. For example, an obvious food crisis when crops fail in the Southwest may have traditionally indicated periods of famine in the following year. Another type of crisis is a revitalization movement, particularly in the midst of a sense of loss of traditional purpose within a society. Hypotheses about the modes of storage and reliable transmission of successful technologies from one generation to the next are critical with respect to food preparation. This may depend on having reliable knowledge that is carefully evaluated and overdetermined in terms of knowing what to do and considering it important enough to repeat in exquisite detail.

In the case of maize the processing typically makes dried maize kernels from storage, which are very hard (and basically too hard to crush in the mouth), into a soft and slippery texture that is easy to grind to a finished food. While this explanation seems to account for the origins of this processing technology as having to do much more with ease of food preparation than any nutritional value the technique produced, other societies practiced different methods that tend not to support a simple food processing advantage. Among the populations of the Southwest, especially the Hopi, the blue corn tradition written about earlier demonstrate the use of alkali after the corn is ground and hence after the energy is expended in grinding. In this case the corn is *not* first softened and yet alkali is still added. While it is possible that the Hopi and related Indians of the Southwest were already taste sensitive to the type of corn flavor changes involved, since many of their languages suggest a Uto-Aztec origin where alkali processing was associated with the Mayan tortilla makers, their food processing technology is still remarkably divergent and hence requires careful exploration for how these cause-and-effect discoveries evolved.

The data also beg questions about the structure of history, mythology, folklore, and religion that is present in the cultural information system that reinforces the rationale for maintaining the food preparatory behaviors necessary for survival. This relates to questions about food traditions since those food processing technologies that have developed, such as bread, beer and tofu, to name a few, have become breakthroughs in terms of enhancing the nutrient values of major staples in the human diet. Although I have worked to document many of these, much work remains to be carried out in this realm, and such work could be used to develop more complete models of the biocultural evolutionary process.

Maize is particularly complicated because serious symptoms of the deficiencies associated with inappropriate processing that lead to pellagra do not become expressed until weeks after the deficiency begins. The usual proximal feedback mechanisms of sight, taste, smell, proprioception, sense of specific hunger, stomach malaise, and diarrheal disease and so forth do not show up soon enough to make the associations that other food based disorders often produce. Thus, this distal association between eating maize and illness is not nearly as likely to become expressed as something that tastes bad or makes the person sick from food poisoning a few hours after consumption.

There are also some examples of foods that were exchanged in post-Colombian times, where there was no evolutionary discovery about how to process the food when the effects were distal to the act of consumption. In the case of maize, alkali processing never developed in the Old World, but many populations quickly abandoned this source of nutrition in favor of other foods. Those populations that continued to consume maize continued to do so largely because of economics and continued to suffer from high rates of pellagra. Other similar historic examples are the introduction of cassava into Africa by the Portuguese during early contact in the sixteenth century, where numerous people died from eating cassava that did not have the cyanate removed by processing. However, this example does not fit the same distal association of cause and effect that maize consumption fits, since it is clear that the source of the poisoning was closely connected to the consumption of this root crop. It would be very helpful for model building if there were additional examples of other foods that had these intermediate effects.

NEXT STEPS

To move to the next steps, we need to be careful to formulate the models that generate meaningful hypotheses about significant human problems. This is in part because it is more likely that selection will heavily favor cultural evolution where, for example, survival is at stake. Several broad issues seem to be emerging. There is evidence of a biocultural evolutionary process that does occur at a significant level with respect to nutriculture. But ways of generating testable hypotheses about the units are not understood well enough to model it; nor are the connections between the units of cuisine practice within societies well understood. There are currently no good models to account for independent invention of nutricultural events. When it comes to empirical databases there is probably no area of greater factual content (and more survival value in the basic cultural information and practices) than the nutrient base of a society. If the nutrient needs are not continuously met, the society will not survive for long.

The feedback relationship between what we eat and how we feel and behave should provide a "fruitful" avenue of approach. There is a causal linkage between what we eat and the nutritional and psychosocial effects it has on us. There are proximal effects and there are distal effects that need to be brought into focus. Proximal effects because they deal in part with prewired factors that all of us share and are easier to understand. For example, we see, smell, or taste something that is off and we choose not to eat it because it could make us ill. On the other hand, we eat something else and we feel fine, and the effects of eating the wrong thing do not become expressed for weeks or months later. The connections between how we feel and what we ate are so remotely connected that we do not have the same feedback relationship to the cause-and-effect relations we had when a food did not look good or taste right.

Given the distal nature of the deficiencies concerning maize consumption with and without alkali, the question arises if there is a blind evolutionary process governing evolution of this phenomenon? If so, it is likely to lead to a wide variety of new kinds of biocultural evolutionary questions about food practices. This blind process might need to be facilitated by all of the developed abilities that we have and is discovered and encoded at a different level of society. We know when we ask traditional Mayans why they use alkali, in their response they will often report that it makes the maize soft and slippery. Is this response an "emic" marker for the appropriate behavior, which, in turn, is maintained because of traditions that everyone maintains about how they survived adversity the last time they were starving? Was it that the food was prepared that way and it tasted good, made them feel good? Or did they "believe" and it was the "believers" in the tradition that survived? Or is it some other process following the rules of a game or of some fundamental sex difference in actual subtle perception in the delectability of the alkali-treated corn?

In these cases, is it reasonable to hypothesize that those who practiced something that no one still understands became the basis for survival of the entire culture? Do societies survive because of the accumulation of information that codes for survival under extreme conditions, just as there are genes that do this? Are there cultural behaviors that do this; and, if so, how are they maintained in complex patterns? Are they socially linked in counter intuitive ways that do not follow the rules of genetics for the orderly errorless translation and transmission of information from one generation to the next? These are just a few of the interesting and significant questions that need further exploration and are generated by a data driven approach to developing biocultural evolutionary models.[19]

SUMMARY

This chapter has briefly reviewed the history of the concept of cultural evolution and has explored heuristically an information theory model of the concept of biocultural evolution using the new concept of nutriculture as a means to demonstrate and define the advantages of a data-driven, hypothesis-testing approach to develop new models of biocultural evolution. The advantages of this nutricultural approach are severalfold:

1. Food is critical for the survival of the population and there are basically no exceptions to this rule. Food is a first priority for all humans throughout all time; it transcends all social and biological issues and is a relative constant need with respect to meeting specific nutrient requirements for health, reproduction, growth, development, and survival. Hence, it is central to all economies and the successful procurement and production of food has provided the foundation upon which all human civilizations are based.

2. Food also involves universal human behaviors that all societies practice every day of their lives. There are also life history variations according to the periods of development and aging as well as sex differences that make for differential survival based on the outcomes of the quantity and quality of nutrients consumed.

3. The study of food has a very solid empirical base for purposes of measurement. There is a whole field of nutritional science from which we can judge the adaptability of the food practice. We know a great deal about human nutritional needs, and this knowledge can be used as a scientific data base

from which we can test hypotheses about the cultural evolutionary significance of the adaptive strategies used by various populations through time and space.

4. There are long recorded and prehistoric records of what people consumed that are steadily being developed. Also, there is a substantial ethnographic literature and cross-cultural literature and databases concerning folk cooking practices that allow tests of very specific hypotheses about food processing.

5. The sciences of food technology, nutrition, medicine, nutraceutics, dietary reconstruction, and neurobiology are also growing all of the time. These new developments from various inferential methodologies are allowing us to become more precise, and there is an industrial literature that allows for a very substantial depth of understanding about the details of the physics, chemistry, and biology of cooking practices.

6. There is a very rapid growth of literature on the medical effects of disease that appear to be related to diet; and there is an excellent and growing literature on the pharmacology of food that helps to explain other critical non-nutritive but important pharmacological advantages of certain dietary practices.

7. There is a literature on the psychotropic effects of various foods that will help build more complete models of the use of these substances from foods in the diet and ritual of the societies, and there is rapidly expanding literature on the physiology and endocrinology of digestion that integrate the gastric feedback effects on the cause and effect relations to foods.

8. Among nonhuman primates there is also a comparative database from field observations, which are beginning to make more complete models available for our biocultural evolutionary database. Thus, the prospect for increasing the scientific refinement of the models of evolutionary explanation is promising and may provide many different new directions for hypothesis testing and model building.

9. Integrating the data-driven approach to nutriculture will enable us to ask relevant questions in a variety of other important areas that focus on the evolutionary interface of biology and culture in which culture is evolving to provide our principle means of survival.

NOTES

1. In order to make this chapter less technical and also to keep it brief, I will footnote extensively to other papers I have published on this topic so the interested reader can follow up with a more complete perspective on the arguments presented. An overview to many of the introductory issues can also be found in S. H. Katz (1999), "Toward a New Concept of Global Morality," *Zygon* 34: 237–254.

2. This is wonderfully illustrated in the great art of the times, which becomes "free" of the previous religious restraints on convention so that Michelangelo re-creates the biblical "David"

from a boy and to a giant who is still recognizable but transformed by this new found freedom. Of course, this is in wonderful contrast to the slightly earlier rendition of David by Donatello, which was petit by comparison.

3. For a more detailed tracking of the intellectual history of this concept until the early 1970s, see S. H. Katz (1974), "Unity and Diversity of Man from the Point of View of Social and Cultural Anthropology," *Unity of Man,* Seuil, Paris, Chapter II, pp. 515–545 (French). Also translated and separately published in German, Spanish, and Japanese editions.

4. See Loren Eiseley's *Darwin's Century* (Garden City, NY: Doubleday, 1958) for an excellent discussion of these trends and counter-trends on the place of evolution in the late nineteenth century.

5. See S. H. Katz (1981), "Evolutionary Considerations of the Is/Ought Relationship," *Zygon,* 12: 124–145 (also in J. Miller, ed., AAAS 1998, *An Evolving Dialogue: Scientific, Historical, Philosophical and Theological perspectives on Evolution,* pp. 501–516).

6. For a discussion of this topic, see S. H. Katz (1974), "The Dehumanization and Rehumanization of Science and Society," *Zygon,* 9: 126–138, especially pp. 126–129.

7. Steven Toulmin, in his review of Monod in *The Return to Cosmology* (University of California Press, 1985), states that Monod "gave an inaugural lecture at the College de France in November, 1967 which was all that such a lecture should be: a striking call for the reintegration of fundamental biological theory with a purified 'natural philosophy,' and for its application to human affairs. 'A natural history of the selection of ideas,' and so make the evolution of human culture as intelligible, in its own way, as Darwinism made organic speciation and evolution." (p. 141)

8. One of the first papers I wrote was a theoretical analysis of the implications of Ross Ashby's *Design for a Brain: The Origin of Adaptive Behavior* (London: Chapman and Hall, 1960) in "A Review and Critical Extension of Amos Hawley's: Human Ecology," *Northeastern University Sociological Review,* 10 to 1962.

9. For a more complete discussion of these heuristic models, see the Symposium on Human Adaptation in S. H. Katz (1970), "Editors Introduction to the Symposium on Human Adaptation" *American Journal of Physical Anthropology* 32: 225–226; 265–266. Note page 303 in S. H. Katz and E. F. Foulks (1970), "Mineral Metabolism and Behavior: Abnormalities of Calcium Metabolism," *Am J. of Phys. Anthropology* 32: 299–304.

10. For an exploration of the complexity of cognitive function of the human cerebral cortex, see S. H. Katz (1975), "Toward a New Science of Humanity," *Zygon,* 10: 12:31–52. Also reprinted in 1980, *UROBROS* 3(5–6):80–110.

11. S. H. Katz (1973), "Evolutionary Perspectives on Purpose and Man." Symposium on Human Purpose. *Zygon,* 8: 325–340. And S. H. Katz (1974), "The Dehumanization and Rehumanization of Science and Society," *Zygon,* 9: 126–138. Also see S. H. Katz (1999), "Toward a New Concept of Global Morality," *Zygon* 34: 237–254.

12. See the discussion of the decrease in crop variability and increase in recipe variabilty in S. H. Katz and M. Voigt (1987), "Bread and Beer: The Early Use of Cereals in the Human Diet," *Expedition* 28, 2: 23–34.

13. See discussion of the "lock and key" hypothesis in S. H. Katz, "Food and Biocultural Evolution: A Model for the Investigation of Modern Nutritional Problems," in *Nutritional Anthropology,* F. E. Johnston, ed. (New York: Allen Liss, 1987), pp. 41–66.

14. See S. H. Katz, "The Role of 'Nutriculture' in The Evolution of Human Diet," in the Symposium on the Contribution of Biology to Our Understanding of Culture (in press, Am. Anthro Assn Annual Meetings, 1999). See also the *Encyclopedia of Food and Culture,* S. H. Katz, ed., Introdution to Vols. 1–3 (2003) (New York: Scribners).

15. See S. H., Katz, M., Hediger, and L. Valleroy, (1974), "Traditional Maize Processing Techniques in the New World: Anthropological and Nutritional Significance," *Science,* 184: 765–773.

16. Ibid.

17. See, B. P. Brenton's dissertation, "Hopi Foodways: Biocultural Perspectives on Change and Contradiction (1994, University of Massachusetts).

18. S. H. Katz, "The Biocultural Evolution of Cuisine," R. Shepard, ed., *Handbook of the Psychophysiology of Human Eating* (New York: Wiley, 1989), pp 115–140. See also K. Kaiser and S. H. Katz (1992), "Nourriture et symbole. Le maïs bleu chez les Hopi." *Anthropologie et Sociétés* 16(2): 55–66.

19. S. H. Katz (1990), "An Evolutionary Theory of Cuisine," *Human Nature* 1: 233–259.

13 The Origins of Religion: Cosmology and Cultivation[1]

Mary Evelyn Tucker *Department of Religion, Bucknell University*

Religion begins and ends in mystery, as many have noted. To speak of its origins with any pretension of certainty is to enter the realms of conjecture or imagination. Surely no one knows definitively how or when or where religion arose. Perhaps we could turn to poetry, art, or music for guidance here; for clearly nothing short of a time machine can ensure us of discovering an origin moment for religion.

Alternatively, we might consult various scholars who have elaborated particular theories on the subject, especially in the late nineteenth century and early twentieth century. These include Lucien Levy-Bruhl (1857–1939), who wrote *How Natives Think* (1910) and *Primitive Mentality* (1922). His conclusion was that early peoples were mystical and prelogical. Moreover, he believed they had a sense of "feeling participation" with the natural and the human world. Max Mueller (1832–1930), who edited the *Sacred Books of the East*, held that the earliest understanding of the divine was in the personifications of natural phenomenon such as are seen in the Hindu scriptures called the Vedas. James Frazer (1854–1941), who published twelve volumes of *The Golden Bough* between 1907 and 1915, suggested that religion arose in sympathetic magic and progressed eventually to science. For E. B. Tyler (1832–1917) there was also a developmental context from the animist consciousness he describes in *Primitive Cultures* (1873) to so-called "higher civilizations." For him, the generative source of religion lay in the idea of animism—that the universe is alive with spiritual beings. These are only some examples of the various themes of the origins of religion—most fed into the later twentieth-century Western Enlightenment version of the progress of civilizations from religion toward science.

This developmental reading of history in the West began with Antoine Nicholas de Condorcet (1743–1794), who believed humans would progress from "superstition and barbarism to an age of reason and enlightenment."[2] It included Count de Saint Simon's (1760–1825) view of religion as moving through stages of polytheism, monotheism, and metaphysics toward positivistic science. This was further elaborated by August Comte (1798–1857), who felt human consciousness progressed through three stages; namely, theology, metaphysics, and science. In this theory theology is a necessary first step but will be inevitably surpassed by science.

Even in the twentieth century many contemporary sociologists of religion predicted that with the advances of science and technology, religion would become less necessary. In other words, modernity would usurp religion. This has proven to be a drastically inaccurate prediction. We see this with the resurgence of traditional religions in Russia and China, with the rise of fundamentalisms around the world, and with the remarkable interdisciplinary dialogue that has been taking place between religion and science in the last few decades. It is my assumption that this latter dialogue will spark the most significant evolution of religious thinking in the last several thousand years.

Nonetheless, a significant sector of the modern West has inherited and further developed Enlightenment attitudes that privilege rational thought and under-value spiritual experience and that, in certain circles, see religion as eventually being superseded by science. A post-Enlightenment version of religion values individualism and personal salvation and sees God as like a clock maker and removed from creation. In this scenario religion in the West has become the province of the individual and of a creator God, while science has moved into the arena of the relationship with nature. Western religions have become concerned with matters of conscience in the human order and matters of salvation in the af-terlife. They have largely retreated from the natural world and become locked into traditional concerns with redemption rather than creation. Except for the process theologians and evolutionary theologians mentioned by John Haught, they have, until recently, ignored or rejected real engagement with scientific cos-mologies. This book represents an important effort to overcome this split. So does the research of countless historians and anthropologists of religion, who in the last hundred years have helped us to understand other religious worldviews be-yond the West. I would like to underscore here again the importance of seeing re-ligion in its multicultural forms not only its Western modes, so that the dialogue of science and religion is more than an interaction between science and the bibli-cal traditions.

To return then to the search for the origins of religion, it is not like discovering in this century, because of certain empirical evidence, that Fred Hoyle's steady-state theory of the universe has been seen as less credible than the Big Bang the-ory. As Joel Primack mentioned, the affirmation of the Big Bang theory occurred first in the theories of Edwin Hubble and other scientists and then in the back-ground radiation heard by Robert Wilson at the Bell Labs in New Jersey, and was finally mapped out in exquisite patterns by the Cosmic Background Explorer in 1989 under the supervision of scientists from Berkeley. Evidence for the Big Bang also remains in the fossil records of the first three minutes, namely in hydrogen, helium, and lithium.

In seeking the origins of religion, we will never be ensured of such extraordinary discoveries as science has given us in this century. And yet is this not somehow consoling? Yes, we can certainly outline patterns of religion from personal religious experience to its communal institutionalization. This was one of the contributions of the distinguished historian of religion, Mircea Eliade, at the University of Chicago. But ultimately this great mystery at the heart of things lies just beyond the vision of even our most powerful microscopes and telescopes—something like dark matter, eluding detection. It is as elusive as the human heart, as stunning as the discovery of relativity, as unique as a fleeting snowflake, as alluring as a loon's call, as beautiful as clouds at sunset, and as haunting as a forest at night.

What is this thing called religion and from whence does it arise? I should say, as I have already said, no one knows, although many have surmised. But perhaps I can begin with two stories from Loren Eiseley.* One is his experience described in his book, *The Immense Journey,* of floating on his back in the Platte River on a spectacular sunny, summer afternoon. Suddenly he was transported into the river and into all its connecting tributaries—melting, moving, gliding down the Missouri River into the great Mississippi and into the vast currents of ocean beyond. He moved from the particular place and moment of the high plains to a sense of the whole and holy other; he was transported from the skin of his body to the skinless identity with the earth's body. For Eiseley this was an experience involving both the power of water and the flow of evolution. He writes,

> Once in a lifetime, perhaps, one escapes the actual confines of the flesh. Once in a life-time, if one is lucky, one so merges with sunlight and air and running water that whole eons, the eons that mountains and deserts know, might pass in a single afternoon without discomfort. . . . [O]ne can never quite define this secret; but it has something to do, I am sure, with common water. Its substance reaches everywhere; it touches the past and prepares the future; it moves under the poles and wanders thickly in the heights of air.[3]

> I, too, was a microcosm of pouring rivulets and floating driftwood gnawed by the mysterious animalcules of my own creation. I was three fourths water, rising and subsiding according to the hollow knocking in my veins: a minute pulse like the eternal pulse that lifts Himalayas and which, in the following systole, will carry them away.[4]

This flowing of the self toward the world, this feeling of the microcosm toward the macrocosm, this relation of the part to the whole is one of the most fundamental movements of the human that we may call religious. Indeed, this urge to be identified with something larger than oneself—the lure of the universe itself and what is beyond—is, in some profound sense, religious.

A second story of Loren Eiseley, also in his book *The Immense Journey,* comes to mind. This one is called "The Judgment of the Birds." Eiseley has fallen asleep by a stump on the edge of a glade. Suddenly he is awakened by the cries of two birds, parents to a captured nestling. A huge black raven is devouring the small red nestling. The other birds, not daring to attack the raven, nonetheless join in the anguished chorus of the parents. Then, after the loss is over the birds quiet down. And suddenly one by one in the silence of the woods, the birds begin to sing. Eiseley describes it this way:

> The sighing died. It was then I saw the judgment. It was the judgment of life against death. . . . For in the midst of protest, they forgot the violence. There, in that clearing, the crystal note of a song sparrow lifted hesitantly in the hush. And finally, after painful fluttering, another took the song, and then another, the song passing from one bird to another, doubtfully at first, as though some evil thing were being slowly forgotten. Till suddenly they took heart and sang from many throats joyously together as birds are known to sing. They sang because life is sweet and sunlight beautiful. . . . In simple truth they had forgotten the raven, for they were the singers of life, and not of death.[5]

---

*Excerpts from *The Immense Journey,* Loren Eiseley (New York: Vintage Books, 1946).

As Eiseley suggests, there is affirmation and continuity in the face of death and struggle, even in the animal kingdom. Life itself is utterly precious, inexplicably valuable, and worthy of survival. And here is our second experience of the religious—affirmation in spite of all. Affirmation in the face of apparent meaninglessness, continuity in the midst of death, joy juxtaposed to sorrow. It is here that the great movements of human aspiration and struggle occur; and it is here that the religious instinct is forged.

For if the first story illustrates the desire in the human to move outward and to identify with all that is larger, grander, more mysterious, the second story calls us to move inward and to affirm life in its vulnerable manifestations.

To identify with the all and to affirm in spite of all—these are two key instincts that we may describe, in some sense, as religious or spiritual. And I am speaking here of the experience not of the institutions that bind that experience into rigid stories, scriptures, or codes, but of the powerful, ever-renewing sense of awe and assent. The pull outward and the call inward—these are mechanisms for situating ourselves in a universe of vast beauty, awesome mystery, and inexplicable suffering. What draws these two instincts together is patterning and organization. The inward pull and outward identification are linked by patterns that connect. As Eiseley describes it,

> Men talk much of matter and energy, of the struggle for existence that molds the shape of life. These things exist, it is true; but more delicate, elusive, quicker than the fins in water, is that mysterious principle known as "organization," which leaves all other mysteries concerned with life stale and insignificant by comparison. . . . That principle—I am beginning to suspect—was there before the living in the deeps of water.[6]

He continues to reflect on the meaning of his experience in the Platte River, where he has returned in the winter season and it is snowing:

> The temperature has risen. The little stinging needles have given way to huge flakes floating in like white leaves blown from some great tree in open space. In the car, switching on the lights, I examine one intricate crystal on my sleeve before it melts. No utilitarian philosophy explains a snow crystal, no doctrine of use or disuse. Water has merely leapt out of vapor and thin nothingness in the night sky to array itself in form. There is no logical reason for the existence of a snowflake any more than there is for evolution. It is an apparition from that mysterious shadow world beyond nature, that final world which contains—if anything contains—the explanation of men and catfish and green leaves.[7]

We may speak, then, of religion as a means of orientation in the midst of the powers of the universe and a means of relationship in the midst of human affairs. Yet it is always contained in the mystery of the patterning of life itself—that patterning is embedded in chaos as well.

We seek to connect to the deep inner patterning of things—in nature and in human life. This drive to see and understand pattern, coherence, and chaos in the universe is in part what motivates many scientists. It moves the astronomers and the microbiologists to seek the mysteries of matter in its far reaches and in its inner depth. Religions promise something of that connecting link through myths and symbols, rituals and prayers. They seek to weave a web (like a spider) from our inner structures to those complex structures that hold life together. This patterning is called by many names in various religions. In Hinduism and Buddhism it is *Dharma* or law; in Confucianism it is *Li* or principle; in Taoism it is the *tao* or the way; in Judaism it is *seder bereishit* or order of creation; in Christianity it is *Logos* or word.

To apprehend and support this patterning we balance ourselves between the outward pull of cosmological processes and the inward pull of the well springs of personal authenticity and collective communion. Many sources organize themselves around the patterns they perceive in nature. For example, indigenous peoples seek to embody the cosmos in their own person as well as in the structures they create in bioregions, such as subsistence activities and organization of habitat.[8]

Hindu society has organized itself into sacrificial ritual patterns analogous to the great sacrifice at the origin of the world, and Chinese religious thought has developed complex rules of correspondences based on how to live in relation to the patterns of nature. Religions, thus, mediate between the patterns of nature and the individual by creating stories of our origins, rituals to ensure continuity through the various stages of life from birth to death, and codes of behavior that aim to maximize harmonious relations and thus survival itself. In its simplest form, then, religion consists of a worldview embracing cosmology and cultivation. These are linked by patterns (or rituals) connecting self, society, and nature.

In further defining our terms it may be helpful to distinguish here between *worldview* (*weltanschauung*) and *cosmology*. Although these are sometimes used interchangeably, we take *worldview* to be a more general and less precisely defined perspective, while *cosmology* is a more specific, focused description of reality often associated with story or narrative. Thus, *worldview* refers to a broad set of ideas and values that helps to formulate basic perspectives of societies and individuals.[9] Cosmology is more specifically linked to an explanation of the universe (mythical or scientific) and the role of humans in it. Cosmology may or may not include cosmogony (a story of origins). Cosmologies of particular world religions, however, usually include explanations for the way things are in the universe or the way things ought to be. Science includes the former but not the latter. Cosmologies of world religions, however, imply a metaphysics and/or an ethics that give both orientation and meaning to human life. In this sense, cosmologies of religions contain "principles of order that support integrated forms of being"[10] and thus give moral direction to a person's life.[11] This is true because of the orientation that religious cosmologies provide for self-cultivation, the term from Chinese religion that I am defining as means of personal development that unify inner and outer lives.

In attempting to formulate the theoretical grounds for describing cosmology and its functions, Gregory Schrempp writes,

> What do we mean by 'cosmology'? In part we seem to point toward formulations that involve a quest for ultimate principles and/or grounds of the phenomenal world and the human place in it. But cosmology often—and this aspect stems perhaps from the Greek notion of kosmos—seems to carry for us a concern with wholeness and integrat-

edness, as if cosmological principles are not only ultimate principles, but also principles of order in the broadest sense, that is, principles engendering and supporting a way of being that is cognitively and emotionally integrated and whole. In these two kinds of concerns—the impetus to seek the 'ground' of the present order, and the impetus toward integratedness and wholeness—there is already a potential tension, since the quest for a ground is implicitly a resting of one thing on another, and thus involves a regression from any given state, whereas the impetus toward wholeness may engender the task of finding closure, as a condition for wholeness.[12]

Something of this tension between "grounding" and "growing" is what interests me in proposing a dialectic of cosmology and cultivation. If cosmology in Schrempp's sense has within it an is/ought tension, then cultivation is the working toward resolving that tension or living that tension through an ongoing deepening and broadening of one's personhood. The deepening is the inner grounding while the broadening is the growing outward.

More than ever before our contemporary challenge is to reorient ourselves to the universe—to know its vastness and its limits and to attune our rich inner space to the rhythms of this universe—that is, in essence, a religious act of boldness, of imagination, and of courage in the midst of staggering odds and enormous obstacles. This is the challenge of the evolution of religion to respond to the complex story of the universe.

In short, we are seeking to reattune our cultural coding and religious symbol systems to be in touch with the genetic coding and natural systems of the universe. We are struggling to reorient social, economic, and political systems to know the boundaries and potential of nature. For, as Thomas Berry has noted, all human activities need to be re-viewed as a subsystem of earth's system. What does this mean in practical terms?

It means we need to seek out the deep, abiding patterns within things. From the wings of a butterfly, to the veins of a leaf, to the seeds of fruit—there is a profound imprinting evident in nature. We can see it in the complex organizational structures of physics, chemistry, biology, and geology that have shaped this evolutionary process. This imprinting is part of the very structure of the universe that reveals its intelligibility, its luminosity, its energy. And it is to that patterning and energy that we need to respond for guidance and for survival. With enormous confidence in the mystery that has guided this process, we seek out the patterns that connect us to this web of life, knowing that deep in our own genetic coding are the links that do connect us to other forms of life. What is imprinted in us is our cosmological heritage—our birth right—our own story. It is the threads of the story we are gathering here, it is the weaving we are beginning to do, but it is the patterning for which we are still searching.

The search for that patterning is part of the religious quest—from earliest times until the present day humans have sought the means of orienting themselves to a universe of meaning and mystery through uncovering patterns that connect. This is essentially the function of myth and ritual in religion. These, then, become embedded in scriptures and in ethics, giving a meaningful context to daily action. It is the broader cosmological context of evolution that we are absorbing now; it is the deeper ecological ethics we seek in relation to nature's patterns. It is the reading not only of written scriptures, but of the natural scriptures that we need to foster. This has implications for education, social systems, economics, and even politics.

COSMOLOGY AND CULTIVATION IN THE WORLD'S SCRIPTURES

When we examine the early scriptures of many of the world's religions, we can see that they were inspired by the great cosmological movements of the universe—that nature was both teacher and guide. Even as historical traditions arose in certain contexts, such as the Middle East, they were always seen in relation to the larger dynamics of nature and seasonal cycles.

As we read these early scriptures we see into the world of nature not simply as backdrop to human action but as inspiration and animator, as the vehicle for seeing deeper truths, for exploring greater mysteries. The natural world is not only that which has given humans birth and sustenance; it is that which sustains humans psychically and spiritually in very tangible ways. It is, indeed, the container of mystery that is both here and beyond, luminous as a bright winter day, illusive as spring rain, and always captivating us with the promise of transformation.

So we return to these two fundamental directions of the religious experience—toward resonance with the universe, which lures us forward, and toward resilience within ourselves in the midst of constant change.

We link ourselves, sometimes unwittingly, to an emerging evolving universe, and yet we also draw back into the pulsations of the personal and communal where we find rest. As we look at the scriptures of the world's religions, we sense this inner and outer dynamic joined by patterns. The Psalms in Israel, the Vedas in India, and the *Book of Changes* in China are some of the oldest written scriptures known to the human community dating back to the first and second millennium B.C.E. They reflect a sense of longing for identification with a larger cosmology, and at the same time they signal the needed component of personal or communal cultivation. They suggest that early river civilizations that were undertaking agriculture were concerned not just with dominion, as has often been suggested, but with cooperation and harmony with nature as well.

At the heart of all of these early scriptures is a profound sense of the dynamic flow of life in the midst of both change and continuity. It is harmonizing with this life pattern, which is both within things and yet beyond, that characterizes these scriptures. How to affect reciprocal relations with the transformations of life is the challenge they present—and this is underscored by rituals that mitigate the unseen forces and that call forth sustaining energy. To open up the transformative powers of the universe in the midst of change is part of the challenge of these early scriptures and the concurrent ritual practices for social organization. In this context, human history fits into this great sweep of cosmic powers, not the other way around.

COSMOLOGY AND JUSTICE: ISRAEL

The Book of Psalms contains 150 prayer-poems probably intended to be sung or accompanied by music. In Hebrew the Book of Psalms means "Praises" (*tehillin*), reflecting affirmation or trust in God even in the midst of sorrow. Although most likely complied in the postexilic period (550 B.C.E.) for temple rituals, many of the themes stretch back much earlier.

As we look at the Psalms we see these songs of nature—worshipping, praising, and invoking the creator and his creation. These are profoundly linked concepts here that go beyond constructed dualisms of Western monotheism that divide God and humans. Instead, there is in the Psalms a lively dynamic exchange of creator, creation, and creatures. There is a sense of dependence of the creatures on both creation and creator. This is more than simply a static monotheism within a historical trajectory. It is a worldview showing us a God of care and compassion as well as omnipotence and justice. But it is a God deeply engaged in creation, not simply directing it from afar. This is a God involved in both cosmos and history. It is a God who offers justice to his chosen people, who in turn yearn for affirmation, mercy, and forgiveness. Thus, there is a sense of Israel's history as woven into a "co-existence with God" (Abraham Heschel). For the Israelites, history was seen as the epiphany of God and Israel was chosen for "converse" with Yahweh.[13] All of this is set against the background of Yahweh as cosmic king and creator, as enthroned over all of creation, yet, intimately connected with it. Indeed, this is celebrated in the enthronement psalms, which were part of the cult establishing a throne-ascension festival. This was held each New Year when Yahweh's rule over Israel, over other nations, and over the cosmos was celebrated with hymns and rituals.

The Psalms are divided into hymns of praise, of lament, and of thanksgiving. In terms of Psalms of praise we have a striking depiction of the creator and creation as deserving utmost respect, wonder, and awe.

> to the One who alone does great wonders,
> > *response*
> who by understanding made the heavens,
> > *response*
> who spread out the earth upon the waters,
> > *response*
> who made the great lights,
> > *response*
> the sun to rule over the day,
> > *response*
> the moon and stars to rule over the night,
> > *response*
>
> Psalm 136:4–99[14]

The order of creation is celebrated and the power and majesty of the creator is underscored. Yet God's continual creativity in history is noted.

All of them [animals and humans] look to you
  to give them their food in its season.
When you give to them, they gather up,
  when you open your hand, they are satisfied to the full.
When you hide your face, they are disturbed,
  when you take away their breath, they expire
  and return to their dust.
When you send forth your spirit, they are recreated,
  and you renew the surface of the soil.

Psalm 104:27–30[15]

The Psalms that reflect lamentation and thanksgiving might be seen as part of the cultivation side of the dyad. As injustice occurs there is a call for deliverance and as blessings are received thanksgiving pours forth. Justice and mercy are reasserted against the forces of oppression and sorrow.

In short, the cosmological world is the container of the history of the chosen people. As the people cultivate their relationship with the creator of the cosmos, they will experience justice and peace. While in this model history becomes a key element, nonetheless, maintaining a proper relationship to creation and the cosmic order is the container for all the history of the chosen people.

COSMOLOGY AND SACRIFICE: INDIA

This cosmic container is present in the Vedas in India, as well, which are hymns to celebrate the gods of nature. Here we have a richly textured universe presided over by a variety of Gods. This is not a model of monotheism as we see in the Psalms, but rather henotheism as described by Max Mueller. This term describes a worldview in which there is a pantheon of gods with no strict hierarchy.[16] While there is more emphasis on cosmos than on history, still there is a sense that the gods are involved in human concerns and need sacrifices to maintain order in the universe and to support human action. The sense of the awesome powers of nature as depicted in these Vedic hymns resonates down to the present period in India, where the hymns are still recited and Vedic sacrifices are still offered. In fact, sacrifice is the structured pattern of the universe itself.

The Vedic hymns were composed between 1600 and 600 B.C.E. and thus constitute the oldest written literature in India. They were transmitted orally for almost 3000 years until some brahmins in Calcutta were reluctantly persuaded to write them down in the 1780s. There are four principal texts, the oldest of which is the Rig Veda, a collection of over 1000 hymns. The Vedas are attributed to the Aryans, a nomadic and horse-riding people who moved into central Europe and India during the second millennium. As they settled in the Indus Valley region they gradually took up agriculture. Thus, these hymns are a fascinating collection of a people moving from pastoral pursuits to farming.

In relation to our overarching theme of the interaction of cosmology and culti-vation, we might say that there are two types of cosmological hymns in the Vedas, hymns of creation and hymns celebrating natural phenomena. There is one type that, broadly speaking, deals with cultivation, in this case sacrificial rituals.

The first kinds of cosmological hymns are those that deal with creation and origins. In other words, they are cosmogonic hymns. One of enormous impor-tance is the Maha purusha, which describes the birth of the universe from the sacrifice of a great person. This becomes a key link to modes of communal culti-vation in sacrifice. (Figure 13.1)

When they divided the Man,
    into how many parts did they divide him?
What was his mouth, what was his arms,
    what were his thighs and feet?

The brahman was his mouth,
    of his arms was made the warrior,
his thighs became the vaisya [peasant]
    of his feet the sudra [serf] was born.

The moon arose from his mind,
    from his eye was born the sun,
from his mouth Indra and Agni,
    from his breath the wind was born.

From his navel came the air,
    from his head there came the sky,
from his feet the earth, the four quarters from his ear,
    thus they fashioned the worlds.

With Sacrifice the gods sacrificed to Sacrifice—
    these were the first of the sacred laws.
These mighty beings reached the sky,
    where are the eternal spirits, the gods.[17]

Another origin hymn reflects the picture of the universe as emerging neither from being nor nonbeing. The power of this hymn is that it conveys a remarkable sense of speculation, questioning, and wonder. Here again we have a sense of the religious instinct resting in mystery, uncertainty, and awe.

Then even nothingness was not, nor existence.
    There was no air then, nor the heavens beyond it.
What covered it? Where was it? In whose keeping?
    Was there then cosmic water, in depths unfathomed?

Then there was neither death nor immortality,
    nor was there then the touch of night and day.
The One breathed mindlessly and self-sustaining.
    There was that One then, and there was no other.

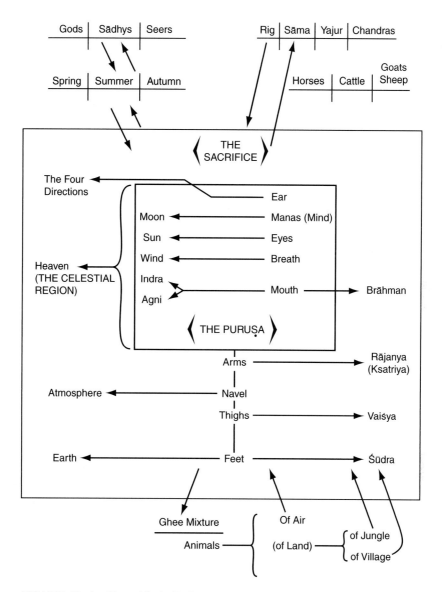

FIGURE 13–1   From Hindu Religious Tradition *1st edition by HOPKINS. ©
1971. Reprinted with permission of Wadsworth, division of Thomson Learning:
www.thomsonrights.com. Fax 800 730-2216.*

At first there was only darkness wrapped in darkness.

All this was only unilluminated water.

That One which came to be, enclosed in nothing,

arose at last, born of the power of heat.

In the beginning desire descended on it—

that was the primal seed, bom of the mind.

The sages who have searched their hearts with wisdom
   know that which is kin to that which is not.

And they have stretched their cord across the void,
   and know what was above, and what below.
Seminal powers made fertile mighty forces.
   Below was strength, and over it was impulse.

But, after all, who knows, and who can say
   whence it all came, and how creation happened?
The gods themselves are later than creation,
   so who knows truly whence it has arisen?

Whence all creation had its origin,
   he, whether he fashioned it or whether he did not,
he who surveys it all from highest heaven,
   he knows—or maybe even he does not know.[18]

A second major type of cosmological hymn are those celebrating the power of natural phenomena. In these Vedic hymns there are three kinds of deities: those of the heavenly, atmospheric, and earthly realms. These include Indra, the god of war and rain, who overcomes the evil serpent to release the waters for the benefit of humans. Varuna is the sky deity who restores and guards the order of the universe (*rta*). Also significant are the earthly deities of Agni, the god of fire, and Usas, the goddess of dawn, who brings refreshing hope and renewal to each day.

This light, most radiant of lights, has come; this gracious one who illumines all things, is bom. As night is removed by the rising sun, so is this the birthplace of the dawn.

The fair-shining dawn has come, bringing forth the sun. The darkness of night has given up her domain. Related to each other, immortal, succeeding one another, mutually exchanging appearances, they move across the heavens.

Munificent dawn awakens men curled up asleep; one of enjoyment, another for devotion, another to seek for wealth; they who could scarcely see, now see clearly. All living beings are now awakened.

We behold her, daughter of the sky, youthful, robed in white, driving forth the darkness. Princess of limitless treasure, shine down upon us throughout the day.

Rig-Veda I, 113[19]

Finally, in terms of cultivation there are hymns that define and celebrate ritual sacrifice as key to the maintenance of cosmological order in the natural and human realms. The power of ritual action is evident throughout these hymns. The early creation hymn of sacrifice previously mentioned sets the stage for the importance of ritual in this worldview. Prayers and offerings are key to placating the powers of the universe, such as wind and rain, thunder and lighting. Moreover, there is a need to maintain balance and order through correct speech, through the sacrifices of the present, through the consecration of the kings, through the great horse sacrifice, through the offerings of ghee (clarified butter), of soma (intoxicating drink), and of fire itself.

To placate the powers of nature, to maintain order, and finally to obtain material benefits—all of these are reasons for the importance of ritual sacrifice. While this is true in many early societies, it takes on a particular importance in India in relation to the cosmos itself.

COSMOLOGY AND HARMONY: CHINA

Finally, in turning to the East Asian world of China we see in the *I Ching* (*The Book of Changes*) the dynamics of change and continuity in the universe celebrated not as gods of nature but as patterns, namely hexagrams, which can be read as symbols guiding human affairs. To discern correct action humans must be in relationship to the movements of the universe. The first hexagram, the creative, *Ch'ien*, illustrates this well.

> COMMENTARY ON THE TEXT Vast indeed is the sublime Creative Principle, the Source of All, co-extensive with the heavens! It causes the clouds to come forth, the rain to bestow its bounty and all objects to flow into their respective forms. Its dazzling brilliance permeates all things from first to last; its activities symbolized by the component lines, reach full completion, each at the proper time. (The Superior Man), mounting them when the time is ripe, is carried heavenwards as though six dragons were his steeds! The Creative Principle functions through Change; accordingly, when we rectify our way of life by conjoining it with the universal harmony, our firm persistence is richly rewarded. The ruler, towering above the multitudes, brings peace to all countries of the world.[20]

The creativity of the universe is manifest throughout the natural order. For a society deeply engaged with agriculture such as China was, the changes of the seasons were seen as key cyclical patterns mirroring transformation in human life. They were revelatory of the birth and death processes of nature and of humans. The constancy of the seasons gave guidance to human affairs. Indeed, it was often said that the seasons do not err and that therefore the great person takes them as a model for action and behavior.[21] Thus, the emperor, for example, was considered as a pole star, the exemplar, for the entire society in this regard. He offered sacrifices at the great temples of Heaven and Earth in Beijing. He ritually planted the rice in the fall and harvested it in the late summer. (This still takes place for the Japanese emperor in Tokyo.) Moreover, throughout Asia there are elaborate systems of geomancy (*feng shui*) that orient persons, houses, public buildings, even graves to the most auspicious direction and balance with nature.

In terms of the broad dialectic of cosmology and cultivation, Chinese religious thought concentrates on connecting biological processes of growth and transformation with particular virtues to be cultivated. The attributes of creativity are four, namely, sublimity, success, furtherance, and perseverance. These are metaphors for the life process of beginning, duration, advantage, and flourishing. They are linked to the virtues of humaneness, faithfulness, righteousness, and wisdom. Thus to be receptive to these cosmological processes of the life cycle one must cultivate virtue. The result of this dynamic process of cosmological creativity finds its counterpoints in the receptive cultivation of the individual. The person is linked to the cosmos through life-generating patterns reflecting both order and change in the universe. A person can thus penetrate the Tao of Heaven and Earth.

The Book of Changes contains the measure of heaven and earth; therefore it enables us to comprehend the Tao of heaven and earth and its order.

> Looking upward, we contemplate with its help the signs in the heavens; looking down, we examine the lines of the earth. Thus we come to know the circumstances of the dark and the light. Going back to the beginnings of things and pursuing them to the end, we come to know the lessons of birth and death. The union of seed and power produces all things.[22]

The result is not only the growth of knowledge but also the growth of virtue:

> Since in this way man comes to resemble heaven and earth, he is not in conflict with them. His wisdom embraces all things, and his Tao brings order into the whole world; therefore he does not err. He is active everywhere but does not let himself be carried away. He rejoices in heaven and has knowledge of fate, therefore he is free of care. He is content with his circumstances and genuine in his kindness, therefore he can practice love.[23]

The result of this penetration of the changes in the cosmos and the cultivation of virtue in the self is that humans are able to both cooperate and collaborate with heaven and earth. In this way they form a triad with heaven and earth—completing their transforming and nourishing powers.

Indeed, the sense of completing and harmonizing with the fecundity of life that underlies the *I Ching* is at the heart of this dynamic system of cosmology and cultivation. For what the *I Ching* aims at is how to release the transformative energies in nature so as to be resonant with the creativity of human energies. Here the overflowing power of material force or *ch'i* comes into play.

Ch'i is that which unites all life from atoms, plants, animals, and humans, to the cosmos itself. This vitalistic principle of life holds within it the great transformative potential of life. These are the patterns that connect, buried deep within the storehouse of human knowing. Our genes contain these patterns of knowing that link us to all other atoms in the universe.

CONCLUSION

To reignite that link between our inner patterned genetic storehouse and that of the natural world is what is needed in all the major religious traditions. It is what is called for now from out of the fire of chaotic groping toward patterns of order and meaning and purpose. These ancient scriptures are examples of how that linkage was fostered in earlier times. Now we need to weave new linkages to both time and space within the context of the epic of evolution. If the epic is the warp, religions may be seen as the woof, as Phil Hefner suggests. The patterns and design are still emerging. In terms of developmental time, we are seeking our place in this vast sweep of evolution.

In terms of space, we are seeking appropriate modes of ecological design—how to live with the river patterns, how to tap into solar energies, how to flow with the rhythms of water, how to move with the currents of air. All of this means harmonizing with the deep inner rhythms in nature—not controlling them or harnessing them in a manipulative way, but learning once again nature's inner ordering principles—understanding the patterning imprinted in the cosmos and cultivated in ourselves. This is the way of religious inspiration—from its earliest pulsations to the present.

Can we listen, can we see, can we feel, can we touch anew with a feeling for the organism, with a deep resonance without and abiding reverence within?

If so, not only will we survive but the planet itself will flourish. And it will do so if we trust the transforming and nourishing powers of the cosmos.

I close with the words of Thomas Berry, who wrote at the conclusion of his essay on "The New Story":

> The basic mood of the future might well be one of confidence in the continuing revelation that takes place in and through the earth. If the dynamics of the universe from the beginning shaped the course of the heavens, lighted the sun, and formed the earth, if this same dynamism brought forth the continents and seas and atmosphere, if it awakened life in the primordial cell and then brought into being the unnumbered variety of living beings, and finally brought us into being and guided us safely through the turbulent centuries, there is reason to believe that this same guiding process is precisely what has awakened in us our present understanding of ourselves and our relation to this stupendous process. Sensitized to such guidance from the very structure and functioning of the universe, we can have confidence in the future that awaits the human venture.[24]

NOTES

1. A version of this paper was published as "Religion and Ecology: The Interaction of Cosmology and Cultivation" in Stephen R. Kellert and Timothy J. Farnham, *The Good in Nature and Humanity: Connecting Science, Religion, and Spirituality with the Natural World* (Washington, DC: Island Press, 2002).

2. Walter Capps, *Religious Studies: The Making of a Discipline* (Minneapolis: Fortress Press, 1995), p. 58.

3. Loren Eiseley, *The Immense Journey* (New York: Vintage Books, 1946), p. 16.

4. Ibid., p. 20.

5. Ibid., p. 175.

6. Ibid., p. 26.

7. Ibid., p. 27.

8. Eugene N. Anderson, *Ecologies of the Heart.* (New York: Oxford University Press, 1996).

9. In using *worldview* I am indebted to Clifford Geertz's articulation of worldview and ethos as well as Ninian Smart's use of the idea of worldview to describe religious traditions.

10. Marshall Sahlins, Foreword to Gregory Schrempp, *Magical Arrows* (Madison: University of Wisconsin Press, 1992).

11. Robin Lovin and Frank Reynolds have edited a volume of provocative essays from cross cultural perspectives on this topic titled *Cosmogony and Ethical Order* (Chicago: University of Chicago Press, 1985).

12. Gregory Schrempp, op. cit., p. 4.

13. Bernhard W. Anderson, *Understanding the Old Testament*, 4th ed. (Englewood Cliffs, NJ: Prentice Hall, 1986), p. 541.

14. Ibid., pp. 550–551.

15. Ibid., p. 551.

16. Kenneth G. Zysk, ed., A. L. Basham: *The Origins and Development of Classical Hinduism.* (Boston: Beacon Press, 1989), pp. 10–11.

17. Ibid., p. 25.

18. Ibid., p. 23.

19. Thomas Berry, *Religions of India: Hinduism, Youga, Buddhism* (Beverly Hills, CA: Bruce Publishing Co., 1971), p. 22.

20. John Blofeld, trans. and ed., *I Ching: The Book of Change* (New York: E. P. Dutton & Co., Inc., 1965), p. 85.

21. Helmut Wilhelm, *Heaven, Earth, and Man in the Book of Changes* (Seattle: University of Washington Press, 1977), p. 18.

22. Helmut Wilhelm, *Change: Eight Lectures on the I Ching,* trans. Cary F. Baynes (New York: Harper Torchbooks, 1960), p. 69.

23. Ibid., p. 69.

24. Thomas Berry, *The Dream of the Earth* (San Francisco: Sierra Club Books, 1988), p. 137.

14 The Spiritual Task of Religion in Culture

Philip Hefner *Zygon Center for Religion and Science*
Lutheran School of Theology

Culture and religion are deeply rooted in our very constitution as human persons. In this chapter, it is my task to understand how that is so and what difference it makes.

WHAT IS CULTURE? WHY IS IT IMPORTANT?

We use terms like *high culture/low culture, women's culture, African American culture.* I am speaking of culture in a different way. Let me explain. We humans require information in order to live (we are fundamentally dependent on information). There are two basic kinds of information without which we would not even be here on this planet. The first is genetic information, the information carried in our DNA, which provides for the making of proteins that, in turn, are essential in fashioning the shapes of our noses, the color of our eyes, the formation of our internal organs, and everything else about us. Genetic information is not all there is, but it is everywhere in our bodies. DNA has been likened to a library of construction manuals, inside every cell of our bodies.

The second kind of information on which we are dependent is cultural information. Genes alone do not a human being make. It is genetic information that directs the fertilizing of an egg and the nourishing of the growing embryo and fetus until a baby is born. But it is another kind of information that determined how that baby was conceived, whether by safe sex or not, whether by in vitro fertilization, egg or embryo transplant, or surrogate motherhood. It is another type of information that made prenatal care possible for mother and child. That information is cultural, and by that we mean that this information is not a programmed input that comes with its own operating instructions, but it is learned and taught. A lot of learning and teaching goes into the final action of safe sex or embryo transplants. There would be no hospitals or birthing centers apart from much learning and teaching. And when the newborn goes home from the hospital, that baby will not survive unless a great deal about nurturing and raising infants has somehow been learned and taught. This learning and teaching we call culture. There is a difference between a calf being born in the barnyard, struggling within a few minutes to get to its feet and amble beside its mother, and the birth of a human baby with expert care and assistance as it learns within the first year of life to walk—and the difference is that humans are creatures of culture in ways and to a degree that cows are not. From the moment you awaken in the morning to an alarm clock or radio, decide whether to eat a low-fat, high-fiber breakfast or poptarts and donuts, jump in a car or take a train to work, you are living in utter dependence on cultural information. And you hope that the learning and teaching has taken hold well enough that when you flip the switch, the lights go on, and when you turn the faucet, water comes out. It is culture that has reshaped the shore of Lake Michigan to create this beautiful museum and its setting. And as a Chicagoan, I can tell you that it is culture that, within the past two years, completely redesigned the system of roads by which we drove to this museum today.

In one sense of the word, culture is what takes place in the Chicago Symphony Orchestra's new center a few blocks north of here. In another sense, the one I am using here, culture is also what got you here this afternoon, and culture is what is happening between us right now, as we assemble and communicate and reflect afterward on what has happened.

STORIES AND CULTURE

The calf and its mother do not have to understand in a self-aware way very much about the process of a calf's birth and its ungainly attempts at walking. The human mother, father, nurse, midwife, and physician have to be aware of a great deal more. Culture has to be constructed, and—strangely and marvelously—it has to be surrounded by embellishing stories. It takes a lot of story construction and storytelling to sustain safe sex. It takes even more to sustain in vitro fertilization, and there are large segments of our society that condemn IVF as unnatural— they have counterstories that say this cultural development should not happen. The lucrative IVF clinics of our major hospitals are banking on a totally different set of stories, to clarify and support their work.

Or take house-building. Birds build nests, for example, much more on the basis of genetic inputs, and less on the basis of self-aware learning, it seems, so that we have tended to say that they do it by instinct. We humans learn how to build our houses, and we teach what we have learned. It's a dynamic process, since house construction is always changing—using new materials and designs. Furthermore, we seem to have to explain and justify our house-building; hence the rather powerful stories we tell. We used to say that "a man's home is his castle," and we back that up by allowing homeowners to shoot intruders, in self-defense within their castles. We speak nowadays about home ownership as the right of every person, and we say that the American Dream is fading, because houses are too expensive for many young persons to buy. Does the bird have a sense of a nest as "every Robin's right"? Does a robin need to? Why do we humans need to tell stories to explain and justify our culture? Is it because we cannot reasonably supply every person his or her own house? Why should owning one's house be more desirable than renting an apartment? The answers to these questions lead to interesting and important understandings of how and why we put our systems of cultural information together as we do. They also reveal that different societies construct their cultures on the basis of differing stories.

THE CHALLENGE OF CULTURE

Culture, in the light of what I have just said, requires a certain amount of awareness and decision making. Buildings like the one we are in did not just happen; they are the end product of much planning and decision making. The same can be said of the processes of in vitro fertilization and the existence of neonatal clinics in the large hospitals that are close to where we are night now. Culture requires a certain kind of freedom, freedom defined as obligation to make decisions if we are to construct the cultural systems that our lives depend on.

Today, virtually all of the major crises that confront us are crises of culture—that is why I speak of culture as a challenge. Global warming, environmental abuse, our proper relationship to the rest of life on the planet, inadequate schools, confusion concerning proper family life, poverty, violence in the streets, conflict between ethnic groups, confusion in the application of reproductive technologies—these are all rooted in our inability to construct and conduct adequate systems of cultural information. We do not know how to build an economy of full employment and fair distribution of wealth that can at the same time live in wholesome relationships with our natural environment. We are culturally incompetent at this point and also at many others.

This incompetence in our culture is potentially lethal. Our culture, in the form of technology, has been responsible for the great population increase on our planet. Now technology not only has enabled the present population size, it is also a necessity, if the population is to survive. Cultural incompetence, then, cannot be tolerated with indifference as if it were simply inherent human fallibility, because the incompetence reduces life chances for large segments of society, and it threatens all of the human population, directly or indirectly. We live in the first era of human evolution, in which culture and population exist in this complex interrelationship on a planetary scale. Prior to this time, errors in our conduct of culture were less critical on the planetary, specieswide scale.

The challenge of culture, the critical moment in which we now live, is a chapter in the epic of evolution, because it is in the process of biological evolution that culture has emerged as a fundamental element of human life. Culture is a natural phenomenon, an evolutionary phenomenon, and the crises we presently face are crises of nature and evolution. The culture-embracing stories that I spoke of, explaining and justifying our culture, are also part of the evolutionary epic. We are searching mightily today for adequate stories and new cultural forms. Since this very conference, as a matter of fact, is part of that search, we must also say that conferences like this are part of the epic of evolution.

CULTURE AND NATURE

There is no dualism between culture and nature, except perhaps at the level of surface appearance—that is why we speak of biocultural evolution. When I say this, I recognize fully that I am flying in the face of a fundamental strand of our Western traditions that hold nature and culture, nature and human spirit, nature and human persons to be two separate realms (the well-known spirit/nature dualism that has haunted us at least since Plato's creation story in the *Timaeus,* in which he asserted that the deficiencies of matter successfully thwarted God's intention to create the kind of world that God really wanted). The testimony of contemporary scientific research rejects such dualisms, since we know that our culture, which is also the seat of the human spirit, has emerged within biological evolution, in the wake of the formation of the human central nervous system.

Culture, therefore, is a happening within nature. Culture belongs to nature. It is, in a metaphorical sense, nature's organ. If we bring into play what I have said about culture, then we must conclude that culture is nature's own process of being self-aware, of being aware of itself, of trying to understand itself and its world, and of trying to discharge fundamental processes of evolution under the condition of free choice and decision making. There have been articulations of this understanding in our recent past: The poet Gerard Manley Hopkins spoke of humans as the "eye, ear, tongue" of nature; Teilhard de Chardin (like Hopkins, a Jesuit) referred to the human species as "evolution become aware of itself"; cosmologist John Wheeler hinted at the essential feature of cosmic evolution as the emergence of the universe viewing itself; medical writer Lewis Thomas developed an image of humans as the reflective agency for nature. Thomas Berry suggests that we are the dream of the earth; Berry and Brian Swimme speak of us as the "eyes of the Milky Way looking at itself." The dynamics and significance of this conference on the Epic of Evolution are misunderstood if we do not understand that we, in these very days, exemplify nature's attempt to understand itself.

CULTURE AND THE ORGANIZATION OF CONSCIOUSNESS

I hope that at least two ideas have implanted themselves firmly in your cerebral cortex, if not in your very souls: (1) that it is impossible to consider the epic of evolution and the nature of human persons by attempting to leapfrog over culture and establish some direct relation between cosmic and biological evolution without taking culture into consideration; and (2) that culture holds an incredibly significant place within the structures of nature, as the epic of evolution portrays nature (cosmic, physical, and biological).

What, then, is the central human issue of culture, viewed scientifically, within the epic of evolution? It is the issue of what some psychologists, like Mihaly Csikszentmihalyi, call the organization of our consciousness. This is another way of saying that the central issue is as follows: What should guide us in the construction and conduct of our culture? The values we hold to, the worldviews we live in, the decisions we make all flow from the ways in which our consciousness is organized. In scientific terms, it is the psychological dimension of our personality that plays the role of gatekeeper between our genetic and cultural inputs, on the one hand, and what we shall select to pay most attention to and therefore act on, on the other hand. This gatekeeper function and decision making rest on the foundation of how consciousness is organized. Our common language recognizes this in such popular sayings as these: "It's all in your head," "mind control," "messing with your head," "playing head games," "get your head together." All of these sayings speak in terms of there being something mental that we need to organize, in order to live our lives adequately.

It is how our consciousness is organized that tells us whether animals are fellow creatures, or just meat on the hoof, or just suppliers of milk and eggs, and we act accordingly. It's the organization of our consciousness that tells us whether ancient forests are so many board feet of lumber or so many rolls of newsprint, or whether they are to be respected and preserved as natural treasures. It is how our consciousness is organized that tells us whether women and men are equal, whether persons of a different skin color are second-class citizens, whether persons are to be more highly valued if they produce more goods and consume more goods than if they do not. Another word for organization of consciousness may be what is now widely referred to, both within religious circles and outside them, in the term *spirituality*.

I am here merely rephrasing Csikszentmihalyi's discussion of spirituality as constituted by memes (the cultural counterpart to genes), which take our genetic evolution into account, but "at the same time point to possibilities to which our biological inheritance is not yet sensitive." Spirituality is not some supernaturally oriented package of ideas—it is a close-to-the-ground perspective that is deeply immersed in the particularities of our evolving world, but that focuses on what those particularities can become. This is the most important component for organizing our consciousness, our focus on what these very natural bodies and brains, in this most natural world, can become.

Roger Sperry, a Nobel laureate in brain research, gave expression to this insight when he said that the most powerful thing in the world's not the nuclear armaments of the nations, it is rather the values that inhabit the minds of those whose hands are on the switches that release those armaments. Those values, which image so concretely what the minds believe the world can become, are the centers of power. He might have said that the ways in which the consciousness of those minds are organized is the key factor, because it determines how the nuclear warheads will be employed.

RELIGION IN THE EPIC OF EVOLUTION

Culture is where religion happens; religion is located within human culture. Religion has emerged within the cultural phase of evolution. What does religion do, what is it for, in the cultural realm? It is a primary force for the organization of consciousness and therefore for the worldviews and values, and decisions that drive culture. Religion is above all concerned with what the natural world can become, its possibilities. Religion's adaptive success in strengthening individual psyches and mobilizing group spirit flows from its vision of what the world can become. You will note that with these words, I am accounting for the place of religion and its function in terms of evolution.

This evolutionary interpretation leads us to say that religion, too, is an information system within culture. Religion is one of those elements in our culture that carries the information that constructs our culture, and it bears core information for culture.

The characteristics that we associate with religion all have to do with the effort of nature to understand itself and conduct itself in freedom to make the choices that sustain evolution in the deepest sense. The myths and doctrines of religion are the stories we have referred to; they try to embrace our culture, explain it, and justify it. The rituals set forth how the stories might shape our lives; the moral codes are literal attempts to shape our daily living. Myths, doctrines, rituals, moral codes—these are not above nature or even alongside it; these are emergent forms that nature itself takes in its effort to understand nature's own meaning, including the meaning of human nature.

In order to play its role, religion must generate the stories, rituals, and moral codes of meaning on the basis of its heritage, but in the currency of the present moment. To invoke the genetic metaphor, our genome is a heritage that we bring with us into the present, but the organism that carries that heritage will die unless it successfully negotiates a passage into the next generations—that is what the term inclusive fitness is all about. Negotiating meaning in the present time, that is at the heart of religion's task. Or, we might say that organizing consciousness in viable ways for passage into the next generation is religion's contribution to the epic of evolution. Since spirituality is another term for this, we can call this the spiritual challenge of our phase of the evolutionary epic.

It amounts to this: In every era and in every situation, religion seeks to serve nature's self-understanding and thereby serve to the conduct of culture in ways that will negotiate the rapids of evolution's future. And as the eye, ear, tongue, and dream of nature, we must develop for ourselves the criteria of what adequate negotiation of the future amounts to. Among both traditional religionists and posttraditionalists, there can be much bad, demonic religion that must be rejected in favor of good religion—and we are the ones who must determine what *good* and *bad* mean.

All persons face this religious challenge, and it is a challenge that is central to the survival of all persons and all particular cultures, even as it is decisive for the future of the planet, although we do not know what that future is.

Many persons share in this religious dimension of nature's evolution as members of traditional religious communities (Jews, Christians, Muslims, Buddhists, Hindus, Sikhs, primordial religions). Even restricting ourselves to the population of this city, the religious affiliations are too numerous to catalogue. For these persons, the traditions of their religious communities are the chief resource for organizing consciousness, their main entree to spirituality for our times.

Those persons who believe in God will hold that God gave religion to the human *race,* and gave revelations to the religions for precisely this purpose, that the most viable organization of consciousness might take place, for the future of God's plans for the evolutionary creation.

All of these religious folk, however, face the incredible task of rendering their tradition for the evolutionary rigors of the present time, looking forward to the next generations. Since those traditions have been transmitted to our time in forms that were adaptive for culture's basic information in previous situations, that are vastly different from our present context, and since we face a crisis of culture that is almost incomprehensibly deep and broad, the task facing the traditional religions is staggering. Nevertheless, religious persons are committed to the hard path that lies ahead for them: transforming their traditions from the past into forms that are life giving for our transition into the future.

There are many others, however, who believe that traditional religions have run their course, that they have come to the end of their string and are incapable of meeting the spiritual challenge of the present moment in the epic of evolution. These persons are equally dedicated to the hard path of spirituality. These persons, no less than the traditional religionists, are engaged in the religious dimension of human culture, namely the formation of the worldviews and values, and the making of decisions for culture that are adequate to the future. These persons seek alternative frameworks of meaning, new stories and rituals. In fact, the theme of this conference, The Epic of Evolution, suggests an image that is new and is a prime candidate to become the creation story for this era of the epic.

This second group may well be more aware of the need for new viable forms of spirituality, and in this sense their sensibilities are ahead of the traditionalists. However, they face perhaps a much more difficult task of starting from scratch, in a way, to construct the stories, the rituals, and the moral codes that are essential to the organization of consciousness for the cultural phase we live in today. Some of these persons are also involved in weaving together traditions from many religions, in the effort to construct new spiritualities. In their declarations of willingness to start afresh, there is a special kind of courage manifested in this group.

Both of these groups of people (the traditional religionists and the posttraditional religionists) are caught up in the challenge of the epic of evolution, which is also the challenge of this conference: to discover the most fitting organization of consciousness for our time; to discern the most adequate spirituality for this phase of evolution on this planet. This opens up one of the most urgent and exciting frontiers that we can observe just now (the evolution of consciousness itself). There is a triad of elements that belong together: cultural evolution, evolution of consciousness, and religion.

I like to speak of this moment in our evolutionary history and its challenges in terms of weaving. We are, all of us, weavers. The weaver constructs the warp, anchoring it to the loom, and then, by working the weft in and through the warp, creates patterns and the entire tapestry. The Epic of Evolution, in the form that scientists present it in their research papers, is the warp on which all present and future meaning for our lives must be woven. Every one of us and every group represented here seeks, within the terms of their own philosophy of life, to weave their spirituality within the Epic of Evolution. We seek to organize our consciousness through our weaving, in ways that can serve our information function within culture. There is no single correct way in which the weaving will take shape, no single authorized manner in which the Epic must appear in our worldviews. The person who finds traditional wisdom still meaningful will weave with that tradition in mind, while the posttraditionalists will seek to weave their characteristic visions. All of the various weavers of meaning will find a commonality in the warp and in the cultural crisis that faces us all, and each will learn from how others negotiate their visions within the loom's constraints and possibilities. Each weaver will discover resources in the vision they bring with them that they did not appreciate before, and each will find that some precious presuppositions just do not fit.

This is what we are here for, we humans who are the cultural religious animals of evolution on our planet. We are here to weave the spiritualities (the consciousness) that are life giving for our phase of the epic of evolution and for the next generation. This is the significance of this conference, that it is a temporary studio for the weavers. When this studio is dismantled, who will be the next to offer us the resources to come together for the sake of the future?

15 Human Evolution: Biology, Culture, Ethics

Francisco J. Ayala   *University of California, Irvine*

INTRODUCTION

It does not take a great deal of biological expertise to realize that humans have organs and limbs similar to those of other animals; that we bear our young like other mammals; that, bone by bone, there is a precise correspondence between the skeletons of a chimpanzee and a human. But it does not take much reflection to notice the distinct uniqueness of our species. There is the bipedal gait and the enlarged brain. Much more conspicuous than the anatomical differences are the distinct behaviors and their outcomes. Humans have elaborate social and political institutions, codes of law, literature and art, ethics and religion; humans build roads and cities; travel by motorcars, ships, and airplanes; and communicate by means of telephones, computers, and televisions.

I will, first, outline what we currently know about the evolutionary history of humans for the last four million years, from bipedal but small-brained *Australopithecus* to modern *Homo sapiens,* our species, through the prolific toolmaker *Homo habilis* and the continent wanderer *Homo erectus.* I shall, then, identify anatomical traits that distinguish us from other animals, and point out our two kinds of heredity, the biological and the cultural.

Biological inheritance is based on the transmission of genetic information in humans very much the same as in other sexually reproducing organisms. But cultural inheritance is distinctively human, based on transmission of information by a teaching and learning process, which is, in principle, independent of biological parentage. Cultural inheritance makes possible the cumulative transmission of experience from generation to generation. Cultural heredity is a swifter and more effective (because it can be designed) mode of adaptation to the environment than the biological mode. The advent of cultural heredity ushered in cultural evolution, which transcends biological evolution.

I will, finally, explore ethical behavior as a model case of a distinctive human trait and seek to ascertain the causal connections between human ethics and human biology. My conclusions are that (1) moral reasoning (i.e., the proclivity to make ethical judgments by evaluating actions as either good or evil) is rooted in our biological nature; it is a necessary outcome of our exalted intelligence; but (2) the moral codes that guide our decisions as to which actions are good and which ones are evil, are products of culture, including social and religious traditions. This second conclusion contradicts those evolutionists and sociobiologists who claim that the morally good is simply that which is promoted by the process of biological evolution.

APE TO HUMAN

Humankind is a biological species that has evolved from other species that were not human. In order to understand human nature, we must know our biological make-up and whence we come, the story of our humbler beginnings. For a century after the publication of Darwin's *On the Origin of Species* in 1859, the story of evolution was reconstructed with evidence from paleontology (the study of fossils), from biogeography (the study of the geographical distribution of organisms), and from the comparative study of living organisms: their morphology, development, physiology, and the like. Since mid–twentieth century we have, in addition, molecular biology, the most informative and precise discipline for reconstructing the ancestral relationships of living species.

Our closest biological relatives are the great apes and, among them, the chimpanzees, who are more related to us than they are to the gorillas, and much more than to the orangutans. The hominid lineage diverged from the chimpanzee lineage 5 to 7 million years ago (Mya) and it evolved exclusively in the African continent until the emergence of *Homo erectus*, somewhat before 1.8 Mya. The first known hominid, *Ardipithecus ramidus*, lived 4.4 Mya, but it is not certain that it was bipedal or in the direct line of descent to modern humans, *Homo sapiens*. The recently described *Australopithecus anamensis*, dated 3.9 to 4.2 Mya, was bipedal and has been placed in the line of descent to *Australopithecus afarensis*, *Homo habilis*, *H. erectus*, and *H. sapiens*. Other hominids, not in the direct line of descent to modern humans, are *Australopithecus africanus*, *Paranthropus aethiopicus*, *P. boisei*, and *P. robustus*, who lived in Africa at various times between 3 and 1 Mya, a period when three or four hominid species lived contemporaneously in the African continent.

Shortly after its emergence in tropical or subtropical eastern Africa, *H. erectus* spread to other continents. Fossil remains of *H. erectus* are known from Africa, Indonesia (Java), China, the Middle East, and Europe. *H. erectus* fossils from Java have been dated 1.81 ± 0.04 and 1.66 ± 0.04 Mya, and from Georgia between 1.6 and 1.8 Mya. Anatomically distinctive *H. erectus* fossils have been found in Spain, deposited before 780,000 years ago, the oldest in southern Europe.

The transition from *H. erectus* to *H. sapiens* occurred around 400,000 years ago, although this date is not well determined owing to uncertainty as to whether some fossils are *erectus* or "archaic" forms of *sapiens*. *H. erectus* persisted for some time in Asia, until 250,000 years ago in China and perhaps until 100,000 ago in Java, and thus was coetaneous with early members of its descendant species, *H. sapiens*. Fossil remains of Neanderthal hominids (*Homo neanderthalensis*) appeared in Europe around 200,000 years ago and persisted until thirty or forty thousand years ago. The Neanderthals had, like *H. sapiens*, large brains. A few years ago, they were thought to be ancestral to anatomically modern humans, but now we know that modern humans appeared at least 100,000 years ago, much before the disappearance of the Neanderthals. Moreover, in caves in the Middle East, fossils of modern humans have been found dated 120,000 to 100,000 years ago, as well as Neanderthals dated at 60,000 to 70,000 years ago, followed again by modern humans dated at 40,000 years ago. It is unclear whether the two forms repeatedly replaced one another by migration from other regions, or whether they coexisted in some areas. Recent genetic evidence indicates that interbreeding between *sapiens* and *neanderthalensis* never occurred.

There is considerable controversy about the origin of modern humans. Some anthropologists argue that the transition from *H. erectus* to archaic *H. sapiens* and later to anatomically modern humans occurred consonantly in various parts of the Old World. Proponents of this "multiregional model" emphasize fossil evidence showing regional continuity in the transition from *H. erectus* to archaic and then modern *H. sapiens*. In order to account for the transition from one to another species (something that cannot happen independently in several places), they postulate that genetic exchange occurred from time to time between populations, so that the species evolved as a single gene pool, even though geographic differentiation occurred and persisted, just as geographically differentiated populations exist in other animal species, as well as in living humans. This explanation depends on the occurrence of persistent migrations and interbreeding between populations from different continents, of which no direct evidence exists. Moreover, it is difficult to reconcile the multiregional model with the contemporary existence of different species or forms in different regions, such as the persistence of *H. erectus* in China and Java for more than one hundred thousand years after the emergence of *H. sapiens*. Other scientists argue instead that modern humans first arose in Africa or in the Middle East somewhat prior to 100,000 years ago and from there spread throughout the world, replacing elsewhere the preexisting populations of *H. erectus* or archaic *H. sapiens*.

Some proponents of this "African replacement" model claim further that the transition from archaic to modern *H. sapiens* was associated with a very narrow bottleneck, consisting of only two or very few individuals who are the ancestors of all modern humankind. This particular claim of a narrow bottleneck is supported, erroneously as I will soon show, by the investigation of a peculiar small fraction of our genetic inheritance, the mitochondrial DNA (mtDNA). The African (or Middle East) origin of modern humans is, however, supported by a wealth of recent genetic evidence and is, therefore, favored by many evolutionists.

THE MYTH OF THE MITOCHONDRIAL EVE

The genetic information we inherit from our parents is encoded in the linear sequence of the DNA's four nucleotide components (represented by A, C, G, T) in the same fashion as semantic information is encoded in the sequence of letters of a written text. Most of the DNA is contained in the chromosomes inside the cell nucleus. The total amount of DNA in a human cell nucleus consists of six thousand million nucleotides, half in each set of 23 chromosomes inherited from each parent. A relatively small amount of DNA, about 16,000 nucleotides, exists in the mitochondria, cell organelles outside the nucleus. The mtDNA is inherited in a peculiar manner; that is, exclusively along the maternal line. The inheritance of the mtDNA is a gender mirror image of the inheritance of the family name. Sons and daughters inherit their mtDNA from their mother, but only the daughters transmit it to their progeny, just as sons and daughters receive the family name of the father, but only the sons transmit it to their children.

Analysis of the mtDNA from ethnically diverse individuals has shown that the mtDNA sequences of modern humans coalesce to one ancestral sequence, the "mitochondrial Eve" that existed in Africa about 200,000 years ago.[1] This Eve, however, is not the one mother from whom all humans descend, but an mtDNA molecule (or the woman carrier of that molecule) from whom all modern mtDNA *molecules* descend.

Some science writers, and even some scientists, have drawn the inference that all humans descend from only one, or very few women,[2] but this is based on a confusion between gene genealogies and individual genealogies. Gene genealogies gradually coalesce toward a unique DNA ancestral sequence (in a similar fashion as living species, such as humans, chimpanzees, and gorillas, coalesce into one ancestral species). Individual genealogies, on the contrary, increase by a factor of 2 in each ancestral generation: An individual has two parents, four grandparents, and so on.[3] Coalescence of a gene genealogy into one ancestral gene, originally present in one individual, does not disallow the contemporary existence of many other individuals, who are also our ancestors, and from whom we have inherited the other genes.

This conclusion can be illustrated with an analogy. My family name is shared by many people, who live in Spain, Mexico, the Philippines, and other countries. A historian of our family name has concluded that all Ayalas descend from Don Lope Sánchez de Ayala, grandson of Don Vela, vassal of King Alfonso VI, who established the domain ("señorío") de Ayala in the year 1085, in the now Spanish Basque province of Alava. Don Lope is the Adam from whom we all descend on the paternal line, but we also descend from many other men and women who lived in the eleventh century, as well as earlier and later.

The inference warranted by the mtDNA analysis is that the mitochondrial Eve is the ancestor of modern humans in the *maternal line*. Any person has a single ancestor in the maternal line in any given generation. Thus a person inherits the mtDNA from the mother, from the maternal grandmother, from the great grandmother on the maternal line, and so on. But the person also inherits other genes from other ancestors. The mtDNA that we have inherited from the mitochondrial Eve represents one-four-hundred-thousandth of the DNA present in any modern human (sixteen thousand out of six billion nucleotides). The rest of the DNA, 400,000 times more than the mtDNA, we have inherited from other contemporaries of the mitochondrial Eve.

From how many contemporaries? The issue of how many human ancestors we had in the past has been elucidated by investigating the genes of the human immune system.[4] The genes of the human leukocyte antigen (HLA) complex exist in multiple versions, which provide people with the diversity necessary to confront bacteria and other pathogens that invade the body. The evolutionary history of some of these genes shows that they coalesce into ancestral genes 30 to 60 Mya; that is, much before the divergence of humans and apes. (Indeed, humans and apes share many of these genes.) The mathematical theory of gene coalescence makes it possible to estimate the number of ancestors that must have lived in any one generation in order to account for the preservation of so many diverse genes through hundreds of thousands of generations. The estimated effective number is about 100,000 individuals per generation. This "effective" number of individuals is an average rather than a constant number, but it is a peculiar kind of average (a "harmonic mean"), compatible with much larger but not much smaller numbers of individuals in different generations. Thus, through millions of years our ancestors existed in populations that were 100,000 individuals strong, or larger. Population bottlenecks may have occurred on rare occasions. But the genetic evidence indicates that human populations never consisted of fewer than several thousand individuals.

HUMAN UNIQUENESS

The most distinctive human anatomical traits are erect posture and large brain. We are the only vertebrate species with a bipedal gait and erect posture; birds are bipedal, but their backbone stands horizontal rather than vertical. Brain size is generally proportional to body size; relative to body mass, humans have the largest (and most complex) brain. The chimpanzee's brain weighs less than a pound; a gorilla's slightly more. The human male adult brain is 1400 cubic centimeters (cc), about 3 pounds in weight.

Evolutionists used to raise the question whether bipedal gait or large brain came first, or whether they evolved consonantly. The issue is now resolved. Our *Australopithecus* ancestors had, since 4 million years ago, a bipedal gait, but a small brain, about 450 cc, a pound in weight. Brain size starts to increase notably with our *Homo habilis* ancestors, about 2.5 Mya, who had a brain about 650 cc and also were prolific toolmakers (hence the name *habilis*). Between 1 and 2 million years afterward, there lived *Homo erectus,* with adult brains up to 1200 cc. Our species, *Homo sapiens,* has a brain about three times as large as that of *Australopithecus*, 1300 to 1400 cc or some 3 pounds of gray matter. Our brain is not only much larger than that of chimpanzees or gorillas but also much more complex. The cerebral cortex, where the higher cognitive functions are processed, is in humans disproportionally much greater than the rest of the brain when compared with apes.

Erect posture and large brain are not the only anatomical traits that distinguish us from nonhuman primates, even if they may be the most obvious. A list of our most distinctive anatomical features includes the following (of which the last five items are not detectable in fossils):

- Erect posture and bipedal gait (entail changes of the backbone, hipbone, and feet)
- Opposing thumbs and arm and hand changes (make possible precise manipulation)
- Large brain
- Reduction of jaws and remodeling of face
- Changes in skin and skin glands
- Reduction in body hair

- Cryptic ovulation (and extended female sexual receptivity)
- Slow development
- Modification of vocal tract and larynx
- Reorganization of the brain

Humans are notably different from other animals not only in anatomy, but also and no less importantly in their behavior, both as individuals and socially. A list of distinctive human behavioral traits includes the following:

- Subtle expression of emotions
- Intelligence: abstract thinking, categorizing, and reasoning
- Symbolic (creative) language
- Self-awareness and death awareness
- Toolmaking and technology
- Science, literature, and art
- Ethics and religion
- Social organization and cooperation (division of labor)
- Legal codes and political institutions

Humans live in groups that are socially organized, and so do other primates. But primate societies do not approach the complexity of human social organization. A distinctive human social trait is culture, which may be understood as the set of nonstrictly biological human activities and creations. Culture includes social and political institutions, ways of doing things, religious and ethical traditions, language, common sense and scientific knowledge, art and literature, technology, and in general all the creations of the human mind. The advent of culture has brought with it cultural evolution, a superorganic mode of evolution superimposed on the organic mode, which has in the last few millennia become the dominant mode of human evolution. Cultural evolution has come about because of cultural change and inheritance, a distinctively human mode of achieving adaptations to the environment and transmitting the adaptations through the generations.

CULTURAL HEREDITY

There are in humankind two kinds of heredity—the biological and the cultural, which may also be called organic and superorganic, or *endosomatic* and *exosomatic* systems of heredity. Biological inheritance in humans is very much like that in any other sexually reproducing organism; it is based on the transmission of genetic information encoded in DNA from one generation to the next by means of the sex cells. Cultural inheritance, on the other hand, is based on transmission of information by a teaching-learning process, which is in principle independent of biological parentage. Culture is transmitted by instruction and learning, by example and imitation, through books, newspapers, radio, television, and motion pictures; through works of art; and by any other means of communication. Culture is acquired by every person from parents, relatives, and neighbors, and from the whole human environment.

Cultural inheritance makes possible for people what no other organism can accomplish—the cumulative transmission of experience from generation to generation. Animals can learn from experience, but they do not transmit their experiences, their "discoveries" (at least not to any large extent) to the following generations. Animals have individual memory, but they do not have a "social memory." Humans, on the other hand, have developed a culture because they can transmit cumulatively their experiences from generation to generation.

Cultural inheritance makes possible cultural evolution; that is, the evolution of knowledge, social structures, ethics, and all other components that make up human culture. Cultural inheritance makes possible a new mode of adaptation to the environment that is not available to nonhuman organisms—adaptation by means of culture. Organisms in general adapt to the environment by means of natural selection, by changing over generations their genetic constitution to suit the demands of the environment. But humans, and humans alone, can also adapt by changing the environment to suit the needs of their genes. (Animals build nests and modify their environment also in other ways, but the manipulation of the environment by any nonhuman species is trivial compared to humankind's.) For the last few millennia humans have been adapting the environments to their genes more often than their genes to the environments.

In order to extend its geographical habitat, or to survive in a changing environment, a population of organisms must become adapted, through slow accumulation of genetic variants sorted out by natural selection to the new climatic conditions, different sources of food, different competitors, and so on. The discovery of fire and the use of shelter and clothing allowed humans to spread from the warm tropical and subtropical regions of the Old World to the whole earth, except for the frozen wastes of Antarctica, without the anatomical development of fur or hair. Humans did not wait for genetic mutants promoting wing development; they have conquered the air in a somewhat more efficient and versatile way by building flying machines. People travel the rivers and the seas without gills or fins. The exploration of outer space has started without waiting for mutations providing humans with the ability to breathe with low oxygen pressures or to function in the absence of gravity; astronauts carry their own oxygen and specially equipped pressure suits. From their obscure beginnings in Africa, humans have become the most widespread and abundant species of mammal on earth. It was the appearance of culture as a superorganic form of adaptation that made humankind the most successful animal species.

Cultural adaptation has prevailed in humankind over biological adaptation because it is a more rapid mode of adaptation and because it can be directed. A favorable genetic mutation newly arisen in an individual can be transmitted to a sizable part of the human species only through innumerable generations. However, a new scientific discovery or technical achievement can be transmitted to the whole of humankind, potentially at least, in less than one generation. Moreover, whenever a need arises, culture can directly pursue the appropriate changes to meet the challenge. On the contrary, biological adaptation depends on the accidental availability of a favorable mutation, or of a combination of several mutations, at the time and place where the need arises.

BIOLOGY TO CULTURE

Erect posture and large brain are distinctive anatomical features of modern humans. High intelligence, symbolic language, religion, and ethics are some of the behavioral traits that distinguish us from other animals. The account of human origins that I have sketched implies a continuity in the evolutionary process that goes from our nonhuman ancestors of 8 million years ago through primitive hominids to modern humans. A scientific explanation of that evolutionary sequence must account for the emergence of human anatomical and behavioral traits in terms of natural selection together with other distinctive biological causes and processes. One explanatory strategy is to focus on a particular human feature and seek to identify the conditions under which this feature may have been favored by natural selection. Such a strategy may lead to erroneous conclusions as a consequence of the fallacy of selective attention: Some traits may have come about not because they are themselves adaptive, but rather because they are associated with traits that are favored by natural selection.

Geneticists have long recognized the phenomenon of "pleiotropy," the expression of a gene in different organs or anatomical traits. It follows that a gene that becomes changed due to its effects on a certain trait will result in the modification of other traits as well. The changes of these other traits are epigenetic consequences of the changes directly promoted by natural selection. The cascade of consequences may be, particularly in the case of humans, very long and far from obvious in some cases. Literature, art, science, and technology are among the behavioral features that may have come about not because they were adaptively favored in human evolution but because they are expressions of the high intellectual abilities present in modern humans: What may have been favored by natural selection (its "target") was an increase in intellectual ability rather than each one of those particular activities.

I now will briefly explore ethics and ethical behavior as a model case of how we may seek the evolutionary explanation of a distinctively human trait. I select ethical behavior because morality is a human trait that seems remote from biological processes. My goal is to ascertain whether an account can be advanced of ethical behavior as an outcome of biological evolution and, if such is the case, whether ethical behavior was directly promoted by natural selection or has rather come about as an epigenetic manifestation of some other trait that was the target of natural selection.

I will argue that ethical behavior (the proclivity to judge human actions as either good or evil) has evolved as a consequence of natural selection, not because it was adaptive in itself but rather as a pleiotropic consequence of the high intelligence characteristic of humans. However, I will first point out that the question whether ethical behavior is biologically determined may refer either to (1) the capacity for ethics (i.e., the proclivity to judge human actions as either right or wrong), which I will refer to as "ethical behavior"; or (2) the moral *norms* or moral codes accepted by human beings for guiding their actions. I will deal here with the first of these questions and argue that the capacity for ethics is a necessary attribute of human nature, and thus a product of biological evolution. With respect to the second question, I will briefly assert my conviction that moral norms are products of cultural evolution, not of biological evolution.

My thesis is grounded on the argument that humans exhibit ethical behavior because their biological make-up determines the presence of the three necessary, and jointly sufficient, conditions for ethical behavior; namely, the ability to anticipate the consequences of one's own actions, to make value judgments, and to choose between alternative courses of action. I thus maintain that ethical behavior came about in evolution not because it is adaptive in itself, but as a necessary consequence of humankind's eminent intellectual abilities, which are an attribute directly promoted by natural selection. I nevertheless maintain that, contrary to many distinguished evolutionists, the norms of morality are not derived from biological evolution. It is true that both natural selection and moral norms sometimes coincide on the same behavior (i.e., the two are consistent). But this isomorphism between the behaviors promoted by natural selection and those sanctioned by moral norms exists only with respect to the consequences of the behaviors; the underlying causations are completely disparate.

BIOLOGICAL ROOTS OF THE MORAL SENSE

I have noted that the question of whether ethical behavior is biologically determined may refer to either one of the following issues: (1) Is the capacity for ethics—the proclivity to judge human actions as either right or wrong—determined by the biological nature of human beings? (2) Are the systems or codes of ethical norms accepted by human beings biologically determined? A similar distinction can be made with respect to language. The issue whether the capacity for symbolic language is determined by our biological nature is different from the question of whether the particular language we speak (e.g., English, Spanish, or Japanese) is biologically necessary.

The first question posed is more fundamental; it asks whether or not the biological nature of *Homo sapiens* is such that humans are necessarily inclined to make moral judgments and to accept ethical values, to identify certain actions as either right or wrong. Affirmative answers to this first question do not necessarily determine what the answer to the second question should be. Independent of whether or not humans are necessarily ethical, it remains to be determined whether particular moral prescriptions are in fact determined by our biological nature or whether they are chosen by society or by individuals. Even if we were to conclude that people cannot avoid having moral standards of conduct, it might be that the choice of the particular standards used for judgment would be arbitrary. Or that it depended on some other, nonbiological criteria. The need for having moral values does not necessarily tell us what these moral values should be, just as the capacity for language does not determine which language we shall speak.

The thesis that I propose is that humans are ethical beings by their biological nature. Humans evaluate their behavior as either right or wrong, moral or immoral as a consequence of their eminent intellectual capacities, which include self-awareness and abstract thinking. These intellectual capacities are products of the evolutionary process, but they are distinctively human. Thus, I maintain that ethical behavior is not causally related to the social behavior of animals, including sin and reciprocal "altruism."

A second thesis that I put forward is that the moral norms according to which we evaluate particular actions as morally either good or bad (as well as the grounds that may be used to justify the moral norms) are products of cultural evolution, not of biological evolution. The norms of morality belong, in this respect, to the same category of phenomena as the languages spoken by different peoples, their political and religious institutions, and the arts, sciences, and technology. The moral codes, like these other products of human culture, are often consistent with the biological predispositions of the human species, dispositions we may to some extent share with other animals. But this consistency between ethical norms and biological tendencies is not necessary or universal: It does not apply to all ethical norms in a given society, much less in all human societies.

Moral codes, like any other dimensions of cultural systems, depend on the existence of human biological nature and must be consistent with it in the sense that they could not counteract it without promoting their own demise. Moreover, the acceptance and persistence of moral norms is facilitated whenever they are consistent with biologically conditioned human behaviors. But the moral norms are independent of such behaviors in the sense that some norms may not favor, and may hinder, the survival and reproduction of the individual and its genes, which are the targets of biological evolution. Discrepancies between accepted moral rules and biological survival are, however, necessarily limited in scope or would otherwise lead to the extinction of the groups accepting such discrepant rules.

I argue that the question whether ethical behavior is determined by our biological nature must be answered in the affirmative. By "ethical behavior" I mean here to refer to the urge of *judging* human actions as either good or bad, which is not the same as "good behavior" (i.e., *doing* what is perceived as good instead of what is perceived as evil). Humans exhibit ethical behavior by nature because, as stated above, their biological constitution determines the presence in them of the three conditions for ethical behavior. These conditions are (1) the ability to anticipate the consequences of one's own actions; (2) the ability to make value judgments; and (3) the ability to choose between alternative courses of action. I shall briefly examine each of these abilities and show that they exist as a consequence of the eminent intellectual capacity of human beings.

The ability to anticipate the consequences of one's own actions is the most fundamental of the three conditions required for ethical behavior. Only if I can anticipate that pulling the trigger will shoot the bullet, which in turn will strike and kill my enemy, can the action of pulling the trigger be evaluated as nefarious. Pulling a trigger is not in itself a moral action; it becomes so by virtue of its relevant consequences. My action has an ethical dimension only if I do anticipate these consequences.

The ability to anticipate the consequences of one's actions is closely related to the ability to establish the connection between means and ends; that is, of seeing a means precisely as means, as something that serves a particular end or purpose. This ability to establish the connection between means and their ends requires the ability to anticipate the future and to form mental images of realities not present or not yet in existence.

The ability to establish the connection between means and ends happens to be the fundamental intellectual capacity that has made possible the development of human culture and technology. The evolutionary roots of this capacity may be found in the evolution of bipedal gait, which transformed the anterior limbs of our ancestors from organs of locomotion into organs of manipulation. The hands thereby gradually became organs adept for the construction and use of objects for hunting and other activities that improved survival and reproduction; that is, that increased the reproductive fitness of their carriers.

The construction of tools, however, depends not only on manual dexterity but on perceiving them precisely as tools, as objects that help to perform certain actions; that is, as means that serve certain ends or purposes: a knife for cutting, an arrow for hunting, an animal skin for protecting the body from the cold. The hypothesis I am propounding is that natural selection promoted the intellectual capacity of our biped ancestors, because increased intelligence facilitated the perception of tools as tools, and therefore their construction and use, with the ensuing amelioration of biological survival and reproduction.

The development of the intellectual abilities of our ancestors took place over 2 million years or longer, gradually increasing the ability to connect means with their ends and, hence, the possibility of making ever more complex tools serving remote purposes. The ability to anticipate the future, essential for ethical behavior, is therefore closely associated with the development of the ability to construct tools, an ability that has produced the advanced technologies of modern societies and that is largely responsible for the success of humankind as a biological species.

The second condition for the existence of ethical behavior is the ability to make value judgments, to perceive certain objects or deeds as more desirable than others. Only if I can see the death of my enemy as preferable to his or her survival (or vice versa) can the action leading to his or her demise be thought as moral. If the alternative consequences of an action are neutral with respect to value, the action cannot be characterized as ethical. The ability to make value judgments depends on the capacity for abstraction; that is, on the capacity to perceive actions or objects as members of general classes. This makes it possible to compare objects or actions with one another and to perceive some as more desirable than others. The capacity for abstraction, necessary to perceive individual objects or actions as members of general classes, requires an advanced intelligence such as it exists in humans and apparently in them alone. Thus, I see the ability to make value judgments primarily as an implicit consequence of the enhanced intelligence favored by natural selection in human evolution. Nevertheless, valuing certain objects or

actions and choosing them over their alternatives can be of biological consequence; doing this in terms of general categories can be beneficial in practice.

Moral judgments are a particular class of value judgments; namely, those
where preference is not dictated by one's own interest or profit but by regard for
others, which may cause benefits to particular individuals (altruism) or take into
consideration the interests of a social group to which one belongs. Value judgments indicate preference for what is perceived as good and rejection of what is
perceived as bad; *good* and *bad* may refer to monetary, aesthetic, or all sorts of
other kinds of values. Moral judgments concern the values of right and wrong in
human conduct.

The third condition necessary for ethical behavior is the ability to choose between alternative courses of action. Pulling the trigger can be a moral action only
if I have the option not to pull it. A necessary action beyond our control is not a
moral action: The circulation of the blood and the digestion of food are not moral
actions.

Whether there is free will has been much discussed by philosophers, and this
is not the appropriate place to review the arguments. I will only advance two considerations based on our common-sense experience. One is our profound personal conviction that the possibility of choosing between alternatives is genuine
rather than only apparent.[5] The second consideration is that when we confront a
given situation that requires action on our part, we are able mentally to explore
alternative courses of action, thereby extending the field within which we can exercise our free will. In any case, if there were no free will, there would be no ethical behavior; morality would only be an illusion. The point that I wish to make
here is, however, that free will is dependent on the existence of a well-developed
intelligence, which makes it possible to explore alternative courses of action and
to choose one or another in view of the anticipated consequences.

In summary, my proposal is that ethical behavior is an attribute of the biological make-up of humans and is, in that sense, a product of biological evolution.
But I see no evidence that ethical behavior developed because it was adaptive in
itself. I find it hard to see how evaluating certain actions as either good or evil
(not just choosing some actions rather than others, or evaluating them with respect to their practical consequences) would promote the reproductive fitness of
the evaluators. Nor do I see how there might be some form of "incipient" ethical
behavior that would then be further promoted by natural selection. The three
necessary conditions for there being ethical behavior are manifestations of advanced intellectual abilities.

It rather seems that the likely target of natural selection may have been the development of these advanced intellectual capacities. This development was favored by natural selection because the construction and use of tools improved the
strategic position of our biped ancestors. Once bipedalism evolved and tool using
and toolmaking became possible, those individuals more effective in these functions had a greater probability of biological success. The biological advantage
provided by the design and use of tools persisted long enough so that intellectual
abilities continued to increase, eventually yielding the eminent development of
intelligence that is characteristic of *Homo sapiens.*

CONCLUDING REMARKS ABOUT MORAL CODES

There are many theories concerned with the rational grounds for morality, such as deductive theories that seek to discover the axioms or fundamental principles that determine what is morally correct on the basis of direct moral intuition. There also are theories, like logical positivism or existentialism, that negate rational foundations for morality, reducing moral principles to emotional decisions or to other irrational grounds. Since the publication of Darwin's theory of evolution by natural selection, philosophers as well as biologists have attempted to find in the evolutionary process the justification for moral norms. The common ground to all such proposals is that evolution is a natural process that achieves goals that are desirable and thereby morally good; indeed it has produced humans. Proponents of these ideas claim that only the evolutionary goals can give moral value to human action: whether a human deed is morally right depends on whether it directly or indirectly promotes the evolutionary process and its natural objectives.

Herbert Spencer[6] was perhaps the first philosopher seeking to find the grounds of morality in biological evolution. More recent attempts include those of the distinguished evolutionists J. S. Huxley[7] and C. H. Waddington[8] and of Edward O. Wilson,[9,10] founder of sociobiology as an independent discipline engaged in discovering the biological foundations of social behavior. I have argued elsewhere[11] that the moral theories proposed by Spencer, Huxley, and Waddington are mistaken and fail to avoid the naturalistic fallacy.[12] These authors argue, in one or other fashion, that the standard by which human actions are judged good or evil derives from the contribution the actions make to evolutionary advancement or progress. A blunder of this argumentation is that it is based on value judgments about what is or is not progressive in (particularly human) evolution.[13] There is nothing objective in the evolutionary process itself that makes the success of bacteria, which have persisted for more than 3 billion years and in enormous diversity and numbers, less "progressive" than that of the vertebrates, even though the latter are more complex.[14] Nor are the insects, of which more than 1 million species exist, less successful or less progressive from a purely biological perspective than humans or any other mammal species. Moreover, the proponents of evolution-grounded moral codes fail to demonstrate why the promotion of biological evolution by itself should be the standard to measure what is morally good.

The most recent and most subtle attempt to ground the moral codes on the evolutionary process emanates from the sociobiologists, particularly from E. O. Wilson,[9,10] who starts by proposing that "scientists and humanists should consider together the possibility that the time has come for ethics to be removed temporarily from the hands of the philosophers and biologicized."[15] The sociobiologists' argument is that our perception that morality exists is an epigenetic manifestation of our genes, which so manipulate humans as to make them believe that some behaviors are morally "good" so that people behave in ways that are good for their genes. Humans might not otherwise pursue these behaviors (altruism, for example) because their genetic benefit is not apparent except to sociobiologists after the development of their discipline.[16]

As I have argued elsewhere, the sociobiologists' account of the evolution of the moral sense is misguided.[11,17] As I have argued, we make moral judgments as a consequence of our eminent intellectual abilities, not as an innate way for achieving biological gain. Moreover, the sociobiologists' position may be interpreted as calling for the proposition that those norms of morality should be considered supreme that achieve the most biological (genetic) gain (because that is, in their view, why the moral sense evolved at all). This, in turn, would justify social preferences, including racism and even genocide, that many of us (sociobiologists included) judge morally obtuse and even heinous.

The evaluation of moral codes or human actions must take into account biological knowledge, but biology is insufficient for determining which moral codes are, or should be, accepted. This may be reiterated by returning to the analogy with human languages. Our biological nature determines the sounds that we can or cannot utter and also constrains human language in other ways. But a language's syntax and vocabulary are not determined by our biological nature (otherwise, there could not be a multitude of tongues) but are products of human culture. Likewise, moral norms are not determined by biological processes but by cultural traditions and principles that are products of human history.

NOTES

1. A. C. Wilson and R. L. Cann, "The Recent African Genesis of Humans," *Scientific American,* April 1992: 68–73.

2. Lee Berger, a paleoanthropologist at the University of Witwatersrand in Johannesburg, announcing that two fossil human footprints had been discovered along Langebaan Lagoon, 100 km north of Capetown, stated, "Whoever left these footprints has the potential of being the ancestor of all modern humans. If it was a woman, she could conceivably even be Eve." He, of course, was referring to the "mitochondrial Eve," not to the biblical Eve [Rich Gore, "Tracking the First of Our Kind," *National Geographic* 129(3): 92–99, September 1997]. Other examples are cited in note 4.

3. The theoretical number of ancestors for any one individual becomes enormous after some tens of generations, but "inbreeding" occurs: After some generations, ancestors appear more than once in the genealogy.

4. F. J. Ayala, "The Myth of Eve: Molecular Biology and Human Origins," *Science* 270: 1930–1936 (1995).

5. Confucious put it thus: "One may rob an army of its commander-in-chief; one cannot deprive the humblest man of his free will." *The Analects of Confucius,* trans. and notes by Simon Leys (New York: Norton, 1996).

6. H. Spencer, *The Principles of Ethics* (London Willams & Norgate 1893).

7. T. H. Huxley and J. S. Huxley, *Touchstone for Ethics* (New York: Harper, 1947); J. S. Huxley, *Evolution in Action* (New York: Harper, 1953).

8. C. H. Waddington, *The Ethical Animal* (London: Allen & Unwin, 1960).

9. E. O. Wilson, *Sociobiology: the New Synthesis* (Cambridge, MA: Harvard University Press, 1975).

10. E. O. Wilson, *On Human Nature* (Cambridge, MA: Harvard University Press, 1978).

11. F. J. Ayala, "The biological roots of morality," *Biology and Philosophy* 2: 235–252 (1987).

12. The "naturalistic fallacy" consists in identifying what "is" with what "ought" to be (G. E. Moore, *Principia Ethica,* Cambridge University Press, 1903). This error was already pointed out by Hume: "In every system of morality which I have hitherto met with I have always remarked that the author proceeds for some time in the ordinary way of reasoning . . . when of a sudden I am surprised to find, that instead of the usual copulations of propositions, *is* and *is not,* I meet with no proposition that is not connected with an *ought* or *ought not.* This change is imperceptible; but is, however, of the last consequence. For as this *ought* or *ought not* expresses some new relation or affirmation, it is necessary that it should be observed and explained; and at the same time a reason should be given, for what seems altogether inconceivable, how this new relation can be a deduction from others, which are entirely different from it" [D. Hume, *Treatise*

of Human Nature (Oxford: Oxford University Press [1740], 1978].

13. F. J. Ayala, "The evolutionary concept of progress," in G. A. Almond et al., eds., *Progress and Its Discontents* (Berkeley: University of California Press, 1982), pp. 106–124.

14. See S. J. Gould, *Full House: The Spread of Excellence from Plato to Darwin* (New York: Harmony Books, 1996).

15. E. O. Wilson, *Sociobiology: The New Synthesis* (Cambridge, MA: Harvard University Press, 1975), pp. 562.

16. M. Ruse, *Taking Darwin Seriously: A Naturalistic Approach to Philosophy* (Oxford: Basil Blackwell 1986); M. Ruse, "Evolutionary Ethics: A Phoenix Arisen," *Zygon* 21: 95–112 (1986); M. Ruse and E. O. Wilson, "Moral Philosophy as Applied Science," *Philosophy: Journal of the Royal Institute of Philosophy* 61: 173–192 (1986).

17. F. J. Ayala, "The Difference of Being Human: Ethical Behavior as an Evolutionary Byproduct," in H. Rolston, III, ed., *Biology, Ethics and the Origin of Life* (Boston and London: Jones and Bartlett, 1995), pp. 113–135.

16 Sociobiology and Moral Discourse

Loyal Rue   *Luther College*

In the eighteenth century, when Linnaeus was working out the details of his famous system for classifying biological species, he came across a major problem: what to do with human beings! Should he put them into the same category with the great apes, or should he put them in a separate category? At one point along the way he says this: "As a natural historian I have yet to find any characteristics which enable man to be distinguished on scientific principles from the ape."[1]

According to strict anatomical standards, humans belong squarely with the apes. But Linnaeus was a bit uneasy about this kinship because he could see that, judging by behavioral standards, humans belong in a world apart.

Linnaeus, of course, didn't have the benefit of genetic theory to guide him—but even if he did the problem wouldn't have gone away. Today we have firm data to show that humans and common chimpanzees share almost 99 percent of their genetic inheritance. In fact, in genetic terms, humans are more closely related to chimps than gorillas are. And yet there remains that immense divide between human existence and simian existence. As Terry Deacon puts it, "Biologically, we are just another ape. Mentally, we are a new phylum of organisms."[2] So the dilemma persists.

In some ways this dilemma represents the great puzzle of our human condition. My own feeling is that if we could somehow come to terms with, understand, *both* our intimate kinship with the apes *and* our undeniable distance from them, then we might come a long way forward in self-understanding.

It is doubtful that we will ever come the whole way in understanding the human condition, but we have taken a few important steps. And I would like to suggest that the discipline of sociobiology has been one of our most valuable guides.

One of the most interesting things about the discipline of sociobiology is that it results from a huge mistake. The mistake was made by the social sciences in general, which did us all the disservice of failing to take Darwin seriously. Darwin, of course, claimed that humans descended from animals by the process of natural selection. The social sciences don't actually deny this, and they do manage to pay some measure of lip service to the Darwinian revolution, but they have continued to regard the insights of this revolution as trivial with respect to human self-understanding. They have remained aloof, vaguely tolerant yet deeply suspicious.

To take Darwin seriously means, among other things, to place the study of human nature squarely within the context of evolutionary biology—which the social sciences have consistently failed to do. Instead, social science theory has developed in ways totally separate from the evolutionary paradigm. As a result, the social sciences adopted a perspective broadly known as social determinism, a view reflected in these statements by Emile Durkheim, the father of modern sociology: "Human nature is merely the indeterminate material that the social factor molds and transforms. Only social facts can explain other social facts."[3]

The first steps to correct this view were taken by the European discipline of ethology, the systematic study of animal behavior. Ethologists were, basically, zoologists who began to explore animal behavior from an evolutionary perspective. They insisted that many behavioral traits of animals, no less than physical traits, were acquired by genetic inheritance. Behavior, in other words, was subject to evolution by natural selection. Among nonhumans, anyway, some social facts could *not* be explained without a few biological facts. Ethology took Darwin seriously. What ethology did *not* take seriously was the study of human beings. That is, it focused almost exclusively on the behavior of nonhuman animals.

Ethology started things moving, but it was left to sociobiology to apply the full force of the evolutionary perspective to human behavior. Sociobiology insists that we will never have a satisfying account of human nature until we recognize the full extent to which human behavior bears the influence of biological systems. Human nature is far from being indeterminate material, and mere social facts are not sufficient to explain all social facts.

Sociobiologists have pointed to a whole class of social facts that social determinism can't very well explain—that is, all those universal behaviors that show up in every culture despite radical differences in social conditioning. Sociobiology has done a terrific job of identifying several of these invariant human behavior patterns and giving us convincing arguments about how they amount to adaptive biological strategies that come to us by way of genetic inheritance. Many of these patterns have to do with reproductive strategies—for example, the optimal mating strategy for males is to go for quantity, while females go for quality; males tend to engage in mate guarding behavior; parents invest themselves differently with respect to sons and daughters; and so on. These and many other behavior patterns can be shown to conform to the logic of evolutionary biology. The only way to account for these universal social facts is to assume that in some measure they come under the control of genes. This program of seeking out the role of genes in human behavior has been very enlightening. But it hasn't been without problems—not the least of which is that sociobiological explanations are easily construed as arguments for hard-wired genetic determinism, a view that is just as difficult to maintain as extreme social determinism.

So what is sociobiology? Basically, it's an attempt to step into the breech and to put social science back on the track of evolutionary thinking. Sociobiology, properly seen, *is* evolutionary social science. It is evolutionary psychology, evolutionary sociology, evolutionary anthropology, and even evolutionary politics and economics, all rolled into one.

So now the question becomes, How can evolutionary social science help us to come to terms with the persistent problem faced by Linnaeus? As long as we're back on Linnaeus I might just report that he dealt with the problem by tinkering with his categories. In the first edition of his *System of Nature* he put humans together with apes under the grouping he called anthropomorpha, but in later editions this category disappears and he becomes more open to separating humans from the apes. We are, he finally decided, *sui generis*—unique, nothing like us. It was finally the moral aspects of human life that impressed Linnaeus the most. We transcend the conditions of our simian cousins because we alone are moral beings: "I well know what a splendidly great difference there is between a man and a beast when I look at them from a point of view of morality."[4]

For Linnaeus, at least, we are *sui generis* because we are moral. But what does this tell us, really? And come to think of it, is it even true that we alone are moral? There are some pretty serious primatologists out there who think that thievery, cruelty, and injustice are just as irritating to chimps as they are to us. And kindness, generosity, and reconciliation are equally cherished by chimps. Chimps at least have interests, and probably even values. But do they engage in moral behavior? What *is* moral behavior anyway? And how did any creature come to have it? That's the modern form of the Linnaean problem. Evolutionary social science suggests that if we want to understand moral behavior and how we come to have it, then we might begin by asking about the evolution of behavior itself. I'll give you what I take to be the basic outlines of the story.

Let's begin with the painfully obvious point that all living things behave. Bacteria behave. Algae behave. Ants and birds behave. There's no dispute about that. The story gets interesting only when we ask *why* they behave as they do. Evolutionary biologists have a short and simple answer to the why question: Organisms behave in ways that are designed by natural selection to maximize their reproductive fitness. That is, all living things have it in their nature to behave in ways that propagate their own genes, and those of their close relatives, indefinitely into the future. This is far from being a trivial truth—it's what you might call a superordinate truth, an organizing principle in evolutionary biology and evolutionary social science. Moral behavior, then, like *all* behavior, should be viewed under the rubric of fitness maximizing behavior.

Another fairly obvious point is that all behaviors are mediated. Let me introduce a footnote here. It's a fundamental category mistake to suggest that behavior per se is heritable. Nobody inherits behavior. What we inherit are genes that code for proteins that build the tissues of mechanisms that mediate behavior. So the evolution of behavior is really evolution in the *mediation* of behavior—in the organizers, the mechanisms of behavior.

This focus on the mediators of behavior gives us a way of thinking that can make use of sociobiological insights, without getting ourselves trapped in the simplistic and misleading notion that there are genes for behaviors—which there are *not*. There are genes for various mediators, which more or less heavily bias our responses to factors in the environment. That is, the genes make lots of promises for how an organism will behave, but which promises are kept will depend on circumstances in the environment.

Sociobiology helped to bring us to our senses concerning the biology of human behavior, and now we can begin to move forward in telling a more complete story. The general drift of the story is that, over evolutionary time, there has been a gradual process of systematic development in which behaviors become mediated by ever more complicated mechanisms, which enable ever more complicated interactions between organisms and their environments. As the mediation of behavior becomes more complex, we see also greater variability in behavior.

In the simplest organisms behaviors are mediated by straightforward bio-chemical reactions—simple lock and key mechanisms that govern the interactions of molecules. This level of behavior never drops out of the picture. In fact, we can say that all behavior—whether it's an alga swimming after a sunbeam or an ambassador negotiating a treaty—*all* behavior ultimately comes down to lock and key molecular systems. If the biochemistry stops, behavior stops. So it's all locks and keys. But here's the point: There are lots of different systematic ways to orchestrate all these locks and keys. The evolution of behavior is a story about these different ways.

At the level of one-celled organisms the orchestration is described by the dynamics of chemical reactions. But when we get to larger, multicellular organisms you have to add in new levels of orchestration to govern the behavior of lots of different cells. In larger organisms you have lots of different cell lines that get involved in organizing the basic chemistry.

When you get neurons on the scene, this process of systematic modulation can get terribly complex. Take the *reflex system,* for example. A reflex system is still biochemistry, but it's highly organized. A reflex system mediates hard-wired behaviors, such as when the pupil of your eye widens in response to dimming the lights, or when you breathe rhythmically during sleep. Lots of new behaviors become possible once reflex systems get organized. Reflex systems are great, and we've inherited quite a few of them. But if that's all you've got to organize your chemistry, then you won't have a very interesting life. Life gets more interesting when physiological drive systems come on line. These systems, like hunger and sex drives, are much more flexible systems, involving more complicated chains of chemical reactions. When a physiological drive mechanism (hunger, let's say) gets activated then the organism begins to look for food, but its behavior is more variable and not just the hard-wired reflex of a frog stabbing its tongue at a fly.

Mammals, of course, have lots of reflex systems and physiological drive systems to help in the mediation of behavior. But in mammals we also begin to see the evolution of emotional systems, which are even more variable and more learning dependent than drive systems. You find emotional systems regulating all sorts of behaviors, in part because the emotional centers in the brain are well connected to lots of other mediation systems. This is what makes it possible for emotional systems to interfere with drive systems—as, for example, when fear interrupts a search for food. Emotional systems are very important for the regulation of social behaviors such as kin selection and reciprocal altruism—not only in our own species but in several other mammals as well. In fact, it's very likely that emotional systems evolved as mechanisms to enable more complex social arrangements that were called for in response to more demanding ecological constraints.

And then, in addition to emotional systems, we also have the mediating influence of cognitive systems, which make it possible for organisms to construct internal neural maps of things and events and processes in the external world and to use this information in organizing behavior.

Now let's go back and take the story from the very beginning. For the first several eons after the Big Bang the only sensible discipline in the universe would have been physics—it was all physics. You don't get chemistry happening until there are lots of elements around to get involved in chemical bonds. But as soon as galaxies get formed and supernovae start to pop off, then chemistry begins. And then for several more eons it's all physics and chemistry, no biology. As far as we can tell, biology didn't begin to make sense in our universe until about 4 billion years ago, when life emerged out of the chemical soup of our planet. Physics, chemistry, and biology are all disciplines that describe systematic organization in the behavior of matter.

Within biology we find lots and lots of deeply interactive and often competing mediating systems, all of which have an influence on behavior by modulating biochemical reactions, either directly or indirectly. The mediation of behavior in higher mammals is ultimately biochemical, but it's anything but straightforward. It's extremely complex and multidynamic, including various systems for reflexes, drives, emotions, and cognitions.

At this point we are drawn right back to the Linnaean problem. It happens that we share *all* these mediation systems with the chimps. Chimp biochemistry is fundamentally the same as human biochemistry. No one has discovered a hormone or a neurotransmitter that is exclusive to humans. Chimps also have reflex systems, physiological drive systems, emotional systems, and cognitive systems. These are heritable systems—we share them with the chimps because they were passed on to both species by our common ancestors. So why is it that we're not more like the chimps? If we share in common all these systems for organizing behavior, then why is our behavior so radically different? What is it that we have that they don't have? The difference is that we have symbolic systems and chimps don't. And it turns out that symbol systems can function as very powerful instruments for regulating these heritable systems.

There's something quite different about these new, exclusively human symbolic mediation systems—they are constructed by social interactions between individuals, and they exist outside the body. In order for these mediation systems to work they have to be internalized, or learned. The process of learning a symbol system amounts to reprogramming the inherited systems so that their default behaviors can be overridden. This process of symbolic reprogramming varies with respect to the different heritable systems.

Let's look at the cognitive systems first. Here I'm going to make the very large assumption that Terry Deacon's theory of language/brain coevolution tells the correct story. Deacon argues that the newest parts of the brain (those parts that manipulate symbols) actually evolved under the selective pressure of increasingly complex symbol systems. In effect, language helped to shape the cognitive systems of the human brain. More complex language systems created selective pressure for brains that were more symbolically competent—which resulted in still more complex language systems, then bigger brains, and so on. This means that our cognitive systems have been built by heredity to be invaded by and dominated by symbol systems. So with respect to our cognitive systems the process of symbolic reprogramming is almost automatic—kids have a built-in bias to learn language, and they do so with almost no effort at all. This is not the case with chimp cognitive systems. You can get chimps to use language—sort of—but the process of reprogramming is difficult and incomplete. It's easy and cheap for a child to learn language, but it's difficult and expensive for a chimp—and without constant effort the chimp quickly defaults away from language use.

But now let's consider another set of mediating systems, the emotions. These systems, it appears, do *not* have the same openness to symbolic domination that the cognitive systems do. For some reason they did not enter into a coevolutionary contract with symbol systems, which means that we are left with emotional systems that are very close to the ones the chimps have. This does not mean that cultural symbol systems cannot reprogram the emotions at all—they certainly can—it only means that the process of reprogramming will be difficult and costly. The hereditary biases in our emotional systems are so strong that it takes a focused, diligent effort to override them. This is why it's so easy for kids to master a language but so difficult for them to master their emotions. In the case of emotional systems the default behaviors programmed in by natural selection are always very close to the surface.

Now I want to say something about morality. Humans are faced with two forms of morality—the moral code programmed into their emotional systems by heredity (i.e., the default morality), and the moral code reprogrammed into them by their culture (i.e., the override morality). The default morality is rather chimplike, and it is already *in* the mediation system. It consists of many genetic promises about how a human will behave. But the override morality is different. It is constructed outside the body by moral discourse, and it is brought into the body by the process of moral nurturing.

One of the lessons of sociobiology has been that our emotional systems are powerful mediators of behavior, and they resist being dominated by artificial systems. These systems keep on insisting to us that we should keep the promises of the default morality, that we are really intended to live as the apes do—to follow their reproductive strategies, to engage in their territorial behavior, to practice their sexual politics, to form their kind of social order, and so on. But against these apelike emotional urges are placed the moral demands of socially constructed standards of behavior, imploring our efforts to override the default behaviors in favor of artificial behaviors. So we are constantly conflicted between our primate programming and our cultural reprogramming. We *can* reprogram the emotions, but it's a very difficult and labor-intensive undertaking, something like teaching a chimp to use language.

This is one of the principal functions of religious traditions—to reprogram the emotions so that we will be motivated to override our default morality. A religious tradition amounts to a coherent collection of stories, images, standards for behavior, and so on—in other words, a symbolic system that gets involved in the mediation of behavior. All religious traditions have a cognitive component to them, but their primary focus is to reprogram the emotional systems.

Let me mention just a few of these systems and try to show how the central images of a religious tradition are designed to engage and to reeducate them. I will use examples from Christianity, but a similar story can be told for other religious traditions. Bear in mind that the great apes are capable of each of these emotional responses, but they are not, of course, capable of responding to religious symbols. The first emotion is affection. When a person feels affection for another person, he or she is predisposed to make sacrifices for the person. We want to do nice things for those we like. The Christian images of the infant Jesus, Madonna and child, and the good shepherd are particularly effective in eliciting an affectionate response. Sympathy: Higher primates can experience a sense of sympathy, especially when they see a conspecific in a state of suffering. Sympathy elicits a motivation to help—as it does when the Christian is aroused by the image of a helpless and innocent man suffering on a cross at the hands of merciless authorities. Gratitude: Higher primates are capable of gratitude—an emotional bias to repay favors. This is what Christians are moved to feel when they are reminded that Jesus' death was a selfless act undertaken for the sake of others. Jesus' sacrifice is a gift that calls for repayment. Finally, I want to mention resentment, not exactly a positive emotion, but certainly an effective regulator of behavior in many primate species. A symbolic exploitation of resentment is found in the story of Judas, who betrayed the altruistic Jesus. Judas has become a symbol in Christian culture for the self-seeking cheater.

These central images of the Christian tradition play on the emotional systems that we have received from the evolutionary past. They pull the emotional triggers and direct the emotional responses toward service to Jesus. They move people to love Jesus, to have sympathy for Jesus, to be grateful to Jesus, and to resent those who don't. When you love Jesus, feel sympathy for him, and are grateful to him, then you will be moved to follow him—to become Christlike, and to practice the universal brotherhood he practiced and preached. That is, when these symbols have done their job, then Christians will be motivated to override the many temptations to act like chimps and will freely sacrifice and cooperate for the welfare of others.

Chimps can sacrifice and cooperate too, but normally only within the limits of the local group—with kin, primarily. Chimps can't manage anything as global as universal brotherhood. Nor can we, apart from the mediation of symbols to help us override our default morality. It's a matter of keeping old genetic promises by default, or making new promises by design. It's a matter of relaxing to the urges of the evolutionary past, or rising to the challenge of expanding our affections, our sympathies, our gratitude, and even our resentment to achieve a larger sense of solidarity and cooperation that includes not only the local troop, but all of humankind—and even beyond our own kind to include all the form and fountains of life itself. Reeducating the emotions to a larger promise will take a lot of work on the part of teachers and learners alike. And here perhaps is the deepest lesson in self-understanding offered to us by sociobiology: that without constant efforts at moral discourse and emotional nurturing our biology will be our destiny.

NOTES

1. Quoted in: Gunnar Broberg, "Linnaeus's Classification of Man," in Tore Frangsmyr (ed.), *Linnaeus: The Man and His Work* (Berkeley: University of California Press, 1983), p. 172.

2. T. Deacon, *The Symbolic Species* (New York: W.W. Norton & Co., 1997), p. 23.

3. E. Durkheim, *The Rules of the Sociological Method* (Glencoe, IL: Free Press, 1895/1962), p. 103

4. Quoted in: Gunnar Broberg, "Linnaeus's Classification of Man," in Tore Frangsmyr (ed.), *Linnaeus: The Man and His Work* (Berkeley: University of California Press, 1983), p. 167.

17 The Evolutionary Roots of Morality in Theological Perspective

Stephen J. Pope   *Boston College*

For all the controversy over the evolution of morality, introducing the word *theology* adds another level of complexity in that this discipline is as diverse and multifaceted as any other. Theology was classically defined by St. Anselm as "faith seeking understanding." Faith takes on a bewildering variety of forms, reflecting the fact that people are influenced by their own individual life experiences and family backgrounds, but also by different histories, communities of origin, ethnicity, language, and so on, and therefore the reflection on faith generated from these diverse backgrounds will itself be radically diverse. In one sense, then, there is no generic "Christian theology," only Greek Orthodox, Lutheran, my own Roman Catholic, and so forth. And of course a variety of theological perspectives or schools develop within as well as across these different communions.

Theology as an intellectual discipline attempts to help us to think more clearly, more adequately, and more profoundly about God and things related to God. Theology typically reflects on its object, theos, "up close," from a personal point of view characterized by commitment, loyalty, and trust. But because theology engages logos, it also strives to be rigorous, fair minded, and methodologically careful. The depth of the subject matter of theology is matched with its comprehensiveness: God and all things in relation to God. Intellectual honesty requires theology to accept truth from wherever it comes. God is the source of both reason and revelation, and truth from one source cannot contradict truth from the other. Disagreements in science and religion are capable of reconciliation because these sources are two valid but distinct modes of apprehending what is true.

On theological grounds, then, we are required not only to acknowledge but also to appropriate critically the information and insights produced by the life sciences, including those pertaining to morality. The doctrine of creation is expressed in the Nicene Profession of Faith in God as the "maker of heaven and earth, of all things seen and unseen." The doctrine of creation refers not just to the cause of the beginning of the world but, even more important, to a relation between the world and God—that of radical dependence of the former on the latter. It does not offer a final scientific explanation of that relation or of that cause, nor does it produce a scientific theory of how human beings (along with a lot of other things) were produced by the long and halting evolutionary process. Evolutionary theory provides the most plausible scientific framework for understanding the proximate means used by God to generate species, including *Homo sapiens*.

EVOLUTIONARY ROOTS OF MORALITY

How might theological ethics itself approach the evolutionary roots of morality? Resolving this question depends on what theory of evolutionary roots is being proposed. I will mention three distinctive positions.

Let me begin with a few generalizations. First, most evolutionary theorists seem to agree that human communities have evolved to need, in some form or other, the social institution that we call morality. Neuroscientist Antonio Damasio[1] believes that morality has its origin in the emergence of the capacity for suffering and the awareness of significant vulnerability to further suffering, made possible by an evolved ability to remember the past, to anticipate the future, and to make and execute plans affecting the future. The primatologist Frans de Waal[2] suggests that we have evolved, as social animals, to need reasonable degrees of order in community, widely shared moral standards that can organize interactions in a way that minimizes conflict, reliable ways of identifying property ownership, commonly held arrangements regarding mating and the rearing of children, and some trust in that the community will provide justice in cases of intracommunal conflict and necessary defense in the face of intercommunal conflict. These are, not coincidentally, all the object of "second table" of the Decalogue (the Ten Commandments), but also of most other moral codes as well. I take it that there is no specific biological drive for morality, but rather that as social animals we are constituted in such a way that morality is a feature of all human communities.

Second, morality depends on evolutionary roots established in human physiology because everything human depends on the biochemical and neurological substrates that are necessary conditions of human action. Moral nobility need not be identified with disembodied cognition or volition. Love, altruism, or other free acts of the will, Damasio properly notes, are not thrown into doubt by the fact that they are made possible by brain chemistry, any more than they are thrown into doubt by the sheer fact that they contribute to a person's survival or are transmitted by proper social and emotional nurturance in childhood.

Biological substrates can sometimes be much more than "necessary conditions for action," though. They can at times give positive support for what we would consider morally appropriate affections or attitudes. For example, the body produces the chemical substance oxytocin, which influences a wide range of behavior, including maternal caregiving and emotional attachment between sexual partners.[3] More broadly, the performance of altruistic acts can be accompanied by "positive somatic markers."[4] They can also have the opposite, less desirable effect, which I will discuss later.

Disagreements arise over the connection between morality and evolution. Some disputation is occasioned by excessive ambiguity. Damasio, for example, recognizes that while elaborate moral codes are transmitted culturally rather than genetically, "some innate mechanisms . . . are the likely basis for some ethical structures used by humans."[5] At another point he describes feelings as the "base for what we humans have described for millennia as the human soul or spirit."[6] Unfortunately, Damasio is not clear about how exactly this "basis" functions in the moral life or influences human conduct. The word *basis* is itself ambiguous: It can function causally, as in "the basis of Jack's obesity is a physiological disorder," or it can function supportively, as a necessary condition, as in "footwork is the basis for a good three point shot." In the latter case, bad footwork makes a good shot improbable, but good footwork does not necessary guarantee a good shot. Here *basis* is a necessary but not sufficient condition. In the former, it is given much stronger causal attribution.

The reductionist version draws a strong causal connection between evolution and morality. It argues that morality itself has evolved because it is adaptive. This view holds that not only that morality as an institution is adaptive but also that particular moral standards are nothing but strategies that have evolved to promote reproductive interests. For example, Buss, who sometimes fits this type, holds that men are prone to enforce the prohibition on extramarital sex against their mates and to react with passionate jealousy when this norm has been violated. He suggests not only that the relevant norms and emotions serve the reproductive interests of males in our society, but also that they exist because and only because they promote these interests. Philosopher Michael Ruse pushes the morality as adaptive more boldly when he writes that "we believe what we believe about morality because it is adaptively useful for us to have such beliefs—*that is all there is to it.*"[7]

The second position appears to be at the other end of the spectrum. This kind of position is illustrated in the work of evolutionary biologist Francisco J. Ayala, who writes that "ethical behavior is rooted in the biological makeup of man. . . . [It] did not evolve because it was adaptive in itself, but rather as the indirect outcome of the evolution of eminent intellectual abilities."[8] Ayala holds that three evolved capacities, similar to those proposed by Damasio above, provide the basis of morality: "Humans exhibit ethical behavior because their biological constitution determines the presence in them of the three necessary, and jointly sufficient, conditions for ethical behavior. These conditions are: (i) the ability to anticipate the consequences of one's own actions; (ii) the ability to make value judgments; and (iii) the ability to choose between alternative courses of action."[9] This strongly nonreductionist approach to evolution and morality employs the less deterministic notion of basis and acknowledges that something can be supported by (in the weak, nonreductive sense) an evolved base without itself having been directly caused (in the reductive sense) by that base.

Ayala's position, which so strongly emphasizes the cultural basis of morality, seems to be the opposite of Ruse's, but his second condition for morality, that of value judgments, may leave open the possibility that evolved emotional and cognitive predispositions may incline human beings to adopt some courses of action more easily than others. In any case, this is proposed in a third view, that of anthropologist William Irons, who holds that morality came to exist because it allowed the formation of "better and more unified groups on the basis of indirect reciprocity."[10] Irons agrees with Ayala that the evolution of basic human cognitive and emotional capacities was a necessary condition for the appearance of morality, but he also echoes in his own way Ruse's belief that the ought-generating "moral sense" was selected because it helped its agents obtain their reproductive goals, especially in the environments of evolution.[11] Irons's position seems finally closer to Ruse, not in the claim that morality is an illusion but at least in its embrace of the principle that, despite frequent enough divergences, "culture is something individuals use and manipulate in pursuit of the proximate goals that, in the environments of human evolution, were reproductively advantageous."[12]

Is it possible to integrate what is valuable in these three competing perspectives? It seems reasonable to hold that evolution has shaped profoundly some of important levels of our emotional and cognitive constitutions as human beings. At what point morality actually emerged from social life is hard to say, and no one seems to have been able to give a convincing argument that "explains" the origin of morality. We might speculate that emerging social conventions reflecting forms of patterned reciprocity would generate monitoring of compliance, attempts to subvert dominant arrangements, retaliation, and internal acceptance of conventions. But as de Waal points out, it is not possible, at least yet, to identify where fear of punishment and fear of being caught is transcended by a more identifiable and distinctive "moral sense" of being obligated by what is right—if indeed this sense is not a pecularialy Western, and notably Stoic and Kantian, theme that we are projecting onto human nature as such.

In any case, it seems reasonable to hold that, rather than particular moral beliefs or a fixed moral code "engraved" in the psyches of all human beings in all societies, the evolutionary process has created a human emotional constitution characterized by general proclivities, desires, or valuational preferences. Human beings inherit evolved proclivities to learn more easily some things rather than others (the theory of "prepared learning"); for example, a newborn child learns to recognize faces and to feel some things more easily than others (e.g., attachment to parents more readily than hospitality toward strangers). Other things being equal, natural proclivities play a role in loyalty to one's own group more than to others, readiness for altruism to kin more than strangers, a willingness to reward those who cooperate and a tendency to punish those who violate reciprocity, and a general desire to treat others the way they treat us. Particular communities at particular times and places attach moral valuation to these preferential tendencies, some channeling parental investment in one direction, toward immediate offspring, others in another direction, toward overlapping caregiving within an extended family.

This accords with the classical position of Aristotle, who, I think, is generally correct to hold that each child is born with a range of fairly indeterminate natural abilities, powers, or capacities (*dunameis*) that exist in human nature prior to practice and that are gradually shaped by training and instruction (or habituation) to become the adult's "second nature" (i.e., the virtues or vices that constitute character).[13] Biological predispositions tend to be fairly general in their directionality, as in the notion of "open programs."[14] We are capable of experiencing a variety of basic emotions but they can be subject to human evaluation and direction. Our moral responses to these predispositions may often be implementation, but they can also include introspection, criticism, deliberate redirection, and revision of the place they have in our lives.

This generality indicates why we should expect a dazzling variety of moral codes throughout history and between cultures. Our evolved specieswide proclivity to aid closely related kin, for example, takes a wide variety of different expressions in different locales. Moreover, and more disagreeably to the pure sociobiologist, the deeply ingrained specieswide proclivity to maximize inclusive fitness itself is subject not only to delay and redirection but even to abandonment by all sorts of people (e.g., missionaries and utopians, artists and poets, prophets and mystics) because of what they consider to be warranted by the highest good.

IMPLICATIONS FOR THEOLOGICAL ETHICS

I would now like at least to mention if not explicate fully four important ethical implications of this approach to the evolutionary roots of morality. First, natural law theory is the traditional resource for thinking about moral norms in the Catholic tradition. It should be noted that natural law theory itself is not static (except in the minds of some of its proponents), and natural law theory itself is currently undergoing its own significant kind of "evolution." Natural law theory infers from the doctrine of creation that the general principle that natural desires that human beings share with other animals are not only biologically significant or interpersonally gratifying, but morally good when ordered ethically.

In the First Part of the *Summa theologiae,* Thomas Aquinas described the soul as the "form of the body" and rejected the alternative, more dualistic view of the soul as a small "pilot in a ship" inside a body that it controls[15] (see 1, 75–76 in Thomas Aquinas 1946, 363–382). This claim supports the recognition of human beings as biophysical entities rather than isolated ethereal souls only artificially attached for a brief time to material bodies. This is a claim that warrants both a sacramental vision of human desires and an ethical commitment to basic rights of bodily integrity.

This applies to the full range of natural desires, be they social desires for companionship, intellectual desires to know, or sensual desires for food and sex. The good life is guided by reason but allows for the healthy and balanced expression of the full range of human passions. Thus it can take seriously evolutionary psychologist David Buss's analyses of evolved psychological mechanisms and sexual strategies, both for their descriptive and explanatory insights but also for their ability to provide material for ethical reflection on what might constitute positive and negative expressions of human sexuality. Theologians might associate Buss's observations about the relatively indiscriminate nature of sexual desire in males, for example, with the sensitive account of "concupiscence," or disordered sexual desire, classically depicted in St. Augustine's *Confessions.*

Second, evolved natural emotional and mental proclivities are pervaded by a profound moral ambiguity. They are capable of motivating good or bad character and leading to right or wrong behavior, depending on the agent's intentions and other relevant circumstances. Kin altruism can be good if expressed in ordered parental care and filial loyalty but can be evil if leading to moral myopia that is indifferent to the suffering of nonkin or xenophobic suspicion of strangers. This moral ambiguity is characteristic of the juxtaposition of elementary adaptations in modern human psyches. Buss hypothesizes that the relatively stronger indiscriminate male desire for sexual variety was an evolutionary solution to the crucial challenge of gaining sexual access to a variety of women in ancestral conditions. This evolved sexual tendency was highly adaptive in prehistory but causes a great deal of havoc in modern society. "Men [today] do not always act on this desire," Buss argues, "but it is a motivating force."[16]

Third, understanding more fully the evolutionary roots of morality therefore can also serve a critical function. I take it that personal integrity involves evaluating spontaneous objects of desire in light of our comprehensive beliefs about the good life and our fundamental commitments. Evolutionary theory can alert us to obstacles to personal integrity that come from within us, by nature (along side those that come from individual character defects).

For example, it alerts us to innate tendencies to engage in deception, to ignore our own oversights, to minimize our own moral weaknesses and vices, and to justify our biases and those of our friends. Evolutionary psychology, for example, is particularly adept at attending to ways in which professional advertisers manipulate psychological mechanisms and to ways in which morality can be co-opted to provide ideological support for nonmoral ends (e.g., in Buss's analysis, for certain kinds of mating strategies). Evolutionary theory strives to get to the roots of many human disappointments and conflicts and thereby to understand more accurately both the depth of the human predicament and the level of commitment required if our conflicts are to be ameliorated more effectively.

Neurophysiology also alerts us to the dangers of bias. "Somatic markers" facilitate decisions in complex social situations but they can be disordered as well, as in uncritical "obedience, conformity, [and] the desire to preserve self-esteem."[17] Bias can be felt "in the bones," as when a person experiences "unpleasant body states" when she encounters those she finds repulsive, be they mentally ill homeless people asking for aid or an affluent interracial couple on a date. The body's neurally based drive to reduce unpleasant body states can and sometimes does act as a countermoral force that needs to be held in check.

Fourth, understanding the evolutionary roots of morality underscores the value of regarding moral progress in terms of the proper training, directing, and tutoring of the emotions. "Knowledge of the conditions that favor each mating strategy," Buss tells us, "gives us the possibility of choosing which to activate and which to leave dormant."[18] We can employ knowledge to avoid the kinds of conditions that tend to activate what we identify to be undesirable aspects of our evolved "incentive system." Conversely, at least ideally we can deliberately create conditions that elicit desirable kinds of behavior. This is as true of a social ethos and its institutions, or what sociologist Robert Bellah and his colleagues call a community's "social ecology," as it is of personal moral development and individual pursuit of the good life.[19]

In Damasio's feedback loop, cognitive processes are induced by neurochemical substances, but neurochemical substances are also induced by cognitive processes. Habitual action shapes and organizes emotional states and their neurochemical profile.[20] In the language of Thomas Aquinas, then, virtue is not "implanted" in us by nature but formed by habit, and the moral life is a matter of gradually shaping these emotional responses (including what Damasio identifies as their underlying neural machinery), into forms that promote the human good.[21] Moral conversion, moreover, might lead to not only a modification of thoughts, words, and deeds, but also, by the repeated physiological effect of appropriate action, to some extent perhaps even a reordering this neurochemistry, particularly in the prefrontal cortices.[22]

Fifth and finally, understanding the evolutionary roots of morality allows us to see more clearly human transcendence of our evolutionary past, a claim more readily appreciated by the nonreductionist perspective mentioned previously. Human beings do not have unlimited freedom, Damasio writes, but we "do have some room for such freedom, for willing and performing actions that may go against the apparent grain of biology and culture."[23] Clearly, accounting for the origin of some human values, even central values, need not exhaust the full range of all human values.

We would probably all agree that evolution has shaped human nature in a way that set the conditions for the emergence of moral ideals that confirm in a general way what is indicated by "nature," in, for example, self-defense and defense of loved ones, parental care, communal loyalty, cooperation, and reciprocity. Yet human nature also sets the conditions for the emergence of moral claims that transcend what seems to be encouraged by natural selection. We are familiar with the lofty ideals of Henry David Thoreau, Mohandas Ghandi, and Martin Luther King, Jr. They articulated ethical ideals of universal love, the golden rule, renunciation of violent retaliation and revenge, disinterested regard for others, love of enemies, and solidarity with the poor and marginalized. They called people to higher standards than are either ordinarily implemented or motivated by inclusive fitness, but their visions are deeply attractive to most of the human race. Our conduct may reflect the influence of the remote evolutionary past of our species, but we can strive for greater nobility than would be encompassed by natural selection.

CHALLENGES FROM EVOLUTIONARY THEORY

There are obviously many more objections (from both theological as well as evolutionary critics) to the kind of position advanced here than can be considered in a short presentation, but I would be remiss not to at least mention and respond briefly to a couple. I do not mean to appear (or be) glib, so please take the brevity of my response to reflect time constraints more than self-satisfied ignorance.

The first objection is that the reading of the evolutionary roots of morality proposed here is Catholic rather than objective; that is, it is guilty of circularity, in which I select out aspects of evolution with which I am predisposed to approve and ignore aspects with which I am uncomfortable. I am not properly acknowledging what some authors take to be the inescapably materialistic implication of Darwinism. This would be rather like a Marxist selecting out lines from Shakespeare to support an interpretation of Shakespeare as proto-Marxist, all the while ignoring, or at least not noticing (in a negligent way), Shakespeare's pervasive pro-aristocratic conservatism. I hope that I am not engaging in rank ideological distortion, obviously, but there is a way in which each of us thinks in a circular manner, always thinking from within our own particular perspectives with all their strengths and weaknesses. This problem is compounded when someone trained in the humanities thinks about scientifically based theories. Probably the best we can do is to aim for nonvicious circularity by acknowledging the characteristic weaknesses of our perspective, trying to be open to correction from fair-minded people who know better, and making judgments with an appropriate degree of humility and openness to revision—the same kind of traits exercised by responsible scientists when engaged in their own work as well as in speculative enterprises outside their fields of expertise.

.A second criticism is more directly philosophical. Some critics argue that since evolutionary theory provides an account of the origin of morality, it cannot have a divine origin. Morality is generated by emotional predispositions that themselves were caused by natural selection and random variation—by an indifferent universe, not by God. Ruse claims that the very fact that we feel a powerful desire for transcendent justification for our morality is an "illusion of our genes" that is itself a fitness-enhancing product of natural selection. If we seek to know the truth rather than simply justify ourselves, Ruse argues, we ought to employ a scientific understanding of the evolutionary roots of morality and throw out the theological understanding of God as the source of morality.[24]

There are many facets to this important criticism, only a few of which I will take up. First, this reflects the reductionist understanding of the evolutionary roots or morality already called into question. Second, it makes an assumption about how God is properly or at least ordinarily conceived as the source of morality by Christians (I am trying to read between Ruse's lines here) usually on the model of supernaturally implanted conscience or moral sense, brought to full maturity by conforming to Scripture. Ruse assumes that Christians accept what is called a "divine command" theory of ethics, a highly contested position within theology. The revised natural law theory entailed here, on the contrary, understands the authority of moral claims to be warranted not by divine dictates but by their contribution to human flourishing. Third, this objection unnecessarily and artificially separates divine and natural causality. The set of scientific hypotheses and insights regarding the evolutionary roots of morality need not make impossible their religious interpretation, including the claim that God orders the world through the evolutionary process. At times those who insist on understanding human life in terms of nature rather than God take for granted that the only way to think about God is in a naively anthropomorphic way; that is, as the really strong, smart, guilt-inducing, and punitive God of Sunday school, a mythical version of someone on what developmental psychologist Lawrence Kohlberg would describe as the conventional level of moral development with lots of power at his discretion.

In theological terms, though, this God is an idol, a false god, a being in the world. Because idolatry constantly threatens to distort religious thought,

Lutheran theologian Paul Tillich[25] spoke of God as the "ground of being," and Catholic Karl Rahner[26] referred to God as "absolute mystery." God is not a being in the world, somewhere out past Orion, but a transcendent Being that continually sustains the world in being and orders it through the processes and patterns of nature. It is therefore unnecessary and theologically improper to assume that either God or the evolutionary process orders the natural world. This is a false dichotomy based on the assumption that God is an alternative cause of ordering. Theologians Kenneth and Michael Himes, drawing on Thomas Aquinas, explain, "every event is caused . . . completely by both God and natural agencies but in two different ways. The action of God and the natural causal network of creation are distinguished modally, not substantively; certain things are not caused by God and others caused by natural factors; everything is caused by God one hundred percent and caused by natural forces within the world one hundred percent."[27]

From a theological viewpoint, then, it is a mistake to force a choice between religious and biological roots. Biological theories compete with other biological theories and not with theology, unless theology offers biological theory (in which case it is no longer theology) or, more likely, relies on inaccurate biological assumptions. Biblical creationism obscures this distinction in treating Genesis and evolutionary theory as alternate scientific theories. In doing so, creationism ironically joins the skeptics in forcing an unnecessary choice between well-established scientific theory and biblical revelation.

So while it is true that the reductionistic model that equates evolutionary roots with the essence of morality will not be acceptable to believers, it is equally the case that the spiritualistic view that regards God rather than nature as the root of morality is equally suspect. Neither view allows for the possibility that God works in and through the intrinsic ordering of human nature.

CONCLUSION

Perhaps some will take offense at the latter claim, as others take offense at the former. The main thesis of this presentation has been that one can reasonably claim that the "evolutionary roots of morality" examined by scientifically informed sources is not only compatible with theological ethics, but also helps to illumine what, theologically construed, is the human nature that is divinely created, habituated in the moral life, denigrated by sin, and healed by grace. These theological claims are not and cannot be justified by or even be made intelligible to evolutionary theory on its own terms, at least when it functions properly in the domain of science with its own proper standards and procedures. This is as it should be. These kinds of theological claims are apprehended in religious faith, though optimally not by a blind faith but rather one that sincerely appreciates and humbly accepts the insights into the roots of morality provided by evolutionary theory.

NOTES

1. Antonio R. Damasio, *Descartes' Error: Emotion, Reason, and the Human Brain* (New York: Avon Books, 1994).

2. Frans de Waal, *Good Natured: The Origins of Right and Wrong in Humans and Other Animals* (Cambridge, MA: Harvard University Press, 1996).

3. Damasio, 1994, p. 122.

4. Ibid, pp. 176ff.

5. Ibid, p. 261.

6. Ibid, p. xvi.

7. Michael J. Ruse, "Evolutionary Ethics: Healthy Prospect or Last Infirmity?" *Canadian Journal of Philosophy* Supplementary Volume 14: 27–73, p. 42; my emphasis.

8. Francisco J. Ayala, "The Biological Roots of Morality," in Paul Thompson, ed., *Issues in Evolutionary Ethics* (Albany: State University of New York Press, 1995), p. 302.

9. Ibid, p. 297.

10. William Irons, "How Did Morality Evolve?" *Zygon: Journal of Religion and Science* 26 (March), p. 67.

11. Ibid, p. 60.

12. Loc. cit.

13. Aristotle, *Nicomachean Ethics*, trans. Martin Ostwald (Indianapolis: Bobbs-Merrill, 1962), p. 33.

14. Ernst Mayr, *Toward a New Philosophy of Biology* (Cambridge, MA; and London, England: Harvard University Press, 1988), p. 26.

15. Thomas Aquinas, *Summa Theologiae.* Three volumes. Trans. Fathers of the English Dominican Province (New York: Benziger Brothers, 1946), 1, 75–76, pp. 363–382.

16. David Buss, *The Evolution of Desire: Strategies of Human Mating* (New York: Basic Books, 1994), p. 77.

17. Damasio, 1994, p. 191.

18. Buss, 1994, p. 209.

19. Robert Bellah, et al., *Habits of the Heart: Individualism and Commitment in American Life* (San Francisco: Harper and Row, 1986), pp. 284ff.

20. Damasio, 1994, pp. 149–150.

21. See Aquinas, 1946, pp. 820–821.

22. Damasio, 1994, pp. 182–183.

23. Ibid, p. 177.

24. Michael Ruse, "Evolutionary Ethics and the Search for Predecessors," *Social Philosophy and Policy* 8: 59–85 (1990), p. 65; Michael Ruse and E. O. Wilson, "The Evolution of Morals," in *The Philosophy of Biology,* ed. Michael Ruse (New York: Macmillan, 1989); Jeffrie Murphy, *Evolution, Morality, and the Meaning of Life* (Totowa, NJ: Roman and Littlefield, 1982).

25. Paul Tillich, *Systematic Theology.* Three volumes (Chicago: University of Chicago Press, 1951), p. 110.

26. Karl Rahner, *Foundations of the Christian Faith: An Introduction to the Idea of Christianity,* trans. William V. Dych (New York: Seabury Press, 1978), pp. 44ff.

27. Michael J. Himes and Kenneth R., Himes *Fullness of Faith: The Public Significance of Theology* (New York/Mahwah, NJ: Paulist Press, 1993), p. 79; Himes's emphasis.

18 Human Impact on the Evolution of the Environment

Mary Barber *Environmental Consultant*

This chapter addresses the ways in which humans have influenced the evolution of nonhuman organisms. Evolution is the process of change in the inherited characteristics of biological species over the course of geologic time, time measured in tens and hundreds of thousands of years. The changes come about because one genotype represented in a species of animal or plant becomes more frequent in a population than others. Humans are less influenced by evolution because of our ability to adapt to most environments on earth. The luxuries of clothing and energy for warmth or coolness and the availability of advanced medicine make us less sensitive as a species to disease and parasites. Nonhuman biota will continue to evolve, but on a globe that has been dramatically changed and transformed by the human species.

This chapter speaks to this planet's transformation, suggests ways these transformations will interact with the evolution of the nonhuman biosphere, discusses the difficulty of modifying our behavior, and addresses the possibilities available to us to become better stewards of the biota surrounding us.

AN ALTERED PLANET: THE HUMAN ENTERPRISE

Until the last century, human modifications to the landscape evoked images of meadows and pastures, agriculture fields, and villages and cities still relatively contained. Today, the scale of human impact on the environment goes far beyond our more bucolic musings. A desire to visit pristine nature can no longer be met. We have modified much of the land and our living space and our atmosphere. According to ecologist and evolutionary biologist Peter Vitousek, "Human alteration of the earth is substantial and growing. Between 1/3 and 1/2 of the land surface has been transformed by human action." Humans have impacted all areas of the world, from our backyards to its most remote regions.

Agricultural Development

This human enterprise, which we all benefit from and which we all contribute to, is an incredible force for change. Twenty percent of the earth's land surface is used for contemporary agricultural methods (i.e., monocultural row cropping) and urban development. The political walls inhibiting international trade have been lifted, making fields of wheat grown in the United States available for populations elsewhere in the world. For most of the human population the days of hunting and gathering are no longer necessary.

On a grand spatial scale, the change caused by humans is quite obvious. The majority of forest loss on earth has not occurred from timber logging but rather from agricultural land development. The World Resources Institute reported that the world's frontier forests—defined as original forest, not cut over in recent times—are extremely rare. Only 20 percent of original frontier forest exists in small and mostly fragmented regions of Brazil, Canada, and Russia. Everywhere else the extensive original forest, and many of its inhabitants are gone.

Also included under the category of agricultural development are fisheries, harvests from the wild and ponds or pens. In some areas fish farming has replaced existing native habitats; for example, shrimp in former mangrove forests. The wild catch harvest of fish is a long-standing industry that today poses many dilemmas. We are so many and our fishing techniques are so effective that we have critically diminished some fish populations. Our techniques also impact non-targeted fish that get caught up in the net; such as, the huge by-catch that results from our harvest of wild shrimp or the organisms that live in the sediments that are regularly scoured by bottom trawlers.

Landscape fragmentation and the creation of landscape islands are major ecological problems. No longer do we have magnificent stretches of forest. Instead we have isolated patches (i.e., protected parks). Ecological theory provides some understanding about population viability in these smaller spaces versus a broader breadth of habitat. Although our knowledge is still limited, we know that larger organisms and migrating animals are often limited by habitat fragments, and that, even for smaller organisms, gene flow between populations may diminish, resulting in inbreeding.

Urban Sprawl and Water Exploitation

The use of water, an essential biological requirement for all life on earth, is an obvious example of human alteration to natural systems. More than half of all accessible surface fresh water is used by humanity, for irrigation, drinking, and industrial use. With a world population of 6 billion, water exploitation by humans is a major environmental issue. What we use is not available for aquatic systems and organisms.

Sixty percent of humans live within 100 miles of some large body of water. We have been described as a coastal species. Most major cities have been built adjacent to aquatic ecosystems. Coasts and waterways provide opportunities for commerce, major ports, and fisheries. Coastal zones are stressed, physically altered, and biologically threatened because of our innate desire for this habitat.

The growth of our cities around the world demands attention. Urban centers expand into less developed rural space. The spread of urban communities overtakes agricultural areas that have already overtaken nonhuman ecosystems. Policy makers even struggle with the need of cities for more room and the need to maintain agricultural lands.

Biogeochemical Balances

Humans have greatly modified the biogeochemical balance of nature. Biogeochemical cycles are the movement of elements through the earth's hydrosphere, biosphere, and geosphere. The inputs and outputs of these complex processes are characteristic of how nature works and have been clearly documented by scientists. Since the beginning of the Industrial Revolution, the carbon dioxide (CO_2) concentration in the atmosphere has increased by nearly 30 percent. Scientists have used historical changes in CO_2 and climate as well as forecasted changes in climate to indicate the result of global carbon increase. Inputs of carbon into the atmosphere are unequal in distribution. International treaties focusing on carbon emissions attempt to resolve the economic and ecological disparity existing between countries. The politics of carbon and climate change are equally as complex as the natural cycles themselves. Despite attempts to ameliorate the rise in CO_2 concentration, humans are far from achieving and restoring any balance to this natural cycle.

Other cycles, including that for nitrogen, have also been altered. Atmospheric nitrogen introduced by humans exceeds all natural terrestrial sources combined. Human activities such as fossil fuel combustion and agricultural fertilizer application are root causes of this nutrient overload. In coastal systems nitrogen over enrichment results in algal blooms (that are often toxic), reduced oxygen, and diminished light levels. We may be inundating natural biochemical cycles to the point where we exceed the resilience of natural processes.

Exotic Species Introduction

We have also introduced species in our transformation of the land at an alarming rate. Non-native plant species, such as Queen Anne's lace, honeysuckle, and tumbleweed, have been with us long enough that they have become a part of the culture. Newer introductions, such as zebra mussel, kudzu, and cheat grass, have caused millions of dollars in damage. There's a constant influx of new organisms into an environment. Humans both increase the pace of these introductions as well as the number of new organisms that arrive. It's no longer just a seed drifting in, or an organism washing up on a beach. It's a whole ballast load of water with organisms from across an ocean that are flushed into a bay.

An extreme example of an exotic species disaster is the San Francisco Bay, which has few remaining native creatures. If we start in 1850, on average, a new species was established every 36 weeks. If we start in 1970, on average it takes 24 weeks to establish a new nonnative creature. In the 1990s, every 12 weeks, a new nonnative organism became established in the Bay. Approximately 85 to 95 percent of the species within the Bay are exotic.

The basic ecological problem with invasive nonnative species that explains their dominance in new environments is that they lack a set of predators or diseases or competitors that can keep their populations in check. New nonnative species are often so successful that the population of resident native species are diminished resulting in major losses of biodiversity.

Biodiversity Loss

Consider biodiversity in relation to some of the human alterations that have been discussed. Remember that biodiversity encompasses not just species, but also all the varieties below the species level, and all the different genetic compositions that a variety might have. In the other direction, biodiversity encompasses the different populations of a particular animal or plant species as well as the habitats where these populations are found. Diverse habitats and biomes, wetlands, prairies, forests, streams, and coasts are all part of the biodiversity of the planet.

Senseless human activities, such as overharvesting, have resulted in the extinction of species, the classic example being the passenger pigeon. We can also harvest to what is called ecological extinction where that creature is no longer doing or performing the ecological task that it had done in the past. An example is the oyster in the Chesapeake Bay, a species that is not extinct, although overharvesting and disease have made populations extremely small. Oysters are ecologically important to the health of the Bay because of their capacity to naturally filter the water. The populations of oysters in the Bay were so extensive that the entire bay was filtered on a weekly scale, a process that no longer occurs. Light was able to penetrate to deeper sediments and vast acres of aquatic grasses provided habitat for other organisms. Now the bay is cloudy and sea grass meadows and associated biota are limited. Biodiversity is diminished not only by overharvesting, but also by habitat modification due to agriculture, urban and suburban sprawl, and by the introduction of non-native species.

The tragic fact about biodiversity loss is that because we have not documented all species that exist, because we do not know what we have, we have no idea of what we have lost and are losing. Scientists can come up with estimates, but the world is full of undocumented creatures—unidentified, undescribed. Our world and our experience are thereby diminished.

Chemical Pollution

Many aspects of the human enterprise involve chemical waste or by-products that are potentially polluting. Mine tailings may leak arsenic into nearby bodies of water. The paint used to ship hulls may leach a tin compound that disrupts snail development. The plastics industry releases an endocrine disruptor that mimics natural hormones. Electrical transformers often contain PCBs that end up in sediments. Harbors are notorious for the concentrations of heavy metals in dredge spoils. These types of hazardous pollutants are not only of concern for human health, but also wreak havoc with habitats and their biota. Organisms may be killed outright or suffer sublethal effects that reduce growth and fecundity or increase susceptibility to disease. Either effect can lead to local extinctions.

IMPEDIMENTS TO HUMAN BEHAVIORAL CHANGE

There is a tension between our human enterprise and its influence on the rest of the biota. There are uncertainties in our knowledge. We may know that CO_2 has increased; but we are unable to predict the exact consequences. These are uncertainties. There are unknown biotic and physical thresholds.

There are also difficult questions concerning human population growth and our consumption of resources. We have all these cultural institutions we've set up at the national level and the international level. Humans are organized geographically into sovereign nations each having their own position and their own valid say. In each nation there are agencies that have different responsibilities. Each nation has subjurisdictions. There are private lands, there are public lands. These are unavoidable complexities that require complex solutions.

POSSIBILITIES FOR CHANGE

What are the possibilities? Scientists deal with complexity, which is something that needs to be embraced if we want to see change happen. Simple answers to complex problems are most often inadequate. We cannot be afraid and inhibited by this challenge. We need to weave together complex scientific knowledge and new approaches and concepts.

Sustainability

Sustainability establishes a framework to begin to surmount impediments to change. The concept recognizes the profound presence of the human endeavor on the landscape and its effects on the rest of life. Sustainability is based on the combined trio of economics, the environment, and social and cultural systems. An underlying principle of sustainability is that there should be an equitable distribution of resources for present and future generations. Environmental, social and cultural, and economic considerations are all valid and equal. The concept of sustainability is being developed by academics and policy experts around the world. Many governments advocate the goal of sustainability. The difficulty comes in the application of the concept. There is progress around the world as governments require their ministries to develop sustainable plans. Cities and local communities use the concept to increase participation in planning efforts. A new science—sustainability science—may be emerging.

Integrated Problem Solving

Ecologists have often acknowledged that an interdisciplinary approach can more readily address the complexities of anthropogenic stress and ecosystem response. As the theme of sustainable ecological systems becomes more pervasive and environmental problems more complex, the integration of the social, physical, and biological sciences for problem solving will be of great importance.

This integration of disciplines is a relatively new movement. Integrated science truly happens when scientists get together at the beginning of the problem solving process. Chemists, atmospheric physicists, and biologists get together and design new ways of asking questions. This is happening today within academic and government institutions; it's difficult, but it's happening.

We have ecological economics, ecological genetics, and ecological anthropology. We have the beginning of a new way of trying to cross boundaries, trying to understand that there really are goods and services that come from ecosystems: pollination, cleaning of water, recycling of minerals and nutrients, and cleaning of air.

Restoration Ecology/Ecosystem Management

Restoration is occurring on various scales. For instance, in Florida, a huge replumbing of the Florida Everglades is happening. A change in canal structure will likely bring back some biotic structure and ecological function.

Ecosystem management is a component of sustainability. The realization around the world that we have to manage across habitats and across jurisdictions complements the integrated approach of disciplines. We can't just manage a national park as an isolated entity. Park boundaries are not impermeable to life outside of them. There are people living around them, and there are forest lands adjacent that are used for different purposes. These greatly influence the park.

Technological Advances for Change

Technological advances, such as satellite remote sensing tools, allow us to visualize changes in the landscape with high resolution. They are allowing us to visualize alternative scenarios and to approach land managers with future predictions and forecasted change.

A Global Movement for Change

Much activity at the international level is occurring with treaties focusing on major environmental issues that affect all nations (for instance, the Montreal Protocol Ozone Treaty and the Kyoto Climate Change Treaty). These are extremely difficult international negotiations, but already the developing world and the developed world are building partnerships. What are our responsibilities as we move forward with our human enterprise?

We can build on our scientific base and use these tools at our disposal. We can recognize and appreciate a global community and negotiate within its boundaries. But ultimately to be better stewards we need to recognize our responsibilities. The dialogue between religion and science is a dialogue, not a contest. Science will help us understand what to do, and religion will help us know we should do it.

One concept that applies to every human is the concept of stewardship, the idea of the caregiver. It's one that we can continue to rely on and one that people from all walks of life can appreciate.

REFLECTIONS

If we are the eyes for the rest of life on this planet, we must be able to see life's entire sphere, not just our own. We are in essence the floating, blue and white finite planet portrayed by those incredible space photographs. If we acknowledge the extreme influence and the growing scale of our human enterprise on the rest of the biota, where does our responsibility lie? It is certainly clear that science is not going to be the driver that tells us we need to be better stewards. That comes from a deeper sense of moral values.

There is no question that we have transformed the order of the planet and the orderly way in which biological evolution has occurred. We've heard about it as it relates to us, and we've gained a sense that there are some laws and some general principles that we can make about this process. Humans have impacted the evolution of nonhuman organisms by modifying the pace and scale at which it occurs and by changing the positioning of organisms in relation to one another.

Patriarch Bartholomew I, a patriarch of the Greek Orthodox Church, stated that "for humans to cause species to become extinct, and to destroy the biological diversity of God's creation; for humans to degrade the integrity of the earth by causing changes in its climate, stripping the earth of its natural forest, or destroying its wetlands; for humans to contaminate the Earth's waters, its land, its air and its life with poisonous substances, these are sins."

19 Science, Tradition, and the Future

N. Scott Momaday *University of Arizona*

It appears that the venerable dispute between the evolutionists and the creationists has surfaced in a new arena; that of archeological investigation of human remains found on or near American Indian land. Actually, this dispute is not new. But it seems now to be expressed in terms that have only just begun to be defined. For the first time, the archeologists and anthropologists and, by extension, the world of science at large, claim unfair treatment at the hands of the Indians. With the passage of the Native American Graves Protection and Repatriation Act, Indian tribes are allowed to claim the remains of their ancestors. They are doing so with a vengeance, so to speak. And vengeance is, perhaps, a viable a part of the equation. For hundreds of years the remains of American Indians have been taken from the earth and deposited in museums. Presumably, they are removed from the earth in order to be studied. Their remains hold the secrets to the past, we are told. They can tell us much about the origin of peoples in North America. They can tell the Indian who he is, and that is presumably a good and great benefit.

But according to the Indian, he knows who he is. He has always known without benefit of science. This resistance is alien to the public mind and, beyond question, the arguments of science are legitimate. We all know that science has unlocked countless doors of universe. By means of scientific investigation, we have seen ourselves, our limits, and our possibilities as we would not otherwise have seen them. We have seen into the history and prehistory and into our possible future with a clarity not available to our nearest ancestors.

But perhaps science has appropriated, in our time, an authority disproportionate to its rightful purpose in our daily lives. The authority of science is monumental. The results of scientific investigation are considered all but infallible. Religion and the humanities have lost significance in proportion as science has gained. Perhaps we are talking about a proper equation, a matter of balance. The world of the Native American is predicated on the realization of balance. The earth and sky are precisely opposed, and so are sun and moon; the wind and the rain are aligned. All things have place. All things exist within a sacred design. The Indian world is possessed of spirit. The physical is not greater than the spiritual. But the imposition of Western civilization with its emphases on industrialization, technology, and science has not only threatened, but in many cases destroyed, the spiritual life of the Indian, not to say the Indian himself.

The archeologists and anthropologists especially have given science a bad name in the Indian world. Where human remains are concerned, they have often acted without respect or sensitivity, much less reverence. The violation of burial sites and the confiscation of human remains has been shameful and unprofessional at best. The boxes of human bones stacked in the Smithsonian Institution, often unidentified and virtually forgotten, stand as a sad monument to bureaucratic apathy.

Indian creationists, like creationists in general, assume unreasonable attitudes. Reason is on the side of science. We did not come from Asia, we did not come from elsewhere, says a Hopi friend, we were always here. By extension, this is to say that the Indians are not descended from apes. Even so reasonable and an intelligent a man as Vine Deloria dismisses the Bering Bridge crossing as "scientific folklore." But the Bering Bridge theory is not a theory at all. We know on hard evidence that people were migrating from Asia to North America 20,000 years ago.

We know the motives of science in this dispute. What we know less well and need to know are the motives of the Native American. Of all the crimes perpetrated on the American Indian, the most destructive has been the theft of the sacred. The wounds of his spirit are eminently more serious than are the wounds to his body: alcoholism, disease, infant mortality, poverty. These are nothing compared to the destruction of his spirit. The process of that destruction has been in motion for a long time now and is ongoing. The scientific scrutiny of the remains of his ancestors is somehow involved in this process. The Indian will resist because he must. His identity, his dignity, and his spirit are at stake.

*　*　*

EVOLUTION[1]

YAHWEH *and* URSET *sit in chairs facing each other. Behind them is a statue of a man, perhaps a Greek philosopher or an athlete.*

URSET
Yes, Great Mystery, man too. He talks as much as the dogs do.

YAHWEH
With greater measure, I hope. Not incessantly.

URSET
Measure indeed. Sometimes he speaks poetry. It's very pleasant to hear. But it seems to me, well, unnatural. A bit elevated, if you see what I mean. High toned, lofty. Almost exclusive.

YAHWEH
It is the highest of all languages, Urset. Higher even than mathematics. It is on plane with music. Yes, man is the keeper of poetry.

URSET
Is it because, as the dogs say, Man is more highly evolved than the rest of us?

YAHWEH
Yes. In certain respects, and in general, he is more highly evolved.

URSET
Why is that, I wonder?

YAHWEH
My timetables. Man is on a faster track than other animals. At the same time that his brain developed to its present size, he developed a vocal mechanism of

some distinction. These two things enabled him to possess language and speech.

URSET

Language, language. How did it happen? How did it begin?

YAHWEH

Oh, the children made it one day. Poor man, he'd been trying to talk for such a long time. Then the children went out to play together. At the end of the day they had invented language. They went home to their parents and said to them, "This is what you have been trying to say."

URSET

Language is child's play.

YAHWEH

There you have it.

URSET

This business of evolution, Great Mystery. What will come of it?

YAHWEH

The end, surely. Nothing will come of it as it has come from nothing.

URSET

But we shall have had a good run.

YAHWEH

Good beyond the time.

NOTE

1. This dialogue is found in N. Scott Momaday, *In the Bear's House* (St. Martin's Press, 1999), pp. 39–41.

20 The Story and the Dream: The Next Stage of the Evolutionary Epic

Thomas Berry *Greensboro, North Carolina*

Our main concern here is with the universe story and our human role in that story. There is, it seems, such a long way from the vastness of the universe to ourselves gathered here in Chicago in the Field Natural History Museum. Yet this is an appropriate place for our meeting, since the purpose of this museum is to bring our present human venture into an intimate presence to these earlier forms so different from our ordinary experience.

But even while all this is here, it seems to play rather a limited role in any phase of the human project other than the scientific, the academic, or the technological phases. We know more about the universe than any people ever knew. We have more command over the functioning of the earth than any people ever had. Yet we are less intimate with the universe than peoples of prior times. This can be seen in the work of scientists who write with great insight into the earlier phases of the universe and then remark that the more we know about the universe, the less meaning it seems to have.

When we inquire just why scientists devote such intense effort, such enduring dedication to research projects concerned with the story of the universe, one answer might be that scientists are answering the irresistible call of the great self of the universe to the small self of the individual. We are only beginning to be aware that this attraction of the scientist to the study of the universe is itself one of the more fascinating aspects of the universe. Since the universe is the only self-referent mode of being in the phenomenal world, every being in the universe is universe referent for its origin and destiny and its proper role in the great community of existence. If there is such a thing as human intelligence, then it has emerged out of the universe and, in its functioning, it must in some manner be ordered toward the universe. The primary study of human intelligence might be designated as universe study, or in terms derived from the Greek, cosmology. Only through understanding the universe can we understand ourselves or our proper role in the great community of existence.

All human occupations and professions must themselves be expressions of the universe and its mode of functioning. This is especially true of what came to be known as religion, for the term *religion* and the term *universe* are somewhat similar in their meaning. Both are derived from the Latin and both have to do with turning back to unity. Religion, *re-ligare*, is a binding back to origin. Universe, or *universa*, is a turning back of the many to the one. Earlier peoples seem to have understood this. They lived in a pattern of human activities that were validated by their relation with the cosmological sequence. They lived within the covenant of the universe, the ontological covenant whereby each component of the universe experienced itself in intimate rapport with the other components of the universe.

209

They constantly evoked their self-consciousness within their universe conscious-ness. The one had no meaning without the other. They situated themselves at each moment in terms of the four cardinal directions governed by their position in rela-tion to the sun. The sun arose in the east, set in the west. At midday the sun was in the south. The north was where the sun never situated itself. The sky was above, earth below. Each person received a self-validation by this act of knowing exactly where he or she was in the universe. So too with any structures erected on the earth. These could only be authentic, even physically secure, by being ordered in relation to the cosmological directions. This required careful alignment with the celestial world whence the sense of direction as well as the sense of time was de-rived.

In the time sequence, rituals were established to create a consciousness of the moments of cosmological change; the dawn and dusk of the daily sequence of sunlight and dark, the increase and decline in the phases of the moon, the winter solstice especially as the danger moment of the universe, the period of dark de-scent; then came the rise into a world of warmth and light and the blossoming of the plants and the birth moment throughout the animal world. These moments of change were the moments when the shining forth of the phenomenal world was most evident. Such moments were moments of grace, moments when the sacred world communicated itself with special clarity to the world of the human.

This intimacy with the universe can be seen in the initiation ceremony of the Omaha Indians. When an infant is born the child is taken out under the sky and presented to the universe with the invocation: "O Ye Sun, Moon, stars, all ye that move in the heavens, I bid you hear me. Into your midst has come a new life, Consent Ye, we implore, make its path smooth that it may move beyond the first hill."[1] After this invocation to the heavenly powers, the invocation is made to the atmospheric powers, to the clouds, the wind, the rain and the snow, with a simi-lar petition that these powers too would accept the child and guide it on its way. So too an invocation was made to the powers of living beings on the earth and then to the earth and the insects and to all those beings that live within the earth. In this manner the covenant of earth was affirmed. Humans asserted their inti-macy with the earth and acknowledged their dependence on the larger commu-nity for whatever they needed in life.

We witness a similar correspondence of human affairs with the cosmological order in the Great Vision of Black Elk, the Sioux Holy Man, a vision that took place in 1864. He experienced the intimacy of the cosmological and the human or-ders in a special dramatic enactment that took place in the heavens. During the vision the entire universe became a ritual dance. So we are told: "The song that filled the heavens was so beautiful that nothing anywhere could keep from danc-ing. The leaves on the trees, the grasses on the hills and in the valleys, the waters in the creeks and in the rivers and the lakes, the four-legged and the two-legged and the wings of the air—all danced together to the music of the stallion's song."[2] Thus was fulfilled the meaning and purpose of the universe, the exuberant cele-bration of delight in existence.

So too in the Chinese world. There the imperial palace was constructed in such correspondence with the movement of the natural world that the emperor could move from one section of the palace to another with each change of seasons. The colors of the garments worn by the emperor were also coordinated with the changes of the cosmological order. The music was altered to suit the quiet and dark of winter, or the brightness and delight of summer. If these correspondences between the human and the cosmological order were not observed, the entire order of the universe would, supposedly, be thrown into disarray.

Also in Western civilization at an earlier period, the entire structure of Western ritual was cosmologically oriented. This was most obvious in the worship ritual, which was extensively coordinated, especially in the monasteries, with the sequence of changes during the day–night cycle. Psalms and hymns were sung in the middle of the night to celebrate the deep contemplative aspect of the nocturnal hours; then came the dawn rituals, the midday and evening rituals. So too at its highest moment of intellectual development, the entire theological explanation of Western religion was integrated with the physics and metaphysics and cosmology as this was handed down through the Aristotelian tradition. This was the great work of Thomas of Aquin, to restructure all Christian thought within a cosmological perception. That is why he tells us quite clearly in the prologue of his summary of Christian theology that our knowledge of the divine comes to us through two sources, through the order of the universe known by human reason and by biblical revelation known through faith. That is why also he tells us, "The Order of the Universe is the ultimate and noblest perfection in things."[3]

Throughout this premodem period the universe, experienced as a cosmic liturgy celebrating the grandeur of existence, was the ultimate creative force in the phenomenal order, giving shape and resplendence and vigor and meaning to every mode of being. Above all, it was the primary focus, the primary place, for the meeting of the divine and the human. Simply to draw attention to such grandeur of perception and human participation in such ecstatic fulfillment is to awaken a deep wonderment in our modern souls. To ourselves who live in this very secular age, all this appears in a distant, something of a dream world, a world that we cannot experience as entirely real.

We live too deeply alienated from the cosmological order, the phenomenal world, the world of the "shining forth" (for such is the meaning of the word *phenomenon*). We live in a human world, a world where all our values are human. The natural world is experienced as subservient to the human. Its reality has diminished as the human has been magnified. If we give attention to the universe, it is to the scholarly world of scientific equations and of atomic and subatomic particles, to the technological world of mechanistic contrivances, to the economic world of unlimited human use of a collection of natural resources.

We seem not to appreciate the dazzling wonder or the sacred dimension that finds expression in the universe itself, a universe that emerged into being by a creativity beyond anything we can imagine, a world that assumed its present form by an unpredictable self-organizing power. What is truly amazing is that these unpredictable processes, sometimes considered as random, produced a universe so coherent in its structure and so finely ordered in its functioning amid the turbulence of an awesome and relentless inner creative energy.

Even when we penetrate deeply into the reality of the physical and the biological orders, even when we understand clearly that the human story and the universe story are a single story, we somehow fail in our ability to tell the story in a way that would provide a comprehensive meaning for our human mode of being. While in former times a world of meaning was worked out within a universe and a planet moving in ever-renewing seasonal cycles, meaning has not yet been worked out within a universe that has come into being by a primordial flaring forth giving rise to an irreversible sequence of transformation episodes moving in the larger arc of their sequence from a lesser to a greater complexity in structure and functioning and from a lesser to greater consciousness—an unfolding sequence that is self-emergent, self-sustaining, self-educating, self-governing, self-healing, and self-fulfilling. From this source must come all emergence, all nourishment, all education, all governance, all healing, all fulfillment.

Humans, in this earlier period of human cultural development, experienced themselves as owning nothing, as receiving existence itself and life and consciousness as an unmerited gift, as having exuberant delight and unending gratitude as their first obligation. It was a personal universe, a world of intimacy and beauty—a universe where every mode of being lived by a shared existence with all other modes of being. No being had meaning or reality or fulfillment apart from the great community of the universe. This primordial community itself existed through the presence of the indwelling Spirit whence came its sacred character.

Whatever humans needed was supplied by the surrounding world: whatever inspiration for their imagination, whatever awakening of intelligence, whatever personal fulfillment. This joyful fulfillment found expression in poetry and music and song and dance, a fulfillment that continues to find expression in our children running through the meadows, wading in the creeks, playing with animals, or simply sitting with utmost satisfaction in a backyard puddle experiencing the cooling delight of such an environment on a summer's day. Such is the beginning of education, of aesthetic experience, of physical vigor, of acquaintance with the universe. This is the awakening of both the senses and the mind. This is the beginning of poetry and music and literature. It is the beginning of cosmology, of philosophical reflection, of moral perception, of theological insight. It is the beginning of the epic of evolution.

This fulfillment within the capacities of the child is continued on in an unbroken sequence in the life of the adult. The experience deepens, but it is not essentially different. It continues to be delight in the celebration of existence in intimate presence to the comprehensive community of the universe—only deepened in its significance by experience of the tragic, the painful, the sacrificial dimension that is found throughout every realm of existence.

In this child's quest for experiencing the universe, Maria Montessori found the basic guidance that we need for an integral educational program within the epic of evolution. In her 1936 series of essays entitled "Education of the Human Potential," she tells us that the six-year-old child needs to experience its own center at the center of the universe, for the universe is the answer to all questions. That is what the child is seeking in his excited discovery of the surrounding universe. As

Maria Montessori tells us, "Since it has been seen necessary to give so much to the child, let us give the child a vision of the whole universe. The universe is an imposing reality, and an answer to all questions. We shall walk together on this path of life, for all things are part of the universe, and are connected with each other to form one whole unity. This idea helps the mind of the child to become fixed, to stop wandering in an aimless quest for knowledge. He is satisfied, having found the universal center of himself with all things."[4]

Then she describes the security that the child feels within the integral functioning of the natural world as soon as he is assured that the universe is the answer to all questions. In this wandering through the natural world, the imagination is inspired, the mind is activated, the feeling of nobility developed. What Maria Montessori could not experience in her times was the empirical evidence of the intimacy of every phase of the universe with every other phase, such as we now recognize as the basis for all scientific inquiry. Yet she knew that the child needed to know the story of the universe and to grow throughout life with ever greater intimacy with the universe and ever greater delight in celebrating the grandeur of existence within this vast community.

This story of the evolutionary universe she told with amazing detail for the period in which she lived. She recognized that telling the story of the universe should not be a technical explanation of the evolutionary process, nor should it be interrupted by constant reference as to how we discovered the story of the universe. The story needed to be told in direct narrative, even in epic style. So she tells us that "to interest the children in the universe, we must not begin by giving them elementary facts about it, to make them merely understand its mechanism, but start with far loftier notions of a philosophical nature, put in an acceptable manner, suited to the child's psychology."[5]

Then she proceeds to tell the drama of the emergent universe, the formation of the oceans, how the continents came to be, then the origins of life, the biosphere, and the Cretaceous Period. Then a transition moment of great significance, transition to the human: "The Earth was trembling with expectancy and glad foreboding. Her heart moved in sympathy with creation's joy; tremors ran through her frame and emotional tears coursed through her in new streams."[6] How appropriate a way of indicating the moment when the earth was about to reflect on itself, to see itself for the first time within the human mode of intelligence. Then she continues on to the emergence of the human and the sequence of stages of human cultural development and finally to the rise of modem empirical science and our unique experience of the universe in the vast range of its extent and the full sequence of its transformations in time.

This excitement of which she speaks is not the excitement of the builder following a blueprint in building a house. It is rather the excitement of the artist who is designing a painting or a sculpture, or the expectation of a poet as he moves into the most significant lines of a poem to which he has dedicated his effort over a long period of time. This was such a moment as the poet Gœthe referred to when he noted that, in writing his finest lines, it seemed that his spirit guide took over his pen and did the writing. Neither the painter working out his design nor the poet writing out his vision nor the musician writing a symphony knows just what he is about to do. Nor is he totally ignorant. Yet in a way the artist and the musician know exactly what they are working toward: a vision of beauty, a musical phrase that expresses the full depths of some deep human experience. There is at this moment an intensity of feeling, an expectation, a joy of soul—all of which then flows over into the creation that emerges. It is this that Maria Montessori has in mind when she writes such a phrase as we have just read concerning the mood of excitement in the universe at the moment when the human first came into being. The human is the model for understanding the universe, as the universe is the model for understanding the human. For certainly humans have nothing but what they received from the universe.

This beginning account of the epic of the evolutionary universe need only be continued and further developed in order to guide the entire course of human affairs into a more coherent rapport between the universe community and our modern human society. In this context, advanced education at the college and university level would have a unity amid all its differentiation; for all studies would be experienced in their differentiation and yet united as expressions of a single great community of existence. The evolutionary universe would be the primary referent in every field of academic concern as well as in every human concern.

This would be clear especially in economics, where the economic well-being of the human would be sought within the well-being of the natural world whence all human wealth and well-being is derived. The first law of human economy would be to preserve the integral economy of the planet and to seek the well-being of the human within this context.

Sociology would not envisage the human community apart from the larger earth community or apart from the integral bioregional communities into which the functioning of the earth is divided.

In law and government humans would discover their proper role within the governing structures of the surrounding natural world, for the planet earth has a governance with a precision and an efficacy far beyond anything that humans might contrive. Human governance should not seek to override but further to integrate and extend with intellectual understanding and conscious decision the governance of the natural world.

In this governance each form of existence has its own role, for each form brings to the community a perfection of insight found in no other mode of being. The integral evolving community would not be simply the human community but the larger community of the earth. Not only the rights of the human but the rights of every mode of earth being would be recognized. The basic biological law concerning habitat would be recognized as binding also on humans: the law that every species should have opposed species or conditions that limit each species so that no one species or group of species would overwhelm the other species. This law would be recognized as binding also on the human, with the difference that humans need to obey this law by conscious recognition and free compliance whereas the nonhuman species would be more constrained in their modes of action by their genetic coding.

So with medicine. The first recognition would be that there cannot be well humans on a sick planet. The way to human well-being would be to recognize that the earth that brought humans into existence, by that fact, established the conditions for the well-being of the human by an integral relation with the other life systems of the planet. To keep this integral community from becoming toxic due to human interference would be recognized as a primary concern.

In religion and theology the great need is to join in the great liturgy of the universe; not now simply an abiding ever-renewing universe but a universe distinguished as both abiding and transforming. We might think of the threefold evolutionary process: the galactic evolutionary processes of the universe, the geobiological evolutionary processes of the earth, and the cultural evolutionary processes of the human that need to be understood in their sacred dimension. These are the three components of the single evolutionary narrative that needs to be seen and understood and recounted in epic style.

Epic narrative, we might say, is the manner in which a period or a culture articulates its experience in the tragic yet glorious enterprise of survival in the midst of fearsome threats to life, continuance and fulfillment of some destiny. Epics are celebrated in poetry and music especially. The epics that we are best acquainted with are the Homeric epics, the epic story of the Bible, and the epic of Virgil, the *Aeneid.* There are also the Rama story and the account of the great Bharatal, the *Mahabharata* of India. In Europe there are also the epics of the *Song of Roland* and the *Nibelungenlied.* In these stories the ideals of the society are articulated. Personal and community life are revealed in their heroic dimensions. Cosmological forces of the surrounding world are identified. The sense of the sacred is expressed. The rituals of the society are enacted. The ideals of personal conduct are made evident. The community is protected at personal risk of the individual. Above all, the sense of transhuman forces at work throughout the universe is communicated.

But if in the past the great moments in human achievement are presented in epic narrative, we must appreciate that the universe achievements are now the subject of the authentic epic of the late twentieth century. A world of these times is no longer simply the human world, no longer the epic of a nation or even of the assembly of nations. It is rather the epic of an emerging universe that has come into human appreciation for the first time with such intimate knowledge of the turbulent trials through which it has passed. No story of human affairs can begin to compare with this story for its significance throughout the order of earthly affairs. While this narrative does not displace any other religious or literary narrative, this story bears the impress of many sacred values to be identified and celebrated with a new appreciation. Such is the triumph of science to give us this story in infinite detail in its sequence of development.

In this evolutionary story we easily identify the moments of change. These moments of transformation are the mysterious, the sacred moments, the moments when a numinous guidance shows through amid the turbulent course of universe affairs. Such moments we can no longer believe are controlled by purely random consequences out of a roiling sea of conflicting forces. Between the random and the directed, as the geneticist Theodosius Dobzhansky insisted, lies the creative. Randomness can only be another name for mysterious ordering processes that govern all artistic creativity.

The dazzling course of things is exciting indeed. Yet the mysterious moment when the galactic formations took shape and the stars were formed throughout the heavens deserves celebration in liturgies not dissimilar from the liturgies co-ordinating human activities with the transforming moments of the seasons of the year or the transformation of day into night or night into day. Such transforming moments in the evolutionary sequence are too numerous to present here.

Yet as an illustration of how the epic of evolution might be integrated into traditional religious services, I would like to mention the most sacred moment in traditional Christian liturgy, the moment designated as the Easter Vigil. This is the moment when the experience of life renewal is reenacted. This liturgy is to be celebrated in the darkness of night just before the dawn. At this moment the story of the creation of the world is recited as well as the events that have transpired in the historical order until the moment of renewal. What is striking in this narrative is that the story of creation is a very limited narrative, since in earlier times the only account of creation of the universe in the religious traditions of the Western world was contained in the few paragraphs of the book of Genesis. After that the entire story of history was the human story. There was no further story of the galaxies or the formation of the earth or the evolutionary emergence of life. What is now available to us is a more extensive account of the universe and how it came into being through the immense amount of time and through a long sequence of transformation episodes. This, to my mind, needs to be incorporated into the story of the creation of the world as this is narrated in religious liturgy.

Of the possible moments for celebration, one that deserves mention is the galactic formation and the formation of the stars. Another might be the first-generation star that, some 4.5 billion years ago, formed the ninety-some elements in its supernova moment of implosion and then explosion as fragments into space. By gathering these fragments with the aid of gravitational attraction, our own star came into being with the earth as one of its nine planets. Amid the turbulent shaping of the planet we might note the rise of the first living cell becoming possible some 3 billion years ago. Then came sexual reproduction, later photosynthesis. From then on a long choice of possibilities would present itself.

The evolutionary responsibility of the human from a religious perspective is to perceive the epic of the universe as the primary revelatory experience of our times. The natural world as revelatory was in former times understood as an ever-renewing sequence of seasonal change. Today, however, the natural world is seen as the irreversible sequence of change, such as we experience through empirical scientific studies. This is an additional revelation that we are having. Revelation is not something merely of the past. It is the reality of the present.

Just as the universe reveals the basic sources of economic understanding, as the universe is the guide to medical understanding, so the universe is our guide to understanding of the sacred dimension of the universe. For too long a time we have refused to accept the insight into the world of the sacred that is there before us. The scientists themselves have been overwhelmed by their discoveries and have found it difficult to explain themselves in other than scientific equations and mathematical description.

Now that this awareness of the epic dimension of the evolutionary process begins to be seriously considered, a new world of understanding appears on the horizon. My first thought is that we not try to write theology at this moment. My thought is that we celebrate the glory of the universe that is there before us. We need have no doubts of the appropriateness of our celebration of the sacred in this epic narrative. Here we join the great wisdom traditions of the past. In the epic of evolution, science becomes a wisdom.

NOTES

1. George W. Cronyn, ed., *American Indian Poetry* (New York: Liveright, 1934), p. 53.

2. Black Elk, recorded by John G. Neihardt, *Black Elk Speaks* (New York: Pocket Books, 1932), p. 35.

3. Thomas Aquinas, *Summa Contra Gentiles.* Translated by James Anderson (Notre Dame: Notre Dame University Press, 1992), Book Two. Ch. 45. par. 10.

4. Maria Montessori, *To Educate the Human Potential* (Oxford: Oxford University Press, 1989), p. 5f.

5. Maria Montessori, p. 19.

6. Maria Montessori, p. 41.

Index

D

Damasio, Antonio, 114, 190,
194–195
D'Aquili, Eugene, 130
dark matter, 35, 36
Darrow, Clarence, 48, 49
Darwin, Charles, 13–14
American reception of, 45–46
on consciousness, 96–97
goals of, 45
neo-Darwinism, 77–90
religious community responses to,
46–47
religious perspective of, 44–45
Dawkins, Richard, 12–13, 53
on memetics, 128
on natural selection, 77–78
scientific skepticism of, 78–80
Deacon, Terence W., 2, 99–111, 130
Decalogue, 190
decision making, 160, 173, 177
deconstructionism, 43
deforestation, 200
democracy, 40
demographic shift, 126
Descartes, René, 101
The Descent of Man (Darwin), 14
deuterium, 30–31
developmental biology. *See* sociobiology
de Waal, Frans, 190
dialogue, benefits of, 19–20
Dialogue on Science, Ethics, and Religion, 4
diet, 132–140
dinosaurs, 57–58
disconnect because superior, 41–43
Discover, 20
distinctiveness. *See* human distinctiveness
diversity
God as source of, 89
loss of biodiversity and, 201–202
through sexuality, 73–76
divine command theory, 196
Divine Discourse (Wolterstorff), 120–121
DNA, 60, 127
bricolage in, 71, 72
mitochondrial Eve and, 168–170
Dobzansky, Theodosius, 13, 216
Doppler effect, 28–29
Draper, William, 5
dualism, 112–114
Dubois, Eugène, 126
Durham, William, 129
Durkheim, Emile, 181–182
Dyson, Freeman, 8

E

earth, age of, 51–52, 54–55
Easter Vigil, 216
economics, 41, 214
ecosystem management, 204
ecosystems model, 131–133
"Education of the Human Potential"
(Montessori), 212–214
Einstein, Albert, 7, 31–32
Eiseley, Loren, 145–146
Eldredge, Niles, 2, 53–59
electromagnetic symmetry, 32–33
electromagnetism, 36
Eliade, Mircea, 144
emission distance, 27
emotional systems, 184, 186, 194
environmental crises, 8, 199–205
humans in, 41–43
as impetus for evolution, 53–59
Precambrian glaciation, 55–56
enzymes, 60
epic narrative, 215
epidemiological model of information
transfer, 129–130
eschatology, 85–86
ethics, 166, 173–174. *See also* morality
biology in, 173–177
divine command theory of, 196
ethology, 182
eubacteria, 72
eukaryotic cells, 53, 72
evolution of, 55, 73
proteins in, 61–62
evolution
Americans' beliefs on, 16–17
bricolage in, 71, 72
destabilizing events in, 53–59
difficulty of framing, 40
of flagella, 66–70
gene emergence and, 65–67
kinds of, 60
mechanism of, 60–76
mutation in, 63–70
patterns in, 72–76
permanence of, 39
proteins in, 60–62
quantum, 54
receptor proteins in, 61–62,
70–71
self-replication and, 62–63
evolutionary psychology. *See*
sociobiology
evolutionary theism, 80
evolutionary theology, 84–89